The Corvette W9-CEK-412
1953-1997

Published by
Michael Bruce Associates, Inc.
Michael Antonick, President
Post Office Box 396
Powell, Ohio 43065

January 1997

CONTENTS

Michael Bruce Associates, Inc. acknowledges with appreciation the following who contributed their expertise to this and previous *Corvette Black Books*: Noland Adams, Dan Aldridge, John Amgwert, Bob Applegate, Pat Baker, Jane Barthelme, Sanford Block, Michele Boling, Kent Brooks, Barry Brown, Dale Brown, David Burroughs, Steve Dangremond, M. F. Dobbins, Bob Eckles, Sam Folz, Fred Gallasch, Steve Guckenberg, Joe Haase, John Hibbert, Mike Hunt, John Hyland, Rick Johnson, Alan Kaplan, Paul Kitchen, Gary Konner, Jim Krughoff, Gary Lisk, Bill Locke, Bob Lojewski, Bob McDorman, Chip Miller, Bill Mock, Bill Munzer, Brian Pearce, John Poloney, Wes Raynal, Bill Rhodes, Jeffrey Smith, Mark & Dixie Smith, Lou Vitalle, Jerry Wadsworth, Jerry Weichers and Don Williams. Thanks also to Callaway Engineering, Mercury-Marine and to the Chevrolet Division of GM.

Notice: *The Corvette Black Book* and its publisher, Michael Bruce Associates, Inc. have no relationship or connection whatever with Hearst Business Media Corporation, its parent or affiliated corporations, or the *Black Book* published by National Auto Research Division of Hearst Business Media Corporation.

Cover: Design by Dick Yoakam. Front cover photo by Mike Antonick, 1967 Corvette owned by Jerry Johnson. Back cover engine cutaway by David Kimble. Printed and bound in the USA by Banta ISG-Viking Press.

ISBN: 0-933534-39-6

Sponsor

GLOSSARY

ABS: Anti-lock Braking System. Sensors monitor wheel rotation and prevent wheel lockup during braking by modulating hydraulic pressure. Corvette's ABS was standard equipment starting with 1986 models.

ASR: Acceleration Slip Regulation. Engine spark retard, throttle close down, and brake intervention limit wheel spin during acceleration. ASR was standard equipment starting with 1992 Corvette models.

A-Pillar: The post section between the windshield and door glass.

B-Pillar: In Corvettes, the area between the door glass and rear window.

Benchmark: Bloomington award for Corvettes achieving both gold certified and survivor status.

Big Block: Large displacement engines of 396, 427 and 454 cubic inches, optional in Corvettes from 1965 through 1974.

Big Tank: Optional thirty-six gallon fuel tank for 1963 through 1967, or twenty-four gallon fuel tank for 1959 through 1962 Corvettes.

Black Hills: Popular Corvette street show in Spearfish, South Dakota.

Bloomington: A major annual Corvette show, but most known for its certification judging system based on factory originality. Held in Bloomington, Illinois from 1973 through 1992; then in Springfield, Illinois starting in 1993.

Blue Flame: Six cylinder engine for 1953, 1954 and a few 1955 models.

Body Off: Extensive restoration in which a Corvette body is completely removed from its frame.

Bolt On: Optional 1967 cast aluminum wheel.

Bose: Short for a series of optional Delco-Bose stereo systems available starting with the 1984 Corvette.

Bowling Green: Location of the Corvette assembly plant since 1981.

Bucket: Headlight container for 1953, 1954 and 1955 models, 1963 to present models, or the bucket seat for any model year.

Bullet: Individual air inlet for 1953 and early 1954 Corvettes.

Buzzer: Tachometer rpm limit warning device used briefly in 1963; or, the similar speedometer warning device optional in 1967-1969.

Callaway Twin Turbo: Engine conversion by Callaway Engineering, Old Lyme, Connecticut. Available through some Chevrolet dealers from 1987 through 1991.

Carlisle: Major annual Corvette show in Carlisle, Pennsylvania.

Casting Number: Usually refers to the GM number cast into engine blocks, but can refer to cast numbers on other components.

Challenge Cars: Corvettes factory-built for the all-Corvette race series sanctioned by the Sports Car Club of America (SCCA) in 1988 and 1989.

Classic: 1953 through 1962 model Corvettes.

Collector Edition: Specially equipped and trimmed 1982 Corvette model.

Convertible: Soft top Corvettes built between 1956-1975, and starting again in 1986.

Corvette Black Book: Pocket "bible" of Corvette facts.

Coupe: 1963-1967 fixed-top Corvettes; also T-top 1968-1982 models, and removable-roof panel 1984 and newer models.

Cypress: Major January Corvette show in Cypress Gardens, Florida.

Doghouse: Fuel injection plenum chamber, 1957-1965 models.

Duntov: Zora Arkus-Duntov, legendary chief engineer, called "father" of the Corvette; also, National Corvette Restorers Society (NCRS) award.

Drum Brake: All Corvettes built before 1965 have them, but the term usually refers to the few 1965 models without disc brakes.

Elephant Ears: Rubberized canvas front brake air scoops for some 1957 through 1964 Corvettes with heavy-duty racing brakes.

FOA: Factory optional accessory.

Flint: Michigan site of first Corvette assembly facility. Three-hundred 1953 Corvettes were built there. Also, site of GM engine plant.

Four+Three: Doug Nash four-speed manual transmission with three overdrives available in Corvettes from 1984 through 1988.

Fuelie: 1957 through 1965 fuel injected Corvette.

Gold Certified: Top Bloomington award for factory originality.

Gold Line: Optional gold stripe tire for 1965-1966 models.

Gold Spinner: Top award at Vettefest show in Chicago, Illinois.

Gymkhana: Optional 1974 through 1982 suspension package.

Headrest: Optional headrests for 1966 through 1968 models.

King of the Hill: Media terminology for the 1990 Corvette ZR-1.

Knock Off: Cast aluminum wheel optional for 1963 through 1966 models. Evidence suggests 1963 was over-the-counter only.

Knoxville: Major annual Corvette show in Knoxville, Tennessee.

LPO: Limited Production Option.

LT1: High performance engine option for 1970, 1971 and 1972. Also, redesigned base engine starting in 1992.

Mid Year: 1963 through 1967 Corvette.

Multiport: Technically accurate description for the fuel injection of 1985 and newer models, but especially for 1992 and newer.

NCCC: National Council of Corvette Clubs.

NCRS: National Corvette Restorers Society.

NOS: New old stock (brand new old parts).

Numbers Match: Stamped and cast codes indicate original parts.

Over The Counter: Parts sold at Chevrolet dealers' parts departments.

Pace Car: Limited edition replica of the 1978 Indianapolis 500 pace car. Also, all 1986 convertibles were "pace car" replicas.

Pilot: Pre-production prototype built on factory assembly line.

Prefix: Alpha stamping into engine identifying engine build plant.

Red Line: Optional 1967 through 1969 red stripe tire.

Replacement: Part furnished by Chevrolet which fits and functions, but doesn't necessarily duplicate the original.

Roadster: Enthusiast term for 1953 through 1955 Corvette.

RPO: Regular Production Option.

St. Louis: Site of Corvette assembly factory from 1954 through 1981.

Selective Ride: Adjustable shock absorber system first available in 1989.

SIR: Supplemental Inflatable Restraint (airbag).

Side Pipes: Optional 1965 through 1967, and 1969 side-mount exhausts.

Silver Anniversary: Two-tone silver 1978 paint option.

Small Block: V-8 engines of 265, 283, 305 (1980 California only), 327 and 350 cubic-inch displacement.

Solid Axle: 1953 through 1962 Corvette.

Split Window: 1963 Corvette coupe.

Sticker: Price posted on government-required window sticker; retail.

Stingray: 1969 through 1976 Corvette.

Sting Ray: 1963 through 1967 Corvette.

Suffix: Alpha stamping into engine which identifies engine usage.

Survivor: Bloomington award for unrestored Corvette with a majority of original components.

T-top: 1969 through 1982 coupe with two removable roof panels.

Teak: Teakwood steering wheel optional in 1965 and 1966.

Tele: Optional telescopic steering column.

Tonawanda: GM engine plant near Buffalo, New York.

Top Flight: NCRS judging award for factory originality.

Vettefest: Major annual Corvette show in Chicago, Illinois.

Tuned Port: 1985 through 1991 fuel injection with "tuned" runners.

VIN: Vehicle Identification Number.

ZR-1: Corvette model introduced in 1990 with special 32-valve, overhead cam engine; also, 1970 through 1972 engine option (ZR1).

INSTRUCTIONS

The *Corvette Black Book* is designed to help you understand and enjoy Corvettes. It does so by presenting useful and interesting data in a readily accessible format. Perhaps more so than any other auto enthusiast group, Corvette owners are conscious of details. You've seen the term "numbers match" associated with Corvettes. This book will help you understand what those numbers are and what they mean.

But numbers are only part of the story, part of an individual Corvette's history. Each Corvette model year has scores of unique features. Within a model year, the range of colors and options available, except for the first couple of years of Corvette production, permitted thousands of combinations. For most Corvette model years, it was theoretically possible that no two Corvettes were built with exactly the same combination of options, colors and equipment. That wasn't the case, of course, but it was possible. Understanding how to determine what is rare and what isn't is another part of understanding an individual Corvette's mystique. Again, the *Corvette Black Book* can help.

Before explaining how to interpret the data presented here, some words of caution. This book was first published in 1978. It has been updated and refined at least annually since, often several times within a year. It's done by starting with Chevrolet records, documents and personnel, then soliciting the critiques of expert Corvette enthusiasts around the country, including dealers, authors, concours judges, owners, restorers and others. Unsolicited mail from enthusiasts, always welcome, sometimes exposes the possibility of an error or an omission. New data or clarifications are always surfacing. In short, it is a never-ending process. This *Corvette Black Book* you are holding is the most complete and accurate yet published. But next year's will be even better.

Yet this book, or any published material, must not be relied upon as a final, definitive guide, especially for determining a Corvette's authenticity or desirability. A high percentage of data presented here is accurate for a high percentage of Corvettes produced, but nothing is absolute in the world of automobiles, especially Corvettes. Deviations are possible in almost every category. In the end, you must balance published data with good judgement, logic and common sense.

Why these cautions? Because of the nature of auto production, a totally accurate listing of automotive facts, particularly relating to part numbers, is impossible. General Motors does not document every production change made. The replacement parts aspect of any auto company is geared to function, not originality. Parts are interchanged during production when shortages occur. New parts inventories are not always phased in so that all "old" parts are used before the new. Frankly, General Motors and other auto companies have had more important things to worry about than documenting their production practices for the benefit of future enthusiasts, restorers, or historians. It wouldn't be nearly as much fun for all of us now if they had.

Former employes of the St. Louis Corvette plant tell of times when the assembly line was about to run out of parts, door trim screws or bumper bolts perhaps, and someone was dispatched to the closest hardware store to find an acceptable substitute so the line could keep rolling. In your analysis of a Corvette, by all means be very critical and conscious of details. There is no question that accuracy and originality are important

6

factors in a Corvette's desirability. At the same time, keep an open mind. Exceptions to practically every rule are possible.

Use this book as an aid in determining originality and correctness. If you find a discrepancy, don't assume something is wrong, only that it may be. Keep looking. What at first appears incorrect may in fact be legitimate, one of only a handful, and thus very desirable. Or it may be the first thread in the unraveling of a completely bogus Corvette. Bogus as in the Corvette that's been resurrected from the dead, with the majority of its components salvaged from other carcasses. There's nothing wrong with such a rebirth, except when it is being represented as an untouched, low mileage original, or anything else it is not.

In some ways, the emphasis on numbers has run amok. There has been so much emphasis on original Corvette parts and components that serious counterfeiting has resulted. As an owner, understand that what you do with your own Corvette is largely your own business. There are laws regarding safety and emissions, of course, but an owner has every right to change colors, interiors, components and the like. It is the representation of an automobile as something it is not that can constitute fraud. Misrepresentation usually doesn't include the bit of embellishment engaged in by most sellers. It is something like converting a base-engine 1967 Corvette convertible into a 435-horsepower, numbers-matching, low mileage "original" with phony documentation to "prove" it. Be careful in your representations, and in interpreting those of others.

Knowledge is power and the *Corvette Black Book* can put powerful knowledge in your back pocket. The following pages contain graphs of Corvette price and volume trends, and a brief written overview (chronology) of the Corvette's history from 1953 to present. The largest and most useful section is the data section starting on page 20 in which two pages are devoted to each Corvette model year from 1953 to present. A great deal of data is condensed here, and it is important to understand how this information is presented and how to interpret it.

NUMBERS

The most familiar and widely used number appearing on an automobile is its *vehicle number*, or vehicle identification number (VIN). It may also be called the serial number, or body-chassis number. Each automobile's vehicle number is unique to that automobile. Think of the vehicle number as an individual Corvette's fingerprint, something shared with no other Corvette. It is the vehicle number that now appears on automobile titles and registrations, though in the past some states have used other numbers such as engine numbers.

The vehicle number is assigned prior to vehicle assembly. Each car receives its own individual number in sequence. The format of the vehicle number for Corvettes has changed several times over the years, but it will, at the very least, indicate the model year and when the Corvette was assembled relative to others during the same model year. Scrutinizing an individual Corvette's place in the production sequence is simplified by the fact that, except for a two month period in 1981 when Corvettes were built simultaneously at St. Louis, Missouri, and at Bowling Green, Kentucky, all Corvettes during any given model year have been built at one facility.

The vehicle number is stamped or etched into a plate which is attached to the body of each Corvette. The location of the plate itself is different for different years. From 1953 through early 1960, the plate was attached to the driver-side door post. Most 1960 and all 1961 and 1962

Corvettes have the plate attached to the steering column in the engine compartment. The 1963 through 1967 models have the plate attached to the instrument panel support brace, visible under the glove box. For the benefit of police, federal law required that the vehicle number be visible from outside the vehicle starting in 1968. So, for 1968 and newer Corvettes, the plate is attached to the top surface of the instrument panel, or to the A-pillar (windshield post), both locations visible through the windshield from outside the vehicle.

To assist in theft recovery and identification, the vehicle number is also stamped into a Corvette's frame in several locations. And from 1960 on, the sequential portion of the vehicle number is also stamped into the engine block, on a pad just forward of the passenger-side head.

Except for 1955, the vehicle number did not reveal which engine a Corvette had until 1972 when the numbering format was changed to include an engine code. Starting in 1963, all vehicle numbers have carried a code differentiating coupe from convertible.

The *Corvette Black Book* lists the vehicle numbering sequence for all Corvette model years from first vehicle produced to last. In most cases, this was a single sequence for the Corvettes produced during a model year. But there were exceptions, including 1978 when the pace car replicas had a separate sequence, 1981 when two plants produced Corvettes simultaneously, 1986 when coupes and convertibles had separate sequences, 1990-1995 when ZR-1s had separate sequences, and in 1996 when Grand Sports had separate sequences.

Generally, when a single sequence was used for a model year, the last five digits of the last vehicle's number will equal that year's total production. For years with two sequences, the total of the last vehicle numbers in each sequence equals total production. One exception is 1973 when 4,000 vehicle identification numbers were somehow skipped. In 1973, total production was 4,000 units less than the last five digits of the final vehicle. Also, from 1953 through 1956, the first vehicles produced had vehicle numbers ending with 01001. For these years, final production was 1,000 units less than the last five digits of the last Corvette produced.

It is important to know that Corvette "plants" like Flint, St. Louis and Bowling Green refer to Corvette vehicle assembly. Corvette engines have never been built in the same plant as vehicle assembly. Engines are built in dedicated plants which build engines for other vehicles in the GM lineup.

For Corvettes, engine plant location is simple enough. The six-cylinder engines used in 1953, all Corvette "big block" engines, and the 305-cubic-inch engine used in 1980 California Corvettes, were all built at GM's Tonawanda, New York, engine plant. The manufacture of the LT5 engine, used exclusively in ZR-1 models starting in 1990, was subcontracted to Mercury Marine in Stillwater, Oklahoma. The 1954 and 1955 six-cylinder engines, and all other Corvette small block V8s through 1996 were built at the GM V-8 engine plant in Flint, Michigan. Starting in 1997, Corvette engines were built at GM's plant in Romulus, Michigan,

When a Corvette engine is assembled at an engine plant, an important number is stamped into the engine block. For 1953-1955 six-cylinders, the number is stamped on a machined pad just rear of the ignition distributor opening. For others, it is on a machined pad just forward of the cylinder head on the passenger side. For 1953, an "LAY" *prefix* preceded a six digit serial number which didn't match the vehicle number. For 1954 through 1956, a seven digit serial number, again not matching the vehicle number, was followed by an "F" indicating Flint engine build, and two numbers indicating year; for example, F56 for Flint 1956.

Starting in 1957, stamped engine numbers started with an alpha character indicating build plant ("F" for Flint through 1966, "V" for Flint after 1966, and "T" for Tonawanda). The next three or four digits designate date of engine manufacture. The last two (later three) characters are referred to as the *suffix* number, even though these digits are alpha not numeric. The suffix indicates the engine's intended use. An example of F0112RF would translate to be a fuel-injected engine (RF), built on January 12th (0112) at the Flint engine plant (F).

The suffix number is important and one of those that is presumed to be correct in a numbers-matching Corvette. Corvette engine suffix numbers have almost always been exclusive to Corvette usage. The number containing the suffix is hand-stamped into the engine during assembly by a worker using a tool containing the complete number set. The worker has several number sets to select from and constantly changes sets as engines move by on an assembly line. Were engines ever stamped incorrectly? Of course. And what happened if the error was recognized? No, the engine wasn't scrapped. The incorrect number was ground off with a pencil grinder, and the correct number stamped over the mistake.

When a Corvette engine is built, the engine plant knows the intended use of the engine, but not into which individual Corvette it will be installed. So when the engine is mated to a vehicle at the Corvette assembly plant, another set of numbers containing the sequential part of the vehicle identification number is stamped into the engine to key it to its specific body and chassis. The number is stamped into the same pad as the suffix number. This started sometime during 1960 production and has continued since. More than any other single number, it is this engine number's *match* to the vehicle number that constitutes the *matching numbers* terminology. It is also the first number to be forged in a counterfeit Corvette.

The *Corvette Black Book* also lists a *block* number for engines. This refers to a seven or eight digit block casting number which is cast into the block at the foundry. While a Corvette engine suffix is nearly always for Corvette use only, the same basic block casting is often used for other Chevrolet or General Motors products. Nevertheless, this is one more element in authenticating a Corvette. The complete casting number for six-cylinder Corvettes is located forward and just below the fuel pump mounting. For V8 engines, the complete number is located at the top rear of the driver side of the block, near the flywheel attachment. On later V8s, the last three digits of the block casting number are also found in the center side area of the engine on both sides.

The *head* numbers appearing in the *Corvette Black Book* refer to cylinder head casting numbers. These are normally visible only with the valve covers removed.

Other numbers listed include *carburetor, distributor, generator, alternator*, and *starter*. These are all engine components. Because of the probability of failure, it isn't unusual for any of these to have been replaced during a Corvette's lifetime. These are also the most difficult for any publication to document accurately and completely. As a general rule, the older the Corvette, the more accurate the component part listing appearing in the *Corvette Black Book* will be. This is because of the enthusiast interest in older models and the documentation done by enthusiasts and organizations. Later models have had less scrutiny, and the difficulty in seeing component numbers in the crowded engine bays of later Corvettes is another factor in making documentation more difficult.

Another category of numbers shown for some model years is *ending vehicle number*. This is simply the serial number of the last vehicle produced during the last day of the months listed. This information is not available for all years, and for some years only partial data exists. When a particular month is not listed, it means either that no cars were produced that month, or that the production records for that month are unavailable.

An individual Corvette has scores of date-coded parts not specifically listed in the *Corvette Black Book*. But one of particular importance and worthy of explanation here is the block casting date code. This is a date code indicating the date the block was cast in the foundry. Obviously, this does not match either the date of engine manufacture or vehicle manufacture. But it must precede engine and vehicle manufacture. Date codes for six-cylinder Corvette engines are found on the passenger side of the engine, near the starter solenoid. For most Corvette V8 engines, the date code is located at the rear, passenger-side of the block, near the casting number. Exceptions are 1965 through 1968 and early 1969 big blocks which have their date codes forward of the starter on the passenger side by the freeze plug, and 1965 small block #3858180 (cast at Tonawanda but built at Flint) which has its date code adjacent to its casting number.

Block date codes appear as three or four characters, an alpha followed by two or three numeric. The alpha denotes the month, "A" for January continuing through "L" for December. The date is indicated by the next one or two numbers; the year by the last single number. A date code of B129 indicates a block cast on February 12, 1959, 1969, 1979 or 1989.

FACTS

The *facts* section in the *Corvette Black Book* contains some of the details that make each year unique. This section is intended to supplement the hard data presented in the numbers, options, and colors sections. Don't assume a particular Corvette model year with a short facts section is somehow lacking in interest. The size of the facts section is determined by the lengths of the numbers, options and colors sections, not by the availability of unique features. One reason for including the chronology of all Corvette years is to include a more equally balanced presentation for all years, something not possible in the data section due to the long numbers, option and color listings, especially for years such as 1968 and 1969.

OPTIONS

Practically all Chevrolet written promotional literature and advertising over the years has contained some disclaimer like "accurate at press time, but manufacturer reserves the right to change options, colors, and prices without notice." Sure enough, these things do change, and not just at the introduction of new models. Corvette base prices have changed as often as four times in a single model year. Manufacturing problems, both within Chevrolet and at supplying vendors, may cause advertised options never to actually be available to consumers. An option appearing after the start of production may never appear in advertising or promotional brochures.

Understanding the options available during a particular Corvette year, especially what is "rare" and what isn't, is key to comprehending the hoopla surrounding certain Corvette models. The *Corvette Black Book* presents options in an straightforward table, listing the order code (usually Regular Production Option or RPO), a shorthand description of the option, the quantity sold or produced if known, and the retail price. Further explanations of specific option content, order restrictions, or other pertinent data are provided below the tables.

The quoted quantities sold or produced came directly or indirectly from Chevrolet. The methods of tracking Corvette option counts by Chevrolet has varied over the years, as has the accuracy. Some quantities for very early years are simply not available and may never be. Some quantities for specific options vary in different Chevrolet documents. In the current computer age, the counts appear to be precise, but even with the newest models some inconsistencies exist. While it might be tempting to criticize Chevrolet for a lack of absolutely accurate record keeping over the past decades of Corvette production, the reality is that the records are quite good considering the complexity and nature of Corvette production when options and option combinations are factored in.

The prices listed are not current market values. Option costs are retail, or "sticker" prices in effect when these Corvettes were sold new. Generally the prices listed are those in effect at the time of model introduction. Price changes during the year, especially base prices, were uncommon during the early years of Corvette production, but common starting in the sixties. Freight costs are generally not included in base vehicle prices, but dealer handling is.

COLORS

Prior to the 1963 model Corvette, no paint identification coding was affixed to the Corvette body. If an earlier Corvette is repainted carefully, the color can be changed without detection. Easier said than done, and most repaints can be spotted if inspected closely. Still, the lack of positive code verification keeps the color controversy brewing.

The "code" shown in the tables is the exterior color code which appears on a plate or label affixed to Corvette bodies starting in 1963. The plate is on the instrument panel support member under the glovebox for 1963 through 1967 models, on the driver door post for 1968 through 1982 models, and on a label for newer models inside the console glovebox lid.

Chevrolet used lacquer for the exterior body surfaces of Corvettes built in Flint and St. Louis. The 1957 and earlier Corvettes, except for 1957's Inca Silver and it's Imperial Ivory cove, were nitrocellulose lacquer. Inca Silver, its Imperial Ivory cove, and later lacquers were acrylic. The 1981 Corvettes built at Bowling Green and later models have an enamel-type paint with clearcoats.

For refinishing, the newer style paints used by Bowling Green are readily available. The acrylic lacquers are generally available from most paint jobbers. The nitrocellulose colors can be a problem, since many paint formulas for the older colors have been pulled from local suppliers by paint manufacturers. Restorers have the choice of cross-referencing to an acrylic equivalent, or using original nitrocellulose lacquer supplied by vendors servicing the old car market.

The chart paint quantities don't always add correctly due simply to record-keeping glitches. Wheel colors listed are for standard equipment. Interiors are those recommended by Chevrolet. Up until 1989, it had always been Chevrolet's policy to permit customers to override the recommended colors, so remember that different interior-exterior combinations from those shown in the charts are entirely possible. For a few years starting in 1989, Chevrolet removed the color-override option though it still happened in special cases. In 1994, Chevrolet reverted to its policy of generally letting customers choose whatever they wanted.

Interior color codes, added to Corvette bodies starting in 1963 along with exterior coding, are found under the color charts for each model year, along with other pertinent color data.

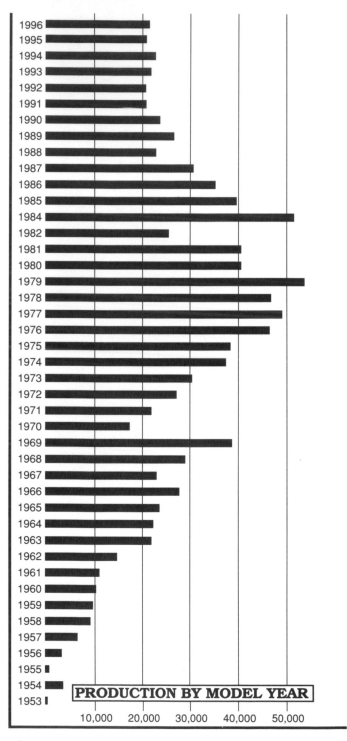

PRODUCTION BY MODEL YEAR

12

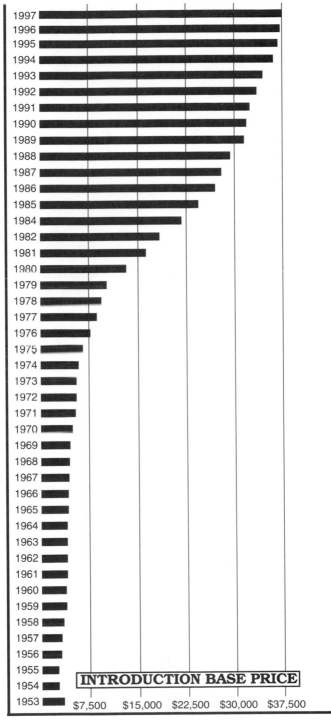

INTRODUCTION BASE PRICE

Year	
1997	
1996	
1995	
1994	
1993	
1992	
1991	
1990	
1989	
1988	
1987	
1986	
1985	
1984	
1982	
1981	
1980	
1979	
1978	
1977	
1976	
1975	
1974	
1973	
1972	
1971	
1970	
1969	
1968	
1967	
1966	
1965	
1964	
1963	
1962	
1961	
1960	
1959	
1958	
1957	
1956	
1955	
1954	
1953	

$7,500 $15,000 $22,500 $30,000 $37,500

CHRONOLOGY

1953: The first public viewing of the Corvette was in January 1953 at the Motorama display at the Waldorf Astoria hotel in New York City. By June, the Corvette was in production at a temporary facility in Flint, Michigan, where 300 Corvettes were built that year. All 1953 models were white with red interiors, and all had Powerglide automatic transmissions mated to 150hp, six-cylinder engines. It is the rarest of all Corvette model years.

1954: Corvette production moved to a renovated facility in St. Louis, Missouri where production started in December 1953. Chevrolet had projected annual sales of 10,000, but this was optimistic as 3,640 1954 Corvettes were built and nearly a third were unsold at year's end.. A mid-year camshaft change increased the six-cylinder engine's horsepower to 155 and all 1954s continued with Powerglide automatics. A beige interior and at least three new exterior colors, blue, red and black, were added.

1955: Next to 1953, this was the lowest volume Corvette with production a mere 700 units. Many predicted this would be the Corvette's last gasp, but Chevrolet held on, perhaps embarrassed by the success of Ford's two-seater 1955 Thunderbird. Nearly all 1955 Corvettes were fitted with Chevrolet's new 265ci, V-8 engine. A three-speed manual transmission was optional along with the Powerglide automatic.

1956: The chassis and interior were little changed, but the 1956 Corvette body was all-new, including roll-up glass windows with optional power assists. Interior choice was limited to red or beige, but six exteriors were available. For the first time, exteriors could be ordered in two-tones with a contrasting color in the side "cove." Engine choices were a base 210hp V8, a 225hp V8 with dual carburetion, and the dual-carb engine with special camshaft (unoffically rated at 240hp). Dr. Dick Thompson and his Corvette won the Sports Car Club of America (SCCA) Class C Production racing title. Sales increased to 3,467.

1957: An American automotive milestone, the 1957 Corvette was the first to combine fuel-injection with a four-speed manual transmission. Engine displacement increased to 283ci, and the most potent fuel-injected engine developed 283hp. Driving a 1957 Corvette, Dr. Dick Thompson and Gaston Audrey won the 12-hour Sebring in March 1957. Corvettes won the SCCA B Sports national title (J. E. Rose), and Class B Production Sports (Thompson). Sales jumped to 6,339.

1958: Design features included new body panels, new instrument panel with a centrally-mounted tachometer, and new upholstery. It was the first Corvette with four headlights and factory-installed seat belts. Corvettes were virtually unchallenged in SCCA Class B Production with Jim Jeffords taking the points championship. Sales increased to 9,168.

1959: The hood louvers and chrome trunk spears from the previous year were removed and a pure black interior color, the Corvette's first, was added. Jim Jeffords and his Corvette again won the SCCA Class B Production points championship. The top twenty positions were all claimed by Corvettes. Sales increased to 9,670, the last time a Corvette model sold less than 10,000 annually.

14

1960: In appearance, the 1960 was very similar to 1959, but 1960 was the first Corvette with an aluminum radiator (limited to high-lift camshaft engines), the last to have taillights formed into the rounded rear fenders, and the first to exclude the combination of automatic transmission and fuel-injected engine. It was also the first Corvette to exceed 10,000 in sales with 10,261. Ferrari offered strong competition in SCCA Class B Production but finished second to Bob Johnson and his Corvette.

1961: The 1961 Corvette had new rear styling, the first to feature the four taillight look that became a Corvette tradition. It was the last Corvette to feature optional two-tone side cove paint treatment and 283ci engines. It was the first with exhaust exits below the body and radiator expansion tanks. Production edged up slightly to 10,939. In SCCA Class B Production, Dr. Dick Thompson and his Corvette won the points championship. Porsche offered the best competition, placing fifth.

1962: Two-tone paint was no longer available for 1962. This was the last Corvette with a conventional trunk and the last with a solid rear axle. Engine displacement increased to 327ci. Powerglide transmissions had aluminum cases for weight savings. Sales jumped sharply to 14,531. Corvettes won the SCCA points championships for A Production (Dick Thompson) and B Production (Don Yenko).

1963: The 1963 Corvette featured a new chassis, including independent rear suspension, and a new body design, available for the first time in both coupe ("split window") and convertible styles. The second genuine Corvette milestone, the 1963 model was a tremendous success with sales of 21,513. Demand exceeded supply and many buyers waited months for delivery. Knock-off wheels were optional, but probably available only over-the-counter. Air conditioning and leather seats (saddle only) were available for the first time. Special racing package RPO Z06 initially included a 36-gallon fuel tank and was limited to coupes. Later, Z06 was available with convertibles and standard fuel tanks. Despite the significant Corvette chassis improvements, Carroll Shelby's Cobra also debuted in 1963 and its higher power-to-weight ratio enabled it to dethrone the Corvette in SCCA racing.

1964: The "split" was removed from coupe rear windows to improve visibility, and some styling details of 1963 were deleted including the simulated air vents in the hood and bright instrument trim. Knock-off wheels were definitely delivered with Corvettes to retail customers. The number of colors available for optional leather seating increased. Sales continued strong, climbing to 22,229.

1965: "Big block" engines made their Corvette appearance as RPO L78 with 396ci and 425hp. Fuel injection was discontinued. Four-wheel disc brakes became standard equipment, but some drum-brake 1965s were built as a delete-cost option. Popular options first available in 1965 included side-mount exhausts, teakwood steering wheels, telescopic steering columns, and goldwall tires. Sales totaled 23,562.

1966: Displacement of optional big block engines increased to 427ci. It was the first year of availability for headrests and shoulder harnesses. It was the last for knock-off wheels, which in 1966 had brush-finish center cones instead of bright. Seats had more pleats to reduce seam splitting. Sales were the highest in the Corvette's history up to that time, 27,720.

1967: Last of the 1963-67 "mid year" series, the 1967 is now an enthusiast favorite, but it was somewhat ignored at the time as buyers awaited the new model coming the following year. The 1967 optional aluminum "bolt on" wheel was unique to the year. The side fender louver treatment was unique, as was the hood for models with optional 427ci engines. Horsepower ratings ranged from the base engine's 300hp to 435hp for the RPO L71 engine. Output of the limited production RPO L88, of which only twenty were sold in 1967, exceeded 500hp but was intentionally understated to restrict its appeal to non-racing customers. Emergency brake handles for 1967 moved to between the seats from under the instrument panel, and this was the first Corvette with standard four-way flashers, dual master cylinders, turn signals with lane-change feature, and folding seatback latches. Sales declined to 22,940.

1968: The chassis remained virtually unchanged, but the body and interior for 1968 were completely new, based on the Mako Shark show car. But it wasn't called a Mako Shark as expected, or a Sting Ray as in 1963 through 1967. For the first time, the coupe featured removable roof panels (T-tops) and a removable rear window. Wheel width increased to seven inches. This was the first Corvette not to have side vent windows and the last with an ignition switch on the instrument panel. For better weight distribution, the battery was moved to a compartment behind the seats. Despite some media criticism of declining quality, 28,566 1968 Corvettes were sold, a new record.

1969: A strike interrupted 1969 production, so when Corvettes started rolling down the line again, Chevrolet's boss, John DeLorean, let them keep rolling for an extra four months. Production for 1969 was 38,762, a level not reached again until 1976. The 1969 looked much like the 1968, but it did have optional side exhausts, the ignition switch was moved to the steering column, map pockets were added to the instrument panel, and the steering wheel diameter was reduced to fifteen inches from sixteen. Wheel width increased from seven to eight inches. The Stingray (one word) name reappeared on the 1969 model. Small block engine displacement increased from 327ci to 350ci.

1970: Optional big block engine displacement increased to 454ci. The small block remained 350ci, but a new high performance RPO LT1 generated 370hp. This was the last year for high compression, full-output engines. The body shape was revised to include fender flares behind the wheels to minimize body damage from wheel-thrown debris. Production for 1970 models didn't begin until January 1970, and sales fell to 17,316, the lowest since 1962.

1971: This was the last Corvette to have the fiber-optics light monitoring system introduced with the 1968 model. Compression ratios were lowered in all engines to permit use of lower octane low lead and unleaded fuels. Production resumed a normal cycle and sales rebounded to 21,801.

1972: Alarm systems were optional on earlier Corvettes, but standard with the 1972 model. This was the last year for a removable rear window in coupes and the last with chrome bumpers front and rear. Horsepower ratings for all engines were reduced due to a change in the way power was measured. Instead of "gross" as before, it became a more realistic "net," which included losses from such things as accessories, air cleaners, and mufflers. Sales increased to 27,004.

1973: This model is easily recognized by its body-color front bumper system combined with conventional chrome rear bumpers. The change in front was dictated by new federal bumper legislation. The 1973 received a new hood which extended over the windshield wipers, eliminating the separate wiper lid used between 1968 and 1972. Also responding to federal requirements, all 1973 Corvettes had metal beams added to the inside of doors for side-impact protection. Sales reached 30,464, with just 4,943 of these convertibles.

1974: This was the first Corvette with body-color bumpers front and rear. These models are distinguished by the vertical split in their rear bumpers, unique to the year. As the last Corvette model without catalytic converters for emission control, it was the last to legally use leaded fuel (other than export). It was also the last year for availability of a "big block" engine. 37,502 were sold, of which 5,474 were convertibles.

1975: It was the first with a one-piece rear bumper skin, the first with catalytic converters, and the first with a pointless (high energy ignition) distributor. Most noteworthy is that the 1975 was the last year for Corvette convertibles in this body style. At the time, most thought it was the last Corvette convertible, period. But resurrection of the convertible in 1986 proved that untrue. Sales increased in 1975 to 38,465, of which 4,629 were convertibles.

1976: The convertible was gone, but that didn't stop 46,558 people from purchasing new 1976 Corvettes. Aluminum wheels were genuinely available after a false start in 1973. An underpan made of steel was added for body rigidity and heat isolation. This was the first Corvette with in-glass heating elements in the rear window defogger, instead of forced air.

1977: The 1977 was the last Corvette with the vertical rear window treatment started in 1968. Vinyl seating surfaces were banished from Corvettes in 1977. Leather was standard, but cloth with leather trim could be substituted at no cost. The console was a new design and accepted a wider variety of radios thanks to its deeper design. Sales were 49,213.

1978: Corvettes were hot topics of conversation in 1978, the marque's twenty-fifth anniversary. Chevrolet offered silver anniversary paint schemes, and "pace car," replicas of the Corvette used to pace the 1978 Indianapolis 500 race. Hoopla prior to the 1978 race boosted pace car prices to double their $13,653.21 sticker prices, but things settled down in time. The 1978 body was redesigned with a fastback rear window, new instrument panel and more. Sales were 46,776, including 6,502 pace car replicas.

1979: New seats, borrowed from the previous pace car replica model, were standard in 1979. Add-on front and rear spoilers, also pace car pieces, were optional in 1979 as RPO D80. Sales soared to 53,807, the highest in the Corvette's history. Even 1984's total, inflated because there was no 1983 model, was less.

1980: Corvettes had a new look in 1980 thanks to new front and rear bumper caps with integrated spoilers. Federal law required that 1980 cars, Corvettes included, have speedometers with maximum readings of 85 mph. Gulp. In an unusual turn of events relating to California's tougher emission standards, Corvette buyers there got a 305ci engine instead of 350ci in 1980, the only year this happened. Sales declined to 40,614.

1981: The St. Louis plant ended production, building its last Corvette on August 1, 1981. The new assembly plant in Bowling Green started production June 1, so for two months both plants built simultaneously. St. Louis built mostly all solid colors using lacquer as it always had, and Bowling Green built two-tones using a new enamel-type paint with clearcoats. A total of 40,606 were built including 8,995 at Bowling Green.

1982: This model ended the body series that began in 1968, and the chassis design that began in 1963. A "collector edition" had silver/beige paint, special trim and a hatchback rear window. At $22,537.59, it was the first Corvette base price to exceed $20K. No manual transmissions were available. Sales were 25,407 including 6,759 Collector Editions.

1984: This new Corvette was introduced as a 1984 model in March 1983. It met all 1984 federal requirements so the expense of a model changeover six months later was saved. Except for its carryover driveline, the 1984 was all new. A coupe with a single removable roof panel, it featured digital instruments, an optional (no-cost) four-speed manual transmission with overdrives in the top three gears, new Girlock disc brakes, single front and rear plastic leaf springs mounted transversely, multi-adjustable seating, and extraordinary handling praised by media worldwide. The extended production run totaled 51,547, second highest in Corvette's history.

1985: Ride quality was improved by reducing spring rates for base and RPO Z51 models. Z51's had thicker stabilizer to compensate for the softer springs. New Bosch fuel injection featured tuned runners, a mass airflow sensor and individual injectors for each cylinder. Power increased from 205hp to 230hp with no fuel economy penalty. Production was 39,729.

1986: Convertible models returned in 1986. Corvette paced the 1986 Indy 500 and all 1986 convertibles were replicas, but didn't have special paint or options. Anti-lock brakes (ABS) were standard. Aluminum heads were introduced during 1986. All convertibles had them; early coupes didn't. All 1986 Corvettes had center, high-mount stoplamps. Production of 35,109 included 7,315 convertibles.

1987: The new RPO Z52 combined elements of RPO Z51 with softer base springs. Roller valve lifters reduced engine friction and added 5hp. Callaway twin-turbo conversions were available through some Chevy dealers as RPO B2K. Not a factory option, B2K triggered a special build at Bowling Green before shipment to Callaway Engineering in Old Lyme, Connecticut for engine conversions. Callaway production for 1987 was 184. Total Corvette production was 30,632, including 10,625 convertibles.

1988: A 35th anniversary edition combined white exterior with white leather and black accents. Suspensions were redesigned for zero scrub to reduce wheel fight. Wheel offsets changed and two new wheel designs were added. Street-legal Corvettes (56) were built for the Corvette Challenge SCCA race series. Callaway built 124 twin-turbos. Black interiors were new. Total Corvette production was 22,789.

1989: Bowling Green built 60 cars for the Corvette Challenge race series, of which just over 30 were converted to race use. A new ZF 6-speed manual transmission was introduced. The RPO FX3 adjustable suspension permitted shock absorber firmness change with a console-mounted switch. Callaway sold 69 twin-turbos. Production totaled 26,412.

18

1990: RPO ZR1 included special rear body panels and an aluminum-block LT5 engine designed by Lotus and Chevrolet. LT5 engines were built by Mercury Marine, but cars were assembled on-line at Bowling Green. Interiors were redesigned with a driver-side airbag, and hybrid instruments (analog tach and secondary gauges; digital speedo). Corvette built 23 special-option cars for the SCCA World Challenge series. Callaway sold 58 twin turbos. Total Corvette sales were 23,646, including 3,049 ZR-1s.

1991: Base and ZR-1 Corvettes had restyled fronts. Rears of base models looked similar to the ZR-1. New RPO Z07 combined elements of discontinued Z51 with the adjustable suspension. Wheels were a new design. Callaway ended twin turbo production with 62 1991 units. Total Corvette production was 20,639, including 2,044 ZR-1s.

1992: The base engine (LT1) was redesigned. It remained 350ci and two valves per cylinder, but output increased to 300hp. All 1992 Corvettes were equipped with traction control called Acceleration Slip Regulation (ASR). It limited acceleration wheel spin with spark retard, throttle closedown and brake intervention. New Goodyear GS-C tires were standard. Total production was 20,479, including 502 ZR-1s.

1993: A 40th Anniversary option had a Ruby Red exterior and interior, and special trim. Cylinder head and valvetrain changes boosted ZR-1 power from 375 to 405hp. A passive keyless entry (PKE) system, had a transmitter to lock and unlock doors by proximity. Base Corvettes had smaller front wheels (8.5x17) and tires (P255/45ZR17) and larger rear tires (P285/40AR17). Total production was 21,590, including 448 ZR-1s.

1994: The interior had a passenger-side airbag, new door trim panels with pockets, and new seat designs. All seats were leather. Convertible rear windows were glass (with in-glass defrosters) instead of plastic. Air conditioning systems were modified to use R-134A refrigerant. Goodyear Extended Mobility (run flat) tires were optional with some models. Electronic control and a brake pedal safety interlock were included with automatic transmissions. Production was 23,330, including 448 ZR-1s.

1995: The exterior was changed with restyling of the front fender vents. It was the ZR-1's last year. Larger brakes, previously included with Z07 and ZR-1 models, were standard. Production of Indy 500 pace car replicas, all Dark Purple over Arctic White convertibles, was limited to 527. Total production was 20,742, including 448 ZR-1's.

1996: Two special models were offered, a "Collector Edition" in Sebring Silver and a limited -production "Grand Sport" in Admiral Blue with white center stripe. The Grand Sport included the new LT4 engine with 30 additional horsepower compared to the base 300hp LT1 engine. LT4 engines required manual transmissions; LT1s required automatics. Production was 21,536 of which 1,000 were Grand Sports.

1997: This was the most-changed Corvette ever with redesigned body, interior, and suspension. The powertrain featured a brand-new aluminum-block, 345-hp pushrod V8 (LS1) driving a rear transaxle with either 4-speed automatic or 6-speed manual. Initially available as a coupe with removable roof panel, this model had 17" wheels in front and 18" in rear. Though wheelbase increased over eight inches and most other dimensions were increased slightly, weight overall was reduced by about eighty pounds.

1953 CORVETTE
Production: 300 roadsters

1953 NUMBERS

Vehicle: E53F001001 through E53F001300

Prefix: LAY: 235ci, 150hp

Block: 3701481: 235ci, 150hp, fd   3835911: 235ci, 150hp, sd

Head: 3836066: 235ci, 150hp,

Carburetor: Carter 2066S #3706151: 235ci, 150hp, fd
Carter 2066SA #3706989: 235ci, 150hp, sd

Distributor: 1112314: 235ci, 150hp

Generator: 1102793: 235ci, 150hp

Starter: 1107109: 235ci, 150hp

Ending Vehicle: Jun 53: 001002
Dec 53: 001300

Abbreviations: ci=cubic inch, fd=first design, hp=horsepower, sd=second design.

1953 FACTS

• The first Corvette was built on June 30, 1953, in Flint, Michigan. The 1953 factory wasn't a factory at all, but a temporary facility in the back of the customer delivery garage, an old building on Van Slyke Avenue. By year's end, 300 1953 model Corvettes were built, much by hand, as production processes were developed for assembling the Corvette's revolutionary fiberglass body. As planned, production for 1954 models moved to St. Louis and began in December 1953.

• Of the 300 1953 Corvettes built, about 225 are accounted for today. The third and fourth Corvettes built at Flint are alive and well in the hands of private owners. Although one theory is that the first two 1953 serial numbers were assigned to Motorama show cars, and that the first Corvette off the line in Flint was actually number three, officially the first two cars built at Flint were engineering prototypes destroyed in testing. Conclusive documentation to support either case has not been found.

• Due to a shortage of Corvette wheel covers, some of the first 1953 Corvettes built were fitted with "dome" wheel covers common to Chevrolet passenger cars. The twenty-seventh Corvette was delivered to its owner with correct Corvette wheel covers, so it is thought perhaps the first twenty-five Corvettes had the temporary dome style. It is possible that dealers replaced some of the dome caps with correct covers.

• Standard 1953 Corvette wheel covers (1953-1955) were single-stamped discs with two chrome "spinner" ornaments attached parallel to a central Chevrolet bow tie emblem. A few early examples, thought to be from a vendor test run, had the spinners mounted perpendicular to the emblem.

• Early wheel disc spinners were plated brass forgings, but vendors later changed to plated zinc die castings.

• Wire wheels were never factory options, but some, both real and simulated, were added by dealers.

• Antennas were standard with all 1953 Corvettes and consisted of a mesh screen fiberglassed into the inside surface of the trunk lid.

• Trunk lids of 1953 models generally did not have the moisture absorbent container for the license recess common to 1954 and 1955 models.

• The starters in all 1953s used two-field ignition coils.

• Early 1953 Corvettes (up to #175) used a foot-operated windshield washer assembly. Later are vacuum operated.

• Three separate "bullet" style air inlets were used for all 1953s.

1953 FACTS

• The 1953 Corvettes all had two interior hood releases, one for each exterior hood latch.
• All 1953s had "short" exhaust extensions.
• The valve cover of the 1953 Corvette was a unique variation of the standard 1953 Chevrolet passenger car cover. The Corvette version was flattened at the forward end for hood clearance. The cover differed from later years by its dual center hold-down bolts. Later covers were held by bolts around the perimeter. The 1953 cover had the words "Blue Flame" on the passenger side and "Special" on the driver side.
• Three gas filler door hinges were used. The first, used to about #20, tended to chip paint. The second corrected that, but limited access. A third design, appearing between #83 and #90, corrected both problems..
• The 1953 brake and fuel lines ran outside the chassis frame. Later models, starting early in 1954 production, ran inboard of the frame.
• Ignition shielding consisted of upper and lower formed metal shields. They were painted, not plated.
• The engine block, head, valve cover, and the intake and exhaust manifolds were painted in blue-green engine enamel.
• The 1953 (and early 1954) radiator surge tank was unique. Its surface was smooth. Later units had two stamped radial rigidity bands.
• The 1953 carburetor connecting linkage was a one-piece stamping.
• The location of the fuel filter in the 1953 model was in the fuel line, just forward of the front carburetor.
• Trunk mats for 1953 models were slightly smaller than later years.
• 1953 engine exhaust valves were shorter than later models.
• The road draft tube in most 1953 models had a smooth top surface. A few 1953s and all later units were stamped with an "X" for rigidity.

1953 OPTIONS

CODE	DESCRIPTION	QTY	RETAIL$
2934	Base Corvette Convertible	300	$3,498.00
101A	Heater	300	91.40
101B	AM Radio, signal seeking	300	145.15

• A 235ci, 150hp engine, Powerglide automatic transmission, vinyl interior trim, whitewall tires, windshield washers, and soft top were included in the base price.
• Prices were effective October 16, 1953. Base price included federal excise tax, and $248.00 delivery and handling. Prices did not include local taxes and other dealer charges. Prices were suggested by Chevrolet and some dealers may have charged different prices.
• Although listed as options, all 1953 Corvettes were built with heaters and radios. Customers could not delete these items.
• The 1953 signal-seeking AM radio was the same as the 1954 unit, except 1953 did not have Conelrad national defense markings.
• Auxiliary hardtops were not available for 1953 models as factory options or as Chevrolet-sponsored dealer accessories. However, aftermarket companies manufactured removable hardtops for 1954-1955 Corvettes and some of these were retrofitted to 1953 models.
• The 1953 heater was not a fresh air type; that is, it recirculated interior cockpit air only.
• All 1953 Corvettes were equipped with tube-type whitewall tires.

1953 COLORS

EXTERIOR	QTY	SOFT TOP	WHEELS	INTERIOR
Polo White	300	Black	Red	Red

• Interior and exterior combination shown was the only one available. There were no exceptions.
• Interiors and exteriors were not coded to individual cars.
• All 1953 Corvette soft tops were black canvas.

1954 CORVETTE
Production: 3,640 roadsters

1954 NUMBERS

Vehicle: E54S001001 through E54S004640

Suffix: YG: 235ci, 150hp, 155hp

Block: 3835911: 235ci, 150hp, 155hp

Head: 3836241: 235ci, 150hp, 155hp

Carburetor: Carter 2066SA #3706989: 235ci, 150hp, 155hp

Distributor: 1112314: 235ci, 150hp, 155hp

Starter: 1107109: 235ci, 150hp, 155hp (early two-coil design)
1108035: 235ci, 150hp, 155hp (later four-coil design)

Ending Vehicle: Dec 53: 001014

Abbreviations: ci=cubic inch, hp=horsepower

1954 FACTS

• Chevrolet started production of 1954 Corvettes in a renovated St. Louis assembly plant in December 1953. The plant was designed to build 10,000 Corvettes annually. Demand was misjudged, as it would be six years (1960) before Corvette exceeded 10,000 in annual sales.

• The Blue Flame Six engines used in all 1954 Corvettes had a power rating of either 150hp or 155hp. The extra horsepower resulted from a camshaft design change made during 1954 production. Externally, the engines looked the same, but the more powerful version can be detected by inspecting the camshaft. Later camshafts had three dots between the fifth and sixth inlet cam lobes.

• Early production 1954 models had two interior hood releases. Later models had a single interior release to activate both hood latches.

• The window storage bag for the 1954 was color-keyed to the car's interior. The design was more square than the 1953. The 1954 type also had a strap to permit anchoring to the forward vertical trunk partition panel.

• The 1954 valve cover was similar to the redesigned 1954 Chevrolet passenger car's cover. Both were attached to the head by stovebolts around the perimeter. The 1954 Corvette's valve cover was either chrome plated or painted engine enamel blue. "Blue Flame" and "150" decals, reading from the passenger side, were affixed to the painted covers.

• Early 1954s had the "bullet" air inlets common to the 1953 model. But 1954s later than #002906 had a dual "pot" apparatus, intended in part to reduce the possibility of engine fires.

• All 1954 Corvettes had six-volt electrical systems.

• Early 1954 Corvettes had short exhaust extensions. Models later than #002523 had longer extensions with built-in baffles. Both styles were originally stainless steel.

• Ignition shielding consisted of upper and lower stamped metal shields, either painted or chromed. Most 1954 Corvettes appear now with both shields painted or both shields chromed, but the factory did not necessarily match the shields on individual cars.

• The 1954 starters had four field coils, except for very early models which had a two-coil style.

• The road draft tube in 1954 models had an "X" stamped in the top surface for rigidity. Most 1953 tubes were smooth.

• The 1954's radiator surge tank, except for very early, had two stamped radial rigidity bands formed in the tank. All were chrome plated.

• The 1954's brake and fuel lines were routed inboard of the frame members, except for very early models.

• The 1954 carburetor linkage was a fabricated, three-piece link.

1954 OPTIONS

CODE	DESCRIPTION	QTY	RETAIL $
2934	Base Corvette Convertible	3,640	$2,774.00
100	Directional Signal	3,640	16.75
101	Heater	3,640	91.40
102	AM Radio, signal seeking	3,640	145.15
290B	Whitewall Tires, 6.70x15	3,640	26.90
313M	Powerglide Automatic Transmission	3,640	178.35
420A	Parking Brake Alarm	3,640	5.65
421A	Courtesy Lights	3,640	4.05
422A	Windshield Washer	3,640	11.85

• A 235ci, 150hp (or 155hp) engine, vinyl interior trim, and soft top were included in the base price.

• Prices included federal excise taxes. Local taxes and dealer charges were not included. Prices were effective October 28, 1954. Initial 1954 pricing was the same as 1953. Prices were suggested by Chevrolet and original customer sales records indicate that the actual prices charged by dealers varied both high and low.

• By listing the Powerglide automatic transmission as an option, the option list implies that a manual transmission was standard equipment. Not true. All 1954 Corvettes had the "optional" Powerglide automatic transmission; in fact, it is nearly certain that all 1954s were built with all options.

• The 1954 signal-seeking AM radio was the same as 1953's, except all but early 1954 radios had 640-kilocycle and 1240-kilocycle Conelrad national defense emergency markings.

• Auxiliary hardtops were not available for 1954 models as factory options or as Chevrolet-sponsored dealer accessories. However, aftermarket companies manufactured removable hardtops for 1954 (and 1953, 1955) Corvettes and some Chevrolet dealers sold them.

• The 1954 heater was not a fresh air type; that is, it recirculated interior cockpit air only.

• All 1954s were built with windshield washer systems. They were vacuum-operated, activated by a button on the windshield wiper switch.

• Tires were changed during 1954 production from tube-type to tubeless. Because different manufacturers supplied tires, it is probable that both types were used simultaneously for some time period.

1954 COLORS

EXTERIOR	QTY(est)	SOFT TOP	WHEELS	INTERIOR
Polo White	3,230	Beige	Red	Red
Pennant Blue	300	Beige	Red	Beige
Sportsman Red	100	Beige	Red	Red
Black	4	Beige	Red	Red

• Exterior color quantities are not from Chevrolet records. These are estimates based on surveys, theories, and other data. They should not be relied upon as precise quantities.

• Suggested interiors shown. Other combinations were possible.

• Interiors and exteriors were not coded to individual cars. The Polo White, Pennant Blue, Sportsman Red, and Black exteriors are those known to have been used during 1954 production.

• Based on original owner reports, there is a reasonable probability that some 1954 Corvettes were painted exterior colors other than Polo White, Pennant Blue, Sportsman Red or Black. Possibilities include, but are not limited to, Metallic Green and Metallic Bronze. Paint vendor documentation confirms the intent to offer additional colors, but production records have not surfaced to positively confirm actual build.

• All 1954 Corvette soft tops were specified to be beige canvas with top bows painted to match, and it is believed all were. However, the owner of a very late 1954 (eight units from the end of production) has reported that based on old home movies, his car appeared to have a white top when purchased new in 1954.

1955 CORVETTE
Production: 700 roadsters

1955 NUMBERS

Vehicle: VE55S001001 through VE55S001700
• For six-cylinder models, "V" is omitted.

Suffix: FG: 265ci, 195hp, at   YG: 235ci, 155hp, at (6-cyl)
GR: 265ci, 195hp, mt

Block: 3703524: 265ci, 195hp   3835911: 235ci, 155hp (6-cyl)

Head: 3703523: 265ci, 195hp   3836241: 235ci, 155hp (6-cyl)

Carburetor: Carter 2066SA #3706989: 235ci, 155hp (6-cyl)
Carter 2218S #3717687: 265ci, 195hp, fd
Carter 2351S #3724158: 265ci, 195hp, sd

Distributor: 1110847: 265ci, 195hp, without vacuum advance
1110855: 265ci, 195hp, with vacuum advance
1112314: 235ci, 155hp (6-cyl)

Generator: 1102025: 265ci, 195hp   1102793: 235ci, 155hp (6-cyl)

Starter: 1107627: 265ci, 195hp, fd   1108035: 235ci, 155hp (6-cyl)
1107645: 265ci, 195hp, sd

Ending Vehicle: Jan 55: 001027   May 55: 001300   Sep 55: 001599
Feb 55: 001110   Jun 55: 001389   Oct 55: 001634
Mar 55: 001150   Jul 55: 001489   Nov 55: 001688
Apr 55: 001200   Aug 55: 001555   Dec 55: 001700

Abbreviations: at=automatic transmission, ci=cubic inch, fd=first design, hp=horsepower, mt=manual transmission, sd=second design.

1955 FACTS

• Outward appearance of the 1955 Corvette nearly duplicated the previous two years, but the big news was the V8 engine under the Corvette's hood. The new 265ci engine that debuted in 1955 Chevrolet passenger cars also found its way into the Corvette. But not all 1955 Corvettes were V8-powered, as a small number of six-cylinder models were also built.
• Electrical systems were changed to 12-volt in 1955 Corvette models, except for the six-cylinder models which continued to use the 6-volt systems common to 1953-54.
• Corvettes with V8s in 1955 were identified by an enlarged gold "V" attached over the small "v" in the Chevrolet script on both front fenders. Also, the vehicle identification number (vin) for V8 models started with a "V." Six-cylinder models had standard scripts and no "V" in their vins.
• Corvette production of 700 in 1955 was second only to 1953 in low annual volume. Poor public acceptance the previous year resulted in over 1,100 unsold 1954 models at the start of 1955 production. Despite the low production, 1955 remains one of the most mysterious Corvette models in terms of accurate documentation.
• Ignition shielding for 1955 consisted of chrome distributor and coil covers with bails, braided and grounded plug wires, and wire carriers behind the exhaust manifolds.
• A manual heater cutoff valve was spliced into the upper heater hose along the inner fender.
• Windshield washer activation was by floor pedal with coordinator.
• Valve covers for V8 models were chrome plated with the Chevrolet script. They were held in place by phillips-head screws. The six-cylinder model valve covers duplicated 1954.
• Shortly after 1955 production began, a new type inside rearview mirror was used which permitted vertical adjustment of the entire mirror unit.

1955 OPTIONS

CODE	DESCRIPTION	QTY	RETAIL $
2934-6	Base Corvette Convertible, six-cylinder	—	$2,774.00
2934-8	Base Corvette Convertible, V8	—	2,909.00
100	Directional Signal	700	16.75
101	Heater	700	91.40
102A	AM Radio, signal seeking	700	145.15
290B	Whitewall Tires, 6.70x15	—	26.90
313	Powerglide Automatic Transmission	—	178.35
420A	Parking Brake Alarm	700	5.65
421A	Courtesy Lights	700	4.05
422A	Windshield Washers	700	11.85

• A 235ci, 155hp six-cylinder engine, 3-speed manual transmission, vinyl interior trim, and a soft top were included in the base price of #2934-6. However, the Powerglide automatic transmission was a required option and no 1955 Corvette with the combination of six-cylinder and manual transmission has ever been documented.

• A 265ci, 195hp V8 engine, 3-speed manual transmission, vinyl interior trim, and a soft top were included in the base price of #2934-8. The Powerglide automatic transmission was a required option with the V8 engine until somewhere past the midpoint of 1955 production when the manual transmission started to be used.

• Most 1955 models had automatic transmissions. Estimates place the number of manual transmissions at 75. Though not necessarily accurate, available records do support a total in the range of 70 to 80 units.

• It is likely that most 1955 options were not really optional, but required. Exceptions may surface, but the list of probable 100% usage includes directional signals, heaters, radios, parking brake alarms, courtesy lamps and windshield washers.

• The 1955 heater was a non-fresh air unit; that is, it recirculated interior cabin air only. The heater itself was the same for six-cylinder and V8 models, except for modifications in the blower motors required by the different voltages of the two models.

• Auxiliary hardtops were not available for 1955 models as factory options or as Chevrolet-sponsored dealer accessories. However, aftermarket companies manufactured removable hardtops for 1955 (and 1953-54) Corvettes and some Chevrolet dealers sold them.

• Corvette tires changed from tube-type to tubeless during 1954, so it is likely, but not certain, that all 1955 models had tubeless tires.

1955 COLORS

CODE	EXTERIOR	QTY(est)	SOFT TOP	WHEELS	INTERIOR
567	Polo White	325	White/Beige	Red	Red
570	Pennant Blue	45	Beige	Red	Dark Beige
573	Corvette Copper	15	White	Bronze	Dark Beige
596	Gypsy Red	180	White/Beige	Red	Light Beige
632	Harvest Gold	120	Dark Green	Yellow	Yellow

• Exterior color quantities are not from Chevrolet records. These are estimates based on surveys, theories, and other data. They should not be relied upon as precise.

• Interiors and exteriors were not coded to individual cars. Only 700 were produced, yet no Chevrolet records have been found to document color usage. The exterior colors are subject to question and conjecture. Records do show Pennant Blue was discontinued in April 1955. Gypsy Red and Corvette Copper are thought to have been offered after Pennant Blue was discontinued. Owners report other color combinations.

• Early 1955 soft tops were made of a canvas material. A vinyl-coated fabric material was introduced after production started. Both materials were used for beige and green soft tops, but all white soft tops were vinyl. Owner surveys have not determined an exact transition from one soft top material to another. Concurrent use was likely.

1956 CORVETTE
Production: 3,467 convertibles

1956 NUMBERS

Vehicle: E56S001001 through E56S004467

Suffix:
FG: 265ci, 225hp, at   GU: 265ci, 240hp, mt
FK: 265ci, 210hp, at   GV: 265ci, 210hp, mt
GR: 265ci, 225hp, mt

Block: 3720991: All

Head: 3725306: 265ci, 210hp, 225hp (2-bolt exhaust manifolds)
3731762: 265ci, 225hp, 240hp (3-bolt exhaust manifolds)

Carburetor: Carter 2362S #3720953: 265ci, 225hp, 240hp, rc
Carter 2366SA #3733246: 265ci, 210hp
Carter 2419S #3730599: 265ci, 225hp, 240hp, fc

Distributor: 1110872: 265ci, 225hp, ep   1110879: 265ci, 225hp, lp

Generator: 1102043: All

Abbreviations: at=automatic transmission, ci=cubic inch, ep=early production, fc=front carburetor, hp=horsepower, lp=late production, mt=manual transmission, rc=rear carburetor.

1956 FACTS

• The Corvette received its first major body redesign in 1956. With the exception of the instrument panel which was nearly identical, the 1956 was visually completely different from the preceding model. The new design featured roll-up windows (glass) with power assist optional, external door handles and locks, exposed headlights with chrome surround bezels (except very early production which were painted), and a sculptured side cove which permitted the Corvette's first two-tone paint combinations.

• Factory auxiliary hardtops were first available in 1956. The anodized header trim made the 1956 tops unique to the year. The anodized trim was, however, painted the same color as the top on some 1956s.

• Seat belts were available for the first time in 1956, but only in kit form as a dealer installed accessory The belts were grey nylon with chrome-plated, quick-release buckles.

• The optional AM radios for 1956 Corvettes were transistorized, another Corvette first. A similar radio was used for 1957, but most 1956 selector bars for the signal-seeking feature were plain. Models not equipped with the radio received a special plate covering the dash mount location.

• All 1956 models with standard transmissions were fitted with a new type clutch which used heat-treated coils to replace the diaphragm-type springs previously used.

• Dual four-barrel carburetors were available on Corvettes for the first time in 1956. The proper air cleaners were buffed aluminum and had an oil-wetted, sealed filter element. A cast aluminum intake manifold was included with dual carburetors.

• Dual point distributors were first used in 1956. All engines except the base 265ci, 210hp unit had the new distributors.

• The windshield washer reservoir for 1956 was a blue vinyl bag.

• Correct 1956 valve covers had staggered hold-down holes and attach with Phillips-head screws. The base 265ci, 210hp engine had painted steel covers with the Chevrolet script. All optional engines had nine-fin cast alloy valve covers.

• Passenger-side seats in 1956 models had fore-aft adjustment rails. Previous Corvette passenger seats were fixed in position.

• A higher-output 12V battery (53-amp hour) was fitted to 1956 models.

1956 OPTIONS

CODE	DESCRIPTION	QTY	RETAIL $
2934	Base Corvette Convertible	3,467	$3,120.00
101	Heater	—	123.65
102	AM Radio, signal seeking	2,717	198.90
107	Parking Brake Alarm	2,685	5.40
108	Courtesy Lights	2,775	8.65
109	Windshield Washers	2,815	11.85
290	Whitewall Tires, 6.70x15	—	32.30
313	Powerglide Automatic Transmission	—	188.50
419	Auxiliary Hardtop	2,076	215.20
426	Power Windows	547	64.60
440	Two-Tone Paint Combination	1,259	19.40
449	Special High-Lift Camshaft	111	188.30
469	265ci, 225hp Engine (2x4 carburetors)	3,080	172.20
471	Rear Axle, 3.27:1 ratio	—	0.00
473	Power Operated Folding Top	2,682	107.60

• A 265ci, 210hp engine, 3-speed manual transmission, vinyl interior trim, and a soft top were included in the base price.
• RPO 449 (Special High-Lift Camshaft) was available only when combined with RPO 469 (225-hp engine with dual four-barrel carburetors). Chevrolet recommended this combination "for racing purposes only" and generally did not specify a horsepower rating. The accepted, though unofficial, power output of RPO 449 is 240hp.
• RPO 469 was often specified by Chevrolet as "dual four-barrel carburetor equipment," rather than as a separate engine. Of the 3,080 RPO-469 quantity, 1,510 were sold with 3-speed manual transmissions, 1,570 with Powerglide automatics.
• The 2,076 RPO 419 auxiliary hardtop quantity included 629 in place of soft tops at no charge.
• RPO 470 permitted selection of beige or white soft tops in place of the standard black soft top at no charge. In 1956, soft top colors sold were 103 black, 1,840 white, 895 beige.
• The Corvette heater was changed from a recirculating-air-only type to a new "outside" air design in 1956. However, the first 145 1956s were built with the old type heater.

1956 COLORS

EXTERIOR	QTY	SOFT TOP	WHEELS	INTERIOR
Onyx Black	810	Bk-W	Black	Red
Aztec Copper	402	Bg-W	Copper	Beige
Cascade Green	290	Bg-W	Green	Beige
Arctic Blue	390	Bg-W	Blue	Beige-Red
Venetian Red	1,043	Bg-W	Red	Red
Polo White	532	Bk-W	Red-Silver	Red

• Suggested interiors shown. Other combinations were possible.
• Interiors and exteriors were not coded to individual cars.
• In 1956 paperwork, code "std" denoted black exterior. All other exteriors, including two-tones, were denoted by "440" followed by one alpha character. Solid colors were denoted by letters R through X (no U). Two-tones were denoted by the letters A through G.
• Exterior color quantity total for 1956 from Chevrolet records equals the 3,467 production total exactly. It appears unlikely that any other exterior colors were possible in 1956.
• The 1,259 quantity for code 440– two-tone paint was split 223 Onyx Black/silver; 166 Aztec Copper/beige; 147 Cascade Green/beige; 172 Arctic Blue/silver, 431 Venetian Red/beige; 120 Polo White/silver.
• Interiors sold in 1956 were: 2,580 red, 887 beige.
• Wheel color with Polo White exteriors depended on interior color. Wheels were red with red interiors, silver with beige interiors.
Abbreviations: Bg=Beige, Bk=Black, W=White.

1957 CORVETTE
Production: 6,339 convertibles

1957 NUMBERS

Vehicle: E57S100001 through E57S106339

Suffix:
EF: 283ci, 220hp, mt
EG: 283ci, 270hp, mt
EH: 283ci, 245hp, mt
EL: 283ci, 283hp, mt
EM: 283ci, 250hp, mt

EN: 283ci, 283hp, mt, ai, uu
FG: 283ci, 245hp, at
FH: 283ci, 220hp, at
FK: 283ci, 250hp, at

Block: 3731548: All

Head: 3740997: 283ci, 220hp, 245hp, 250hp, 270hp
3731539: 283ci, 283hp

Carburetor: Carter 2362S #3720953: 283ci, 245hp, rc
Carter 2366SA #3733246: 283ci, 220hp, fd
Carter 2419S #3730599: 283ci, 245hp, fc, fd
Carter 2613S #3741089: 283ci, 270hp, fc
Carter 2614S #3741090: 283ci, 270hp, rc
Carter 2626S #3744002: 283ci, 245hp, fc, sd
Carter 2627S #3744004: 283ci, 245hp, rc, sd
Carter 2655S #3744925: 283ci, 220hp, sd

Fuel Injection: Rochester 7014360: 283ci, 250hp, 283hp, ep
Rochester 7014520: 283ci, 250hp, 283hp
Rochester 7014800: 283ci, 250hp, 283hp, lp
Rochester 7014960: 283ci, 283hp, lp

Distributor: 1110889: 283ci, 250hp, 283hp
1110891: 283ci, 220hp, 245hp, 270hp
1110905: 283ci, 250hp(mt,at), 283hp
1110906: 283ci, 250hp, at
1110908: 283ci, 283hp

Generator: 1102043: All

Ending Vehicle: Oct 56: 100580   Jun 57: 104924   Sep 57: 106339
Nov 56: 101070   Jul 57: 105584
May 57: 104331   Aug 57: 106229

Abbreviations: ai=cold air induction, at=automatic transmission, ci=cubic inch, fc=front carburetor, fd=first design, ep=early production, hp=horsepower, lp=late production, mt=manual transmission, rc=rear carburetor, sd=second design, uu=uncertain usage.

1957 FACTS

• Although the body for 1957 was a carryover from 1956, the 1957 Corvette was a milestone model due to its optional fuel injection and optional 4-speed manual transmission, both Corvette firsts.
• Fuel injection was available throughout 1957 production, though limited early. A total of 1,040 fuel injected 1957 Corvettes were sold.
• The 4-speed manual transmission was released for sale on April 9, 1957, equating to about vehicle #E57S103500. Sales were 664 for 1957.
• The optional 1957 AM radio was similar to the 1956 transistorized unit, except most 1957 selector bars contained the word "Wonderbar."
• The optional 1957 auxiliary hardtop had stainless steel header trim.
• Correct 1957 valve covers had staggered hold-down holes and attached with Phillips-head screws. The base 283ci, 220hp engine had painted steel valve covers with the Chevrolet script. All optional engines had seven- or nine-fin cast alloy valve covers.
• Seat belts were not factory-installed in 1957 Corvettes, but mounting brackets were provided for optional installation by dealers.

1957 OPTIONS

CODE	DESCRIPTION	QTY	RETAIL $
2934	Base Corvette Convertible	6,339	$3,176.32
101	Heater	5,373	118.40
102	AM Radio, signal seeking	3,635	199.10
107	Parking Brake Alarm	1,873	5.40
108	Courtesy Lights	2,489	8.65
109	Windshield Washers	2,555	11.85
276	Wheels, 15x5.5 (5)	51	15.10
290	Whitewall Tires, 6.70x15	5,019	31.60
303	3-Speed Manual Transmission, close ratio	2,886	0.00
313	Powerglide Automatic Transmission	1,393	188.30
419	Auxiliary Hardtop	4,055	215.20
426	Power Windows	379	59.20
440	Two-Tone Paint Combination	2,797	19.40
469A	283ci, 245hp Engine (2x4 carburetors)	2,045	150.65
469C	283ci, 270hp Engine (2x4 carburetors)	1,621	182.95
473	Power Operated Folding Top	1,336	139.90
579A	283ci, 250hp Engine (fuel injection)	182	484.20
579B	283ci, 283hp Engine (fuel injection)	713	484.20
579C	283ci, 250hp Engine (fuel injection)	102	484.20
579E	283ci, 283hp Engine (fuel injection)	43	726.30
677	Positraction Rear Axle, 3.70:1	327	48.45
678	Positraction Rear Axle, 4.11:1	1,772	48.45
679	Positraction Rear Axle, 4.56:1	—	48.45
684	Heavy Duty Racing Suspension	51	780.10
685	4-Speed Manual Transmission	664	188.30

• A 283ci, 220hp, engine, 3-speed manual transmission, vinyl interior trim, and a soft top were included in the base price.
• RPO 684 included special front and rear springs and shock absorbers, heavier front stabilizer bar, quick steering adaptor, metallic brake facings, finned brake drums, fresh air ducting to rear brakes, and front brake air scoops (elephant ears). Positraction, manual transmission and 270hp or 283hp engines, were required. A version of this option, RPO 581, may have been available earlier without the brake components.
• RPO 276 included hubcaps (small) in place of standard wheel discs.
• The 4,055 RPO 419 (auxiliary hardtop) quantity included 931 in place of soft tops at no charge.
• RPO 579F included fresh air Intake and a mechanical tachometer mounted on the steering column.
• RPOs 287 and 288 for 6-ply blackwall tires were planned but actual delivery to retail customers is uncertain.

1957 COLORS

EXTERIOR	QTY	SOFT TOP	WHEELS	INTERIOR
Onyx Black	2,189	Bg-Bk-W	Black	Bg-R
Aztec Copper	452	Bg-W	Copper	Bg
Cascade Green	550	Bg-Bk-W	Green	Bg
Arctic Blue	487	Bg-Bk-W	Blue	Bg-R
Venetian Red	1,320	Bg-Bk-W	Red	Bg-R
Polo White	1,273	Bg-Bk-W	Red-Silver	Bg-R
Inca Silver	65	Bk-W	Silver	Bg-R

• Suggested interiors shown. Other combinations were possible.
• Interiors and exteriors were not coded to individual cars. In 1957, three Corvettes were painted a non-standard color, combination, or primer.
• The 2,797 quantity for code 440 two-tone paint was split 10 Inca Silver/ivory; 909 Onyx Black/silver; 319 Polo White/silver; 716 Venetian Red/beige; 263 Aztec Copper/beige; 258 Arctic Blue/silver; 319 Cascade Green/beige; 3 uncertain.
• Interiors sold in 1957 were: 5,021 red, 1,315 beige, 3 uncertain.
• Wheel color with Polo White exteriors depended on interior color. Wheels were red with red interiors; silver with beige interiors.
Abbreviations: Bg=Beige, Bk=Black, R=Red, W=White.

1958 CORVETTE
Production: 9,168 convertibles

1958 NUMBERS

Vehicle: J58S100001 through J58S109168

Suffix:
CQ: 283ci, 230hp, mt	CU: 283ci, 270hp, mt
CR: 283ci, 250hp, mt	DG: 283ci, 230hp, at
CS: 283ci, 290hp, mt	DH: 283ci, 250hp, at
CT: 283ci, 245hp, mt	DJ: 283ci, 245hp, at

Block: 3737739 or 3756519: All

Head: 3748770: All (sh)

Carburetor: Carter 2613S #3741089: 283ci, 270hp, fc
Carter 2614S #3741090: 283ci, 270hp, rc
Carter 2626S #3744002: 283ci, 245hp, fc
Carter 2627S #3744004: 283ci, 245hp, rc
Carter 2669S #3746384: 283ci, 230hp

Fuel Injection: Rochester 7014800: 283ci, 250hp
Rochester 7014800R: 283ci, 290hp, ep
Rochester 7014900: 283ci, 250hp
Rochester 7014900R: 283ci, 290hp
Rochester 7014960: 283ci, 290hp
Rochester 7017200: 283ci, 250hp, lp

Distributor:
1110890: 283ci, 230hp	1110914: 283ci, 290hp
1110891: 283ci, 245hp, 270hp	1110915: 283ci, 250hp
1110908: 283ci, 290hp, ep	

Generator: 1102043: 283ci, 230hp, 245hp, 250hp, 270hp
1102059: 283ci, 290hp

Ending Vehicle:
Oct 57: 100486	Feb 58: 104789	Jun 58: 108192
Nov 57: 101443	Mar 58: 105779	Jul 58: 108840
Dec 57: 102511	Apr 58: 106544	Aug 58: 109168
Jan 58: 103677	May 58: 107489	

Abbreviations: at=automatic transmission, ci=cubic inch, fc=front carburetor, fd=first design, ep=early production, hp=horsepower, lp=late production, mt=manual transmission, rc=rear carburetor, sd=second design, sh=staggered valve cover holes.

1958 FACTS

• Extensive redesign for 1958 included new body panels, new instrument panel and new upholstery. External distinguishing features included dual headlights, a Corvette first, non-functional louvers on the hood, and twin chrome trunk spears.
• The interior for 1958 had a large 160-mph speedometer flanked by secondary instruments. The tachometer was relocated from its previous central instrument panel location to just above the steering column. A passenger grab bar was built into the passenger side. A central console was included. Door panels were a two-piece design.
• Seat belts were factory-installed for the first time in 1958 Corvettes. Previously, they had been dealer-installed accessories. However, seat belt anchors were installed in 1956-57 at the factory.
• Correct 1958 valve covers had staggered hold-down holes and attach with Phillips head screws. The base 283ci, 230hp engine had painted steel covers. All optional engines had seven-fin cast alloy valve covers.
• Low-loop rayon pile carpeting was factory-installed in 1958 Corvettes.
• Carbureted engines were equipped with glass fuel filter bowls.

1958 OPTIONS

CODE	DESCRIPTION	QTY	RETAIL $
867	Base Corvette Convertible	9,168	$3,591.00
101	Heater	8,014	96.85
102	AM Radio, signal seeking	6,142	144.45
107	Parking Brake Alarm	2,883	5.40
108	Courtesy Light	4,600	6.50
109	Windshield Washers	3,834	16.15
276	Wheels, 15x5.5 (5)	404	0.00
290	Whitewall Tires, 6.70x15	7,428	31.55
313	Powerglide Automatic Transmission	2,057	188.30
419	Auxiliary Hardtop	5,607	215.20
426	Power Windows	649	59.20
440	Two-Tone Exterior Paint	3,422	16.15
469	283ci, 245hp Engine (2x4 carburetors)	2,436	150.65
469C	283ci, 270hp Engine (2x4 carburetors)	978	182.95
473	Power Operated Folding Top	1,090	139.90
579	283ci, 250hp Engine (fuel injection)	504	484.20
579D	283ci, 290hp Engine (fuel injection)	1,007	484.20
677	Positraction Rear Axle, 3.70:1	1,123	48.45
678	Positraction Rear Axle, 4.11:1	2,518	48.45
679	Positraction Rear Axle, 4.56:1	370	48.45
684	Heavy Duty Brakes and Suspension	144	780.10
685	4-Speed Manual Transmission	3,764	215.20

• A 283ci, 230hp engine, 3-speed manual transmission, vinyl interior trim, and a soft top were included in the base price.
• RPO 684 included special front and rear springs and shock absorbers, heavier front stabilizer bar, quick steering adaptor, metallic brakes, finned brake drums, fresh air ducting to rear brakes and front brake air deflectors (except very early models). Positraction axle, manual transmission and RPO 579D were required.
• RPO 276 included hubcaps (small) in lieu of standard wheel discs.
• The 5,607 RPO-419 (auxiliary hardtop) quantity included 2,215 in lieu of soft tops at no charge.
• The 504 RPO-579 (250hp engine) quantity was split 400 with manual transmissions, 104 with Powerglide automatic transmissions.
• The 2,436 RPO-469 (245hp engine) quantity was split 1,897 with manual transmission, 539 with Powerglide automatic transmissions.
• RPOs 677, 678 and 679 (Positraction) required manual transmission.

1958 COLORS

EXTERIOR	QTY	SOFT TOP	WHEELS	INTERIOR
Charcoal	1,631	Bk-W	Silver	Bg-C-R
Snowcrest White	2,477	Bk-W-Bg	Silver	Bg-C-R
Silver Blue	2,006	Bg-W	Silver	Bg-C
Regal Turquoise	510	Bk-W	Silver	C
Panama Yellow	455	Bk-W	Silver	C
Signet Red	1,399	Bk-W	Silver	C-R
Black	493	Bk-W	Silver	C-R
Silver	193	Bk-W	Silver	C-R

• Suggested interiors shown. Other combinations were possible.
• Interiors and exteriors were not coded to individual cars. In 1958, four Corvettes were painted a non-standard color, combination, or primer.
• The 3,422 quantity for code 440 two-tone paint (contrasting cove) was split 757 Silver Blue/silver; 756 Signet Red/white; 729 Charcoal/silver; 499 Snowcrest White/silver; 252 Regal Turquoise/white; 190 Panama Yellow/white; 199 Black/silver; 36 Silver/black; 4 uncertain.
• The Charcoal exterior color is believed to have been replaced by Black somewhere past the mid-point of 1958 production.
• The wheels of RPO 276 may have been painted black instead of silver.
Abbreviations: Bg=Blue-Gray, Bk=Black, C=Charcoal, R=Red, W=White.

1959 CORVETTE
Production: 9,670 convertibles

1959 NUMBERS

Vehicle: J59S100001 through J59S109670

Suffix: CQ: 283ci, 230hp, mt   CU: 283ci, 270hp, mt
CR: 283ci, 250hp, mt   DG: 283ci, 230hp, at
CS: 283ci, 290hp, mt   DH: 283ci, 250hp, at
CT: 283ci, 245hp, mt   DJ: 283ci, 245hp, at

Block: 3737739: All (ep)   3756519: All

Head: 3748770: All (ep, sh)   3767465: All (lp)
3755550: All (ep, sh)

Carburetor: Carter 2613S #3741089: 283ci, 270hp, fc
Carter 2614S #3741090: 283ci, 270hp, rc
Carter 2626S #3744002: 283ci, 245hp, fc
Carter 2627S #3744004: 283ci, 245hp, rc
Carter 2818S #3756676: 283ci, 230hp

Fuel Injection: Rochester 7014900: 283ci, 250hp
Rochester 7014900R: 283ci, 290hp
Rochester 7017200: 283ci, 250hp
Rochester 7017250: 283ci, 290hp
Rochester 7017300: 283ci, 290hp
Rochester 7017300R: 283ci, 250hp

Distributor: 1110891: 283ci, 245hp, 270hp   1110915: 283ci, 250hp
1110914: 283ci, 290hp   1110946: 283ci, 230hp

Generator: 1102043: 283ci, 230hp, 245hp, 250hp, 270hp
1102059: 283ci, 290hp, fd
1102173: 283ci, 290hp, sd

Ending Vehicle: Sep 58: 100409   Jan 59: 103962   May 59: 107934
Oct 58: 100623   Feb 59: 104921   Jun 59: 108702
Nov 58: 101587   Mar 59: 106033   Jul 59: 109437
Dec 58: 102641   Apr 59: 107144   Aug 59: 109670

Abbreviations: at=automatic transmission, ci=cubic inch, fc=front carburetor, fd=first design, ep=early production, hp=horsepower, lp=late production, mt=manual transmission, rc=rear carburetor, sd=second design, sh=staggered valve cover holes.

1959 FACTS

• Exterior 1959 appearance was similar to 1958, except 1959 did not have the simulated hood louvers or the twin chrome trunk spears.
• Door panels were redesigned by relocating the armrests for additional elbow room, and by moving the door releases forward.
• Instruments were redesigned for better legibility in 1959. This included making the gauge lenses concave for less light reflection, and adding a new tachometer face.
• The "T" shift handle with positive reverse lockout was introduced in 1959 models with 4-speed manual transmissions.
• A storage bin was added under the passenger grab bar. The grab bar itself was more heavily padded than for the previous year.
• The optional 1959 windshield washer reservoir mounted on the left side for all carbureted engines, and on the right side for all fuel injected engines. Right side mountings were protected by heat shields.
• Seat upholstery was smoother than the previous year and the black interior available in 1959 models was the Corvette's first.

1959 OPTIONS

CODE	DESCRIPTION	QTY	RETAIL $
867	Base Corvette Convertible	9,670	$3,875.00
101	Heater	8,909	102.25
102	AM Radio, signal seeking	7,001	149.80
107	Parking Brake Alarm	3,601	5.40
108	Courtesy Light	3,601	6.50
109	Windshield Washers	7,929	16.15
121	Radiator Fan Clutch	67	21.55
261	Sunshades	3,722	10.80
276	Wheels, 15x5.5 (5)	214	0.00
290	Whitewall Tires, 6.70x15	8,173	31.55
313	Powerglide Automatic Transmission	1,878	199.10
419	Auxiliary Hardtop	5,481	236.75
426	Power Windows	587	59.20
440	Two-Tone Exterior Paint	2,931	16.15
469	283ci, 245hp Engine (2x4 carburetors)	1,417	150.65
469C	283ci, 270hp Engine (2x4 carburetors)	1,846	182.95
473	Power Operated Folding Top	661	139.90
579	283ci, 250hp Engine (fuel injection)	175	484.20
579D	283ci, 290hp Engine (fuel injection)	745	484.20
675	Positraction Rear Axle	4,170	48.45
684	Heavy Duty Brakes and Suspension	142	425.05
685	4-Speed Manual Transmission	4,175	188.30
686	Metallic Brakes	333	26.90
1408	Blackwall Tires, 6.70x15 nylon	—	—
1625	24 Gallon Fuel Tank	—	—

• A 283ci, 230hp engine, 3-speed manual transmission, vinyl interior trim, and a soft top were included in the base price.
• RPO 684 included special front and rear springs and shock absorbers, heavier front stabilizer bar, quick steering adaptor, metallic brakes, finned brake drums, fresh air ducting to rear brakes (early only) and front brake air deflectors. RPO 469C or RPO 579D, RPO 675, and manual transmission were required.
• RPO 276 (15x5.5 wheels) included hubcaps (small) in lieu of standard wheel discs.
• LPO 1625 required the hardtop without soft top because the fuel tank occupied part of the folding top storage area.
• The 5,481 RPO 419 quantity included 1,695 in lieu of soft tops at no cost.
• RPO 675 (Positraction) required manual transmission.

1959 COLORS

EXTERIOR	QTY	SOFT TOP	WHEELS	INTERIOR
Tuxedo Black	1,594	Bk-W	Black	B-Bk-R
Classic Cream	223	Bk-W	Black	Bk
Frost Blue	1,024	B-Bk-W	Black	B-R
Crown Sapphire	888	Bk-Tq-W	Black	Tq
Roman Red	1,542	Bk-W	Black	Bk-R
Snowcrest White	3,354	B-Bk-Tq-W	Black	B-Bk-R-Tq
Inca Silver	957	Bk-W	Black	Bk-R

• Suggested interiors shown. Other combinations were possible.
• Interiors and exteriors were not coded to individual cars. In 1959, five Corvettes were painted a non-standard color, combination, or primer. An additional 83 were exported and their colors combinations are unknown.
• Numbers of interiors sold in 1959 are as follows: 1,303 blue, 1,181 turquoise, 5,124 red, 2,062 black.
• The 2,931 quantity for code 440 two-tone paint (contrasting cove) was split 805 Roman Red/white; 535 Snowcrest White/silver; 496 Tuxedo Black/silver; 420 Crown Sapphire/white; 361 Frost Blue/white; 220 Inca Silver/white; 89 Classic Cream/white; 5 other.
• Turquoise soft tops were available only in 1959.
Abbreviations: B=Blue, Bk=Black, R=Red, Tq=Turquoise, W=White.

33

1960 CORVETTE

Production: 10,261 convertibles

1960 NUMBERS

Vehicle: 00867S100001 through 00867S110261

Suffix: CQ: 283ci, 230hp, mt   CU: 283ci, 270hp, mt
CR: 283ci, 250hp, mt   DG: 283ci, 230hp, at
CS: 283ci, 290hp, mt   DJ: 283ci, 245hp, at
CT: 283ci, 245hp, mt

• Suffix codes CY (283ci, 275hp) and CZ (283ci, 315hp) were assigned to aluminum-head versions of two fuel injected engines for 1960. Aluminum heads definitely exist, but delivery of a 1960 Corvette with factory-installed aluminum heads to a retail customer has not been confirmed.

Block: 3756519: All

Head: 3774692: All

Carburetor: Carter 2613S #3741089: 283ci, 270hp, fc
Carter 2614S #3741090: 283ci, 270hp, rc
Carter 2626S #3744002: 283ci, 245hp, fc
Carter 2627S #3744004: 283ci, 245hp, rc
Carter 2818S #3756676: 283ci, 230hp, fd
Carter 3059S #3779178: 283ci, 230hp, sd

Fuel Injection: Rochester 7017200: 283ci, 250hp
Rochester 7017250: 283ci, 290hp
Rochester 7017300: 283ci, 290hp
Rochester 7017310: 283ci, 250hp
Rochester 7017320: 283ci, 290hp

Distributor: 1110891: 283ci, 245hp, 270hp   1110915: 283ci, 250hp
1110914: 283ci, 290hp   1110946: 283ci, 230hp

Generator: 1102043: 283ci, 230hp, 245hp, 250hp, 270hp
1102173: 283ci, 290hp

Ending Vehicle: Oct 59: 101168   Feb 60: 104360   Jun 60: 109149
Nov 59: 101454   Mar 60: 105711   Jul 60: 109846
Dec 59: 102059   Apr 60: 107011   Aug 60: 110261
Jan 60: 103158   May 60: 108167

Abbreviations: at=automatic transmission, ci=cubic inch, fc=front carburetor, fd=first design, hp=horsepower, mt=manual transmission, rc=rear carburetor, sd=second design.

1960 FACTS

• The 1960 exterior appearance continued the smooth-contoured look of the previous years, and the 1960 Corvette was the last to feature taillights formed into the rounded rear fenders. It was also the last with heavy "teeth" in the grill.
• Aluminum radiators (with top tanks) appeared first in 1960 Corvettes, but use in 1960 was limited to 270hp and 290hp engines.
• All 1960 fuel injected engines required manual transmissions. Previously, automatic transmissions could be combined with the lower-horse-power fuel injected engines.
• The base 230hp engines had painted steel valve covers. All optional engines had seven-fin cast alloy valve covers. All covers had straight-across mounting holes and all attached with Phillips-head screws.
• Windshield washer reservoirs mounted on the left side, except for fuel injected engines. For fuel injected engines, reservoirs were mounted on the right side and were protected by heat shields.

1960 OPTIONS

CODE	DESCRIPTION	QTY	RETAIL $
867	Base Corvette Convertible	10,261	$3,872.00
101	Heater	9,808	102.25
102	AM Radio, signal seeking	8,166	137.75
107	Parking Brake Alarm	4,051	5.40
108	Courtesy Light	6,774	6.50
109	Windshield Washers	7,205	16.15
121	Temperature Controlled Radiator Fan	2,711	21.55
261	Sunshades	5,276	10.80
276	Wheels, 15x5.5 (5)	246	0.00
290	Whitewall Tires, 6.70x15	9,104	31.55
313	Powerglide Automatic Transmission	1,766	199.10
419	Auxiliary Hardtop	5,147	236.75
426	Power Windows	544	59.20
440	Two-Tone Exterior Paint	3,309	16.15
469	283ci, 245hp Engine (2x4 carburetors)	1,211	150.65
469C	283ci, 270hp Engine (2x4 carburetors)	2,364	182.95
473	Power Operated Folding Top	512	139.90
579	283ci, 250hp Engine (fuel injection)	100	484.20
579D	283ci, 290hp Engine (fuel injection)	759	484.20
675	Positraction Rear Axle	5,231	43.05
685	4-Speed Manual Transmission	5,328	188.30
686	Metallic Brakes	920	26.90
687	Heavy Duty Brakes and Steering	119	333.60
1408	Blackwall Tires, 6.70x15 nylon	—	15.75
1625A	24 Gallon Fuel Tank	—	161.40

• A 283ci, 230hp engine, 3-speed manual transmission, vinyl interior trim, and a soft top were included in the base price.
• RPO 687 included special front and rear shocks, air scoops/deflectors for front brakes and air scoops for rear brakes, metallic brake facings, finned brake drums with cooling fans, and quick-steering adaptor. RPO 469C or RPO 579D, RPO 675, and manual transmission were required.
• RPO 276 included hubcaps (small) in lieu of standard wheel discs.
• LPO 1625A (24 gallon fuel tank) required hardtop without soft top because the tank occupied part of the folding top storage area.
• The 5,147 RPO-419 (auxiliary hardtop) quantity included 1,641 in lieu of soft tops at no charge.
• RPO 675 (Positraction) required manual transmission.

1960 COLORS

EXTERIOR	QTY	SOFT TOP	WHEELS	INTERIOR
Tuxedo Black	1,268	B-Bk-W	Black	B-Bk-R-T
Tasco Turquoise	635	B-Bk-W	Turquoise	Bk-T
Horizon Blue	766	B-Bk-W	Blue	B-Bk-R
Honduras Maroon	1,202	Bk-W	Maroon	Bk
Roman Red	1,529	Bk-W	Red	Bk-R
Ermine White	3,717	B-Bk-W	White	B-Bk-R-T
Sateen Silver	989	B-Bk-W	Silver	B-Bk-R-T
Cascade Green	140	B-Bk-W	Green	Bk

• Suggested interiors shown. Other combinations were possible.
• Interiors and exteriors were not coded to individual cars.
• The number of interiors sold in 1960 are 3,231 black; 4,920 red; 1,078 turquoise; 1,032 blue.
• The 3,309 quantity for code 440 two-tone paint (contrasting cove) was split 779 Roman Red/white; 572 Honduras Maroon/white; 488 Ermine White/silver; 383 Tasco Turquoise/white; 368 Tuxedo Black/silver; 359 Horizon Blue/white; 280 Sateen Silver/white; 65 Cascade Green/white. Fifteen were a non-standard color, combination, or primer.
• Data suggests all soft top colors were available with all exteriors.
• Blue soft tops were a lighter shade than blue (or blue/gray) interiors.
• Cascade Green was metallic and different than 1956-57 Cascade Green.

Abbreviations: B=Blue, Bk=Black, R=Red, T=Turquoise, W=White.

1961 CORVETTE
Production: 10,939 convertibles

1961 NUMBERS

Vehicle: 10867S100001 through 10867S110939

Suffix:
CQ: 283ci, 230hp, mt
CR: 283ci, 275hp, mt
CS: 283ci, 315hp, mt
CT: 283ci, 245hp, mt
CU: 283ci, 270hp, mt
DG: 283ci, 230hp, at
DJ: 283ci, 245hp, at

Block: 3756519: All   3789935: All (lp)

Head: 3774692: 283ci, 230hp, 245hp, 270hp
3782461: 283ci, 275hp, 315hp

Carburetor: Carter 2613S #3741089: 283ci, 270hp, fc, fd
Carter 2614S #3741090: 283ci, 270hp, rc
Carter 2626S #3744002: 283ci, 245hp, fc, fd
Carter 2627S #3744004: 283ci, 245hp, rc
Carter 3059S #3779178: 283ci, 230hp
Carter 3181S #3785554: 283ci, 245hp, fc, sd
Carter 3182S #3785552: 283ci, 270hp, fc, sd

Fuel Injection: Rochester 7017310: 283ci, 275hp
Rochester 7017320: 283ci, 315hp

Distributor: 1110891: 283ci, 245hp, 270hp   1110915: 283ci, 275hp
1110914: 283ci, 315hp   1110946: 283ci, 230hp

Generator: 1102043: 283ci, 230hp, 245hp, 270hp, 275hp
1102173: 283ci, 315hp, fd
1102268: 283ci, 315hp, sd

Ending Vehicle:
Sep 60: 101052
Oct 60: 102301
Nov 60: 103355
Dec 60: 104306
Jan 61: 105203
Feb 61: 105966
Mar 61: 106889
Apr 61: 107804
May 61: 108960
Jun 61: 110160
Jul 61: 110939

Abbreviations: at=automatic transmission, ci=cubic inch, fc=front carburetor, fd=first design, hp=horsepower, lp=late production, mt=manual transmission, rc=rear carburetor, sd=second design.

1961 FACTS

• Exterior styling was facelifted for 1961. It was the first Corvette without heavy "teeth" in the grill area. The forward headlight bezels were body-color. The rear was completely restyled with four taillights, now a Corvette trademark, but new for 1961.
• Reduction of the transmission tunnel width by twenty-percent increased 1961 Corvette interior space.
• Side-mount radiator expansion tanks began to be used during the 1961 production year.
• Windshield washers, courtesy light, sun shades, temperature-controlled radiator fan, and parking brake warning light all became standard equipment in 1961 models.
• Windshield washer reservoirs mounted on the left side, except for fuel injected engines. For fuel injected engines, reservoirs were mounted on the right side and were protected by heat shields.
• The base 230hp engines had painted steel valve covers. All optional engines had seven-fin cast alloy valve covers.
• Exhausts exited below the body on 1961s, a change from all previous Corvettes which exited through the rear body panel or rear bumper.
• Door sills were redesigned as one-piece, instead of two-piece as in 1960.
• Aluminum cases for 4-speed transmissions were introduced in 1961.

1961 OPTIONS

CODE	DESCRIPTION	QTY	RETAIL $
867	Base Corvette Convertible	10,939	$3,934.00
101	Heater	10,671	102.25
102	AM Radio, signal seeking	9,316	137.75
242	Positive Crankcase Ventilation	—	5.40
276	Wheels, 15x5.5 (5)	337	0.00
290	Whitewall Tires, 6.70x15	9,780	31.55
313	Powerglide Automatic Transmission	1,458	199.10
353	283ci, 275hp Engine (fuel injection)	118	484.20
354	283ci, 315hp Engine (fuel injection)	1,462	484.20
419	Auxiliary Hardtop	5,680	236.75
426	Power Windows	698	59.20
440	Two-Tone Exterior Paint	3,368	16.15
468	283ci, 270hp Engine (2x4 carburetor)	2,827	182.95
469	283ci, 245hp Engine (2x4 carburetor)	1,175	150.65
473	Power Operated Folding Top	442	161.40
675	Positraction Rear Axle	6,915	43.05
685	4-Speed Manual Transmission	7,013	188.30
686	Metallic Brakes	1,402	37.70
687	Heavy Duty Brakes and Steering	233	333.60
1408	Blackwall Tires, 6.70x15 nylon	—	15.75
1625	24 Gallon Fuel Tank	—	161.40

• A 283ci, 230hp engine, 3-speed manual transmission, vinyl interior trim, and a soft top were included in the base price.
• RPO 687 included special front and rear shocks, air scoops/deflectors for front brakes and air scoops for rear brakes, metallic brake facings, finned brake drums with cooling fans, and quick-steering adaptor. RPO 354 or RPO 468, and RPO 675 were required.
• "Wide" whitewall tires (optional) appeared last on 1961 Corvette models.
• RPO 242 (pcv) was specified in order guides for California.
• RPO 276 (15x5.5 wheels) included hubcaps (small) in lieu of standard full wheel discs.
• LPO 1625 (24 gallon fuel tank) required the hardtop without soft top because the tank occupied part of the folding top storage area.
• The 1,458 RPO-313 (automatic transmission) quantity was split 1,226 with 230hp engines, 232 with 245hp engines.
• The 5,680 RPO-419 (auxiliary hardtop) quantity included 2,285 in lieu of soft tops at no charge.
• RPO 675 (Positraction) required manual transmission.

1961 COLORS

EXTERIOR	QTY	SOFT TOP	WHEELS	INTERIOR
Tuxedo Black	1,340	Bk-W	Black	B-Bk-F-R
Ermine White	3,178	Bk-W	White	B-Bk-F-R
Roman Red	1,794	Bk-W	Red	Bk-R
Sateen Silver	747	Bk-W	Silver	B-Bk-R
Jewel Blue	855	Bk-W	Blue	B-Bk
Fawn Beige	1,363	Bk-W	Beige	Bk-F-R
Honduras Maroon	1,645	Bk-W	Maroon	Bk-F

• Suggested interiors shown. Other combinations were possible.
• Interior and exterior colors were not coded to individual cars.
• Number of interiors sold in 1961 are as follows: 4,459 Red; 3,487 Black; 1,662 Fawn; 1,331 Blue.
• Contrasting cove colors were last available in 1961.
• The 3,368 quantity for code 440 two-tone paint (contrasting cove) was split 954 Roman Red/white, 647 Honduras Maroon/white, 429 Tuxedo Black/silver, 419 Jewel Blue/white, 385 Ermine White/silver, 358 Fawn Beige/white, 159 Sateen Silver/white. In 1961, seventeen Corvettes were painted a non-standard color, combination, or primer.
• Jewel Blue was available only in 1961.
Abbreviations: B=Blue, Bk=Black, F=Fawn, R=Red, W=White

1962 CORVETTE

Production: 14,531 convertibles

1962 NUMBERS

Vehicle: 20867S100001 through 20867S114531

Suffix: RC: 327ci, 250hp, mt   RF: 327ci, 360hp, mt
RD: 327ci, 300hp, mt   SC: 327ci, 250hp, at
RE: 327ci, 340hp, mt   SD: 327ci, 300hp, at

Block: 3782870: All

Head: 3782461: 327ci, 300hp, 340hp, 360hp   3795896: 327ci, 250hp
3884520: 327ci, 250hp, uu

Carburetor: Carter 3190S #3788245: 327ci, 250hp, at, ep
Carter 3191S #3788246: 327ci, 250hp
Carter 3310S #3819207: 327ci, 300hp, at
Carter 3269S #3797699: 327ci, 300hp(mt), 340hp

Fuel Injection: Rochester 7017355 (ep)   Rochester 7017360

Distributor: 1110984: 327ci, 250hp,300hp   1110990: 327ci, 360hp,ep
1110985: 327ci, 340hp   1111011: 327ci, 360hp

Generator: 1102174: 327ci, 250hp, 300hp
1102268: 327ci, 340hp, 360hp

Ending Vehicle:

Aug 61: 100443	Jan 62: 106234	Jun 62: 113459
Sep 61: 100827	Feb 62: 107585	Jul 62: 114520
Oct 61: 102065	Mar 62: 109116	Aug 62: 114531
Nov 61: 103465	Apr 62: 110519	
Dec 61: 104766	May 62: 112035	

Abbreviations: at=automatic transmission, ci=cubic inch, ep=early production, hp=horsepower, mt=manual transmission, uu=uncertain usage.

1962 FACTS

• Engine displacement increased in 1962 from 283ci to 327ci. The base engine for 1962 had 250hp. Dual-four barrel carburetor engines available in Corvettes from 1956 to 1961, were not available in 1962.
• Styling for 1962 resembled 1961 strongly, but there were visual differences. The side cove lip on 1962s was formed by the fiberglass body panels, not accented by bright trim as previously. Because the trim was removed, 1962 Corvettes could not be ordered with coves painted to contrast overall body color.
• The simulated vent treatment in the cove area was changed in 1962 to a single louver, replacing the triple-spear vent.
• Conventional trunks last appeared in 1962 Corvettes. Models to follow had no external rear storage access until 1982 when a special "collector edition" model featured a hatch window.
• Other "lasts" for 1962 included last year for exposed headlights, solid rear axle, and optional power top.
• An aluminum case for the Powerglide automatic transmission was first introduced in 1962 Corvettes.
• This was the first year to have tires with narrow whitewalls (optional).
• Tachometers were distributor-driven in all 1962s. Previous use of tach-drive distributors in Corvette V8s was limited to fuel injected engines.
• The 250hp and 300hp engines had painted steel valve covers. The 340hp and 360hp engines had seven-fin cast alloy valve covers.
• Windshield washer reservoirs on 1962s mounted on the left side except for fuel injected engines. For fuel injected engines, reservoirs mounted on the right and were protected by heat shields.

1962 OPTIONS

CODE	DESCRIPTION	QTY	RETAIL $
867	Base Corvette Convertible	14,531	$4,038.00
102	AM Radio, signal seeking	13,076	137.75
203	Rear Axle, 3.08:1 ratio	—	0.00
242	Positive Crankcase Ventilation	—	5.40
276	Wheels, 15x5.5 (5)	561	0.00
313	Powerglide Automatic Transmission	1,532	199.10
396	327ci, 340hp Engine	4,412	107.60
419	Auxiliary Hardtop	8,074	236.75
426	Power Windows	995	59.20
441	Direct Flow Exhaust System	2,934	0.00
473	Power Operated Folding Top	350	139.90
488	24 Gallon Fuel Tank	65	118.40
582	327ci, 360hp Engine (fuel injection)	1,918	484.20
583	327ci, 300hp Engine	3,294	53.80
675	Positraction Rear Axle	14,232	43.05
685	4-Speed Manual Transmission	11,318	188.30
686	Metallic Brakes	2,799	37.70
687	Heavy Duty Brakes and Steering	246	333.60
1832	Whitewall Tires, 6.70x15	—	31.55
1833	Blackwall Tires, 6.70x15 nylon	—	15.70

• A 327ci, 250hp engine, 3-speed manual transmission, vinyl interior trim, and a soft top were included in the base price.
• Heaters became standard in 1962 for the first time, but could be factory-deleted with RPO 610. The 610 code specified "export," but other heater-deletes may have been built for racing.
• RPO 687 included special front and rear shocks, air scoops/deflectors for front brakes and air scoops for rear brakes, metallic brake facings, finned brake drums with cooling fans, and quick-steering adaptor. RPOs 582 and 675 were required.
• RPO 242 (pcv) was specified in order guides to be for California use.
• RPO 488 (24-gallon fuel tank) required hardtop without soft top because the tank occupied part of the folding top storage area.
• RPO 276 (15x5.5 wheels) included hubcaps (small) in place of standard full wheel discs.
• Base 3-speed manual transmissions were split 1,619 with 250hp/300hp engines, 62 with 340hp/360hp engines.
• The 1,532 RPO-313 quantity was split 1,067 with 250hp engines, 465 with 300hp engines.
• The 8,074 RPO-419 quantity included 3,179 in lieu of soft tops.
• The 11,318 RPO-685 quantity was split 5,050 with 250hp/300hp engines, 6,268 with 340hp/360hp engines.

1962 COLORS

EXTERIOR	QTY	SOFT TOP	WHEELS	INTERIOR
Tuxedo Black	—	Bk-W	Bk	Bk-F-R
Fawn Beige	1,851	Bk-W	Bk-Fb	F-R
Roman Red	—	Bk-W	Bk-R	Bk-F-R
Ermine White	—	Bk-W	Bk-W	Bk-F-R
Almond Beige	820	Bk-W	Bk-Ab	F-R
Sateen Silver	—	Bk-W	Bk-Si	Bk-R
Honduras Maroon	—	Bk-W	Bk-M	Bk-F

• Suggested interiors shown. Other combinations were possible.
• Generally, 1962s with whitewall tires had black wheels. Wheels combined with blackwall tires or RPO 276 were painted body color.
• Interior and exterior colors were not coded to individual cars. Other exterior colors, including primer only, were built. For example, Cadillac Royal Heather Amethyst (purple) is documented for a small number of 1962 Corvettes built for the Omaha Tangier Shrine Corvette Patrol.
Abbreviations: Ab=Almond Beige, Bk=Black, F=Fawn, Fb=Fawn Beige, M=Maroon, R=Red, Si=Silver, W=White.

1963 CORVETTE

Production: 10,594 coupe, 10,919 convertible, 21,513 total.

1963 NUMBERS

Vehicle: 30837S100001 through 30837S121513
     • For convertibles, fourth digit is a 6.

Suffix: RC: 327ci, 250hp, mt   RF: 327ci, 360hp, mt
            RD: 327ci, 300hp, mt   SC: 327ci, 250hp, at
            RE: 327ci, 340hp, mt   SD: 327ci, 300hp, at

Block: 3782870: All

Head: 3795896: 327ci, 250hp
        3782461: 327ci, 300hp, 340hp, 360hp

Carburetor: Carter 3460S #3826006: 327ci, 300hp, at
                Carter 3461S #3826004: 327ci, 300hp, 340hp, mt
                Carter 3500S #3826005: 327ci, 250hp, at
                Carter 3501S #3826003: 327ci, 250hp, mt

Fuel Injection: Rochester 7017375

Distributor: 1111022: 327ci, 360hp
              1111024: 327ci, 250hp, 300hp, 340hp

Alternator: 1100628: All without ac
            1100633: All with ac

Ending Vehicle: Sep 62: 100675   Jan 63: 107976   May 63: 116409
                    Oct 62: 102756   Feb 63: 109814   Jun 63: 118524
                    Nov 62: 104047   Mar 63: 111833   Jul 63: 120990
                    Dec 62: 105972   Apr 63: 114128   Aug 63: 121513

Abbreviations: ac=air conditioning, at=automatic transmission, ci=cubic inch, hp=horsepower, mt=manual transmission.

1963 FACTS

• In 1963, the Corvette's body and chassis were completely redesigned. For the first time, a coupe body was available. A center wind split on the coupe roof flowed through the rear glass creating a "split window."
• Knock-off aluminum wheels were introduced as a 1963 option, but actual availability is questionable. Porosity of the aluminum and rim seal difficulty in early wheels caused tubeless tires to leak. Delivery of a 1963 with knock-off wheels to a retail customer has not been confirmed, but wheels were sold over-the-counter. Two bar (early) and three-bar spinner styles were available. Finish between the fins was natural.
• The 1963 exterior doors had raised pads for the door handles. Also, coupes had stainless steel trim forward of the vent window.
• All 1963 Corvettes had built-in adjusting mechanisms for the bottom seat cushions. Early 1963s had under-seat depressions, possibly for tool storage. This feature was removed about midway during the model year.
• Most 1963 Corvettes had fiberglass headlight buckets. Late 1963s and all 1964-67 models had metal buckets.
• Early 1963 models used roller-type catches for the gas filler doors. Later production used nylon slide catches.
• The glove box door in the 1963 Corvette was fiberglass and its face was covered with clear plastic. In early 1963s, the dash surface around the radio and speaker bezel was painted instead of vinyl-covered.
• 1963 hoods had rectangular trim panels glued in two forward recesses.
• 4-speed manual transmissions changed from Borg-Warner manufacture to Muncie during the 1963 model year.
• The outside rearview mirror was revised to a taller design with a shorter base at about the midpoint of 1963 production.

1963 OPTIONS

RPO #	DESCRIPTION	QTY	RETAIL $
837	Base Corvette Sport Coupe	10,594	$4,257.00
867	Base Corvette Convertible	10,919	4,037.00
898	Genuine Leather Seats	1,114	80.70
941	Sebring Silver Exterior Paint	3,516	80.70
A01	Soft Ray Tinted Glass, all windows	629	16.15
A02	Soft Ray Tinted Glass, windshield	470	10.80
A31	Power Windows	3,742	59.20
C07	Auxiliary Hardtop (for convertible)	5,739	236.75
C48	Heater and Defroster Deletion (credit)	124	-100.00
C60	Air Conditioning	278	421.80
G81	Positraction Rear Axle, all ratios	17,554	43.05
G91	Special Highway Axle, 3.08:1 ratio	211	2.20
J50	Power Brakes	3,336	43.05
J65	Sintered Metallic Brakes	5310	37.70
L75	327ci, 300hp Engine	8,033	53.80
L76	327ci, 340hp Engine	6,978	107.60
L84	327ci, 360hp Engine (fuel injection)	2,610	430.40
M20	4-Speed Manual Transmission	17,973	188.30
M35	Powerglide Automatic Transmission	2,621	199.10
N03	36 Gallon Fuel Tank (for coupe)	63	202.30
N11	Off Road Exhaust System	—	37.70
N34	Woodgrained Plastic Steering Wheel	130	16.15
N40	Power Steering	3,063	75.35
P48	Cast Aluminum Knock-Off Wheels (5)	—	322.80
P91	Blackwall Tires, 6.70x15, (nylon cord)	412	15.70
P92	Whitewall Tires, 670x15 (rayon cord)	19,383	31.55
T86	Back-up Lamps	318	10.80
U65	Signal Seeking AM Radio (earlier)	11,368	137.75
U69	AM-FM Radio (later)	9,178	174.35
Z06	Special Performance Equipment	199	1,818.45

• A 327ci, 250hp engine, 3-speed manual transmission, vinyl interior trim, and a soft top (convertible) were included in the base price.
• Z06 was first a coupe-only option. Revision to $1,293.95 excluded knock-off wheels and 36 gallon tank, and was available with convertibles.
• The 5,739 C07 quantity included 1,099 in lieu of soft tops at no extra cost.
• The 2,621 M35 quantity was split 1,116 with 250hp, 1,505 with 300hp.
• RPO U69 radios were phased in around March 1963, but these and RPO U65 radios were available simultaneously as supplies permitted.

1963 COLORS

CODE	EXTERIOR	QTY	SOFT TOP	WHEELS	INTERIORS
900	Tuxedo Black	—	Bk-W-Bg	Bk	Bk-R-S
912	Silver Blue	—	Bk-W-Bg	Bk-Si	Bk-Db
916	Daytona Blue	3,475	Bk-W-Bg	Bk-Db	Db-R-S
923	Riverside Red	4,612	Bk-W-Bg	Bk-R	Bk-R-S
932	Saddle Tan	—	Bk-W-Bg	Bk-S	Bk-R-S
936	Ermine White	—	Bk-W-Bg	Bk	Bk-Db-R-S
941	Sebring Silver	3,516	Bk-W-Bg	Bk-Si	Bk-Db-R-S

• Suggested interiors shown. Other combinations were possible.
• When whitewall tires were ordered, the standard wheels were painted black. With blackwalls, wheels were painted body color (except with white exteriors which may have had black wheels regardless of tire type).

Interior Codes: Std/Blk=Bk, 490A/J/S/XE/XG=Db/V-cpe, 490B/K/T/XF/XH=Db/V-con, 490C/L/Q/XA/XC=R/V-cpe, 490D/M/R/XB/XD=R/V-con, 490E/N/U/XJ/XL=S/V-cpe, 490F/P/V/XK/XM=S/V-con, 898A/E/Q/G/S=S/L-cpe, 898B/F/R/H/T=S/L-con.
• With the exception of "std" or "blk" for black vinyl, codes had three numbers followed by a one or two alpha-character suffix. This was the first year for coding to trim tags and inconsistencies exist.

Abbreviations: Bg=Beige, Bk=Black, con=convertible, cpe=coupe, Db=Dark Blue, L=Leather, R=Red, S=Saddle, Si=Silver, V=Vinyl, W=White.

1964 CORVETTE
Production: 8,304 coupe, 13,925 convertible, 22,229 total.

1964 NUMBERS

Vehicle: 40837S100001 through 40837S122229
· For convertibles, fourth digit is a 6.

Suffix:
RC: 327ci, 250hp, mt
RD: 327ci, 300hp, mt
RE: 327ci, 365hp, mt
RF: 327ci, 375hp, mt
RP: 327ci, 250hp, mt, ac
RQ: 327ci, 300hp, mt, ac
RR: 327ci, 365hp, mt, ac

RT: 327ci, 365hp, mt, ig
RU: 327ci, 365hp, mt, ac, ig
RX: 327ci, 375hp, mt, ig
SC: 327ci, 250hp, at
SD: 327ci, 300hp, at
SK: 327ci, 250hp, at, ac
SL: 327ci, 300hp, at, ac

Block: 3782870: All

Head: 3782461: 327ci, 300hp, 365hp, 375hp
3795896: 327ci, 250hp

Carburetor: Carter 3696S #3846246: 327ci, 250hp, at
Carter 3697S #3846247: 327ci, 250hp, mt
Carter 3720S/SA/SB #3851762: 327ci, 300hp, at
Carter 3721S/SA/SB #3851761: 327ci, 300hp, mt
Holley R2818A #3849804: 327ci, 365hp

Fuel Injection: Rochester 7017375, ep   Rochester 7017380, lp
Rochester 7017375R, lu

Distributor: 1111024: 327ci, 250hp,300hp 1111064: 327ci, 375hp, ig
1111060: 327ci, 365hp, ig   1111069: 327ci, 365hp, lp
1111062: 327ci, 365hp, ep   1111070: 327ci, 375hp, lp
1111063: 327ci, 375hp, ep

Alternator: 1100628: 327ci, ep, lu
1100665: 327ci, 250hp, 300hp, 365hp, ac
1100668: 327ci
1100669: 327ci, 365hp, 375hp, ig
1100684: 327ci, 365hp, ac, ig

Ending Vehicle:
Sep 63: 101741   Jan 64: 110297   May 64: 118805
Oct 63: 104045   Feb 64: 112322   Jun 64: 120920
Nov 63: 106063   Mar 64: 114570   Jul 64: 122229
Dec 63: 108091   Apr 64: 116865

Abbreviations: ac=air conditioning, at=automatic transmission, ci=cubic inch, ep=early production, hp=horsepower, ig=transistor ignition, lp=late production, lu=limited use, mt=manual transmission.

1964 FACTS

· Visible styling clues for 1964 included removal of the window split (coupes) and removal of the hood trim panels. Hood recesses remained.
· A three-speed fan was added to the rear of coupes to help ventilation. The fan pulled air through vents added to the driver side roof panel. The control switch was mounted under the driver's side of the instrument panel.
· Seats in 1964s looked similar to 1963, but 1964 backs were thicker and more square at the top; also, 1964 seats didn't have tilting mechanisms.
· Delivery of the knock-off wheel option during 1964 was certain. Only three-bar spinners were offered and the finish between fins was natural.
· Center recess areas of 1964 instruments were finished in black.
· Steering wheels in all 1964 Corvettes were walnut-grained plastic.
· The exterior door surface of 1964 models had a raised "pad" for the door handle to mount (except for late 1964s).
· Starting in 1964 (through 1967), some Corvette bodies were supplied by Dow-Smith, Ionia, Michigan, a division of A. O. Smith Company.

1964 OPTIONS

RPO #	DESCRIPTION	QTY	RETAIL $
837	Base Corvette Sport Coupe	8,304	$4,252.00
867	Base Corvette Convertible	13,925	4,037.00
—	Genuine Leather Seats	1,334	80.70
A01	Soft Ray Tinted Glass, all windows	6,031	16.15
A02	Soft Ray Tinted Glass, windshield	6,387	10.80
A31	Power Windows	3,706	59.20
C07	Auxiliary Hardtop (for convertible)	7,023	236.75
C48	Heater and Defroster Deletion (credit)	60	-100.00
C60	Air Conditioning	1,988	421.80
F40	Special Front and Rear Suspension	82	37.70
G81	Positraction Rear Axle, all ratios	18,279	43.05
G91	Special Highway Axle, 3.08:1 ratio	2,310	2.20
J50	Power Brakes	2,270	43.05
J56	Special Sintered Metallic Brake Package	29	629.50
J65	Sintered Metallic Brakes, power	4,780	53.80
K66	Transistor Ignition System	552	75.35
L75	327ci, 300hp Engine	10,471	53.80
L76	327ci, 365hp Engine	7,171	107.60
L84	327ci, 375hp Engine (fuel injection)	1,325	538.00
M20	4-Speed Manual Transmission	19,034	188.30
M35	Powerglide Automatic Transmission	2,480	199.10
N03	36 Gallon Fuel Tank (for coupe)	38	202.30
N11	Off Road Exhaust System	1,953	37.70
N40	Power Steering	3,126	75.35
P48	Cast Aluminum Knock Off Wheels (5)	806	322.80
P91	Blackwall Tires, 6.70x15 (nylon cord)	372	15.70
P92	Whitewall Tires, 6.70x15 (rayon cord)	19,977	31.85
T86	Back-up Lamps	11,085	10.80
U69	AM-FM Radio	20,934	176.50

• A 327ci, 250hp engine, 3-speed manual transmission, vinyl interior trim, and a soft top (convertible) were included in the base price.
• The 7,023 C07 quantity included 1,220 in lieu of soft tops at no extra cost.
• The 1,988 C60 quantity was split 1,069 coupe, 919 convertible.
• The 19,034 M20 quantity was split 10,538 with wide ratio 250hp and 300hp engines; 8,496 with close ratio 365hp and 375hp engines
• The 2,480 M35 quantity was split 904 with 250hp, 1,576 with 300hp .

1964 COLORS

CODE	EXTERIOR	QTY	SOFT TOP	WHEELS	INTERIORS
900	Tuxedo Black	1,897	Bk-W-Bg	Black	Bk-R-Si-W
912	Silver Blue	3,121	Bk-W-Bg	Black	Bk-B-W
916	Daytona Blue	3,454	Bk-W-Bg	Black	B-Si-W
923	Riverside Red	5,274	Bk-W-Bg	Black	Bk-R-W
932	Saddle Tan	1,765	Bk-W-Bg	Black	S-W
936	Ermine White	3,909	Bk-W-Bg	Black	Bk-B-R-S-Si-W
940	Satin Silver	2,785	Bk-W-Bg	Black	Bk-B-R-Si-W

• Suggested interiors shown. Other combinations were possible.
• In 1964, 24 Corvettes had non-standard paint, or primer.

Interior Codes: Std=Bk/V, 898A=Bk/L, 490AA/AB/G/H=R/V, 898FA/EA/L/M=R/L, 490BA/BB/J/K=B/V, 898JA/KA/N/P=B/L, 490CA/CB/L/M=S/V, 898CA/DA/G/H=S/L, 491AA/AE=Si+Bk/V, 899AA/AE=Si+Bk/L, 491BA/BE/M/N=Si+B/V, 899BA/BE/M/N=Si+B/L, 491CA/CB/CE=W+Bk/V, 899CA/CB/CE=W+Bk/L, 491GA/GE/R/S=W+B/V, 899GA/GE/R/S=W+B/L, 491DA/DE/P/Q=W+R/V, 899DA/DE/P/Q=W+R/L, 491HA/HE/T/U=W+S/V, 899HA/HE/T/U=W+S/L

• With the exception of "std" for black vinyl, 1964 interior codes consisted of three numbers followed by a one or two alpha-character suffix. In some cases, the suffix differentiated coupe from convertible and/or A. O. Smith body build from St. Louis in-house body build.

Abbreviations: B=Blue, Bg=Beige, Bk=Black, L=Leather, R=Red, S=Saddle, Si=Silver, V=Vinyl, W=White.

1965 CORVETTE
Production: 8,186 coupe, 15,376 convertible, 23,562 total.

1965 NUMBERS

Vehicle: 194375S100001 through 194375S123562
- For convertibles, fourth digit is a 6.

Suffix:
HE: 327ci, 250hp, mt	HO: 327ci, 250hp, at
HF: 327ci, 300hp, mt	HP: 327ci, 300hp, at
HG: 327ci, 375hp, mt	HQ: 327ci, 250hp, at, ac
HH: 327ci, 365hp, mt	HR: 327ci, 300hp, at, ac
HI: 327ci, 250hp, mt, ac	HT: 327ci, 350hp, mt
HJ: 327ci, 300hp, mt, ac	HU: 327ci, 350hp, mt, ac
HK: 327ci, 365hp, mt, ac	HV: 327ci, 350hp, mt, ig
HL: 327ci, 365hp, mt, ig	HW: 327ci, 350hp, mt, ac, ig
HM: 327ci, 365hp, mt, ac, ig	IF: 396ci, 425hp, mt, ig
HN: 327ci, 375ph, mt, ig	

Block: 3782870: 327ci   3855962: 396ci   3858180: 327ci (lu)

Head: 3782461: 327ci   3856208: 396ci

Carburetor: Carter 3696S #3846246: 327ci, 250hp, at
Carter 3697S #3846247: 327ci, 250hp, mt
Carter 3720SB #3851762: 327ci, 300hp, at
Carter 3721SB #3851761: 327ci, 300hp, mt
Holley R2818A #3849804: 327ci, 350hp, 365hp
Holley R3124A #3868826: 396ci, 425hp

Fuel Injection: Rochester 7017380

Distributor: 1111060: 327ci, 365hp, ig   1111076: 327ci, 250hp, 300hp
1111064: 327ci, 375hp, ig   1111087: 327ci, 350hp
1111069: 327ci, 365hp   1111088: 327ci, 350hp, ig
1111070: 327ci, 375hp   1111093: 396ci, 425hp, ig

Alternator: 1100693: 327ci   1100696: 327ci, 396ci, ig
1100694: 327ci, ac   1100697: 327ci, 350hp, 365hp, ac, ig

Ending Vehicle:
Aug 64: 100227	Jan 65: 108442	May 65: 118753
Sep 64: 101425	Feb 65: 111059	Jun 65: 121216
Nov 64: 103347	Mar 65: 113936	Jul 65: 123562
Dec 64: 105754	Apr 65: 116516	Aug 65: 123564

Abbreviations: ac=air conditioning, at=automatic transmission, ci=cubic inch, hp=horsepower, ig=transistor ignition, lu=limited use, mt=manual transmission.

1965 FACTS

- Appearance changes included a restyle of the side front fender louvers as three functional, vertical slots. Hood recesses were removed. Horizontal grill bars changed to black, but outer trim rings remained bright.
- The vehicle identification number (VIN) of the last 1965 Corvette built ended in 23,564, two units higher than the 23,562 total build figure. It isn't certain if the total is wrong, or if two VINs weren't used.
- This was the last year for fuel injection in Corvettes until throttle-body injection in 1982. In mid-March 1965, the big-block option was unveiled, limited to a 396ci, 425hp version which came with a special hood.
- Four-wheel disc brakes were introduced as standard equipment for 1965 Corvettes. Drum brakes were a cost-delete option while supplies lasted.
- Instruments were done in a black, flat-face style. The area around the radio and speaker bezel was painted, rather than vinyl-covered.
- Seats and inner door panels were redesigned for 1965 Corvettes.
- Optional knock-off wheels were dark grey between the fins.

1965 OPTIONS

RPO #	DESCRIPTION	QTY	RETAIL $
19437	Base Corvette Sport Coupe	8,186	$4,321.00
19467	Base Corvette Convertible	15,376	4,106.00
—	Genuine Leather Seats	2,128	80.70
A01	Soft Ray Tinted Glass, all windows	8,752	16.15
A02	Soft Ray Tinted Glass, windshield	7,624	10.80
A31	Power Windows	3,809	59.20
C07	Auxiliary Hardtop (for convertible)	7,787	236.75
C48	Heater and Defroster Deletion (credit)	39	-100.00
C60	Air Conditioning	2,423	421.80
F40	Special Front and Rear Suspension	975	37.70
G81	Positraction Rear Axle, all ratios	19,965	43.05
G91	Special Highway Axle, 3.08:1 ratio	1,886	2.20
J50	Power Brakes	4,044	43.05
J61	Drum Brakes (substitution credit)	316	-64.50
K66	Transistor Ignition System	3,686	75.35
L75	327ci, 300hp Engine	8,358	53.80
L76	327ci, 365hp Engine	5,011	129.15
L78	396ci, 425hp Engine	2,157	292.70
L79	327ci, 350hp Engine	4,716	107.60
L84	327ci, 375hp Engine (fuel injection)	771	538.00
M20	4-Speed Manual Transmission	21,107	188.30
M35	Powerglide Automatic Transmission	2,021	199.10
N03	36 Gallon Fuel Tank (for coupe)	41	202.30
N11	Off Road Exhaust System	2,468	37.70
N14	Side Mount Exhaust System	759	134.50
N32	Teakwood Steering Wheel	2,260	48.45
N36	Telescopic Steering Column	3,917	43.05
N40	Power Steering	3,236	96.85
P48	Cast Aluminum Knock-Off Wheels (5)	1,116	322.80
P91	Blackwall Tires, 7.75x15 (nylon cord)	168	15.70
P92	Whitewall Tires, 7.75x15 (rayon cord)	19,300	31.85
T01	Goldwall Tires, 7.75x15 (nylon cord)	989	50.05
U69	AM-FM Radio	22,113	203.40
Z01	Comfort and Convenience Group	15,397	16.15

- A 327ci, 250hp engine, 3-speed manual transmission, vinyl interior trim, and soft top (convertible) were included in the base price.
- The 7,787 C07 quantity included 1,277 in lieu of soft tops at no extra cost.
- The 2,423 C60 quantity was split 1,551 coupe, 872 convertible.
- The 2,021 M35 quantity was split 663 with 250hp, 1,358 with 300hp.
- The P91 blackwall tire option was a nylon replacement for the standard rayon blackwall. It was available briefly early in production.
- The Z01 option included backup lights and an inside rearview mirror.

1965 COLORS

CODE	EXTERIOR	QTY	SOFT TOP	WHEELS	INTERIORS
AA	Tuxedo Black	1,191	Bk-W-Bg	Black	Bk-B-G-M-R-S-Si-W
CC	Ermine White	2,216	Bk-W-Bg	Black	Bk-B-G-M-R-S-Si-W
FF	Nassau Blue	6,022	Bk-W-Bg	Black	Bk-B-W
GG	Glen Green	3,782	Bk-W-Bg	Black	Bk-G-S-W
MM	Milano Maroon	2,831	Bk-W-Bg	Black	Bk-R-M-S-W
QQ	Silver Pearl	2,552	Bk-W-Bg	Black	Bk-R-Si
UU	Rally Red	3,688	Bk-W-Bg	Black	Bk-R-W
XX	Goldwood Yellow	1,275	Bk-W-Bg	Black	Bk-W

- Suggested interiors shown. Other combinations were possible.
- In 1965, 5 Corvettes had non-standard paint, or primer.

Interior Codes: Std=Bk/V; 402=Bk/L; 407=R/V; 408=R/L; 414=B/V; 415=B/L; 420=S/V; 421=S/L; 426=Si/V; 427=Si/L; 430=G/V; 431=G/L; 435=M/V; 436=M/L; 437=W+Bk/V; 438=W+Bk/L; 443=W+R/V; 444=W+R/L; 450=W+B/V; 451=W+B/L.

Abbreviations: B=Blue, Bg=Beige, Bk=Black, G=Green, L=Leather, M=Maroon, R=Red, S=Saddle, Si=Silver, V=Vinyl, W=White.

1966 CORVETTE
Production: 9,958 coupe, 17,762 convertible, 27,720 total.

1966 NUMBERS

Vehicle: 194376S100001 through 194376S127720
  • For convertibles, fourth digit is a 6.

Suffix: HD: 327ci, 350hp, mt, ar   IK: 427ci, 425hp, mt
HE: 327ci, 300hp, mt   IL: 427ci, 390hp, mt
HH: 327ci, 300hp, mt, ar   IM: 427ci, 390hp, mt, ar
HO: 327ci, 300hp, at   IP: 427ci, 450/425hp, mt
HP: 327ci, 350hp, mt, ps   IQ: 427ci, 390hp, at
HR: 327ci, 300hp, at, ar   IR: 427ci, 390hp, at, ar
HT: 327ci, 350hp, mt   KH: 327ci, 350hp, mt, ar, ac, ps

Block: 3858174: 327ci   3892657: 327ci, lp (uu)
3869942: 427ci   3855961: 427ci, ep (uu)

Head: 3782461: 327ci, 300hp, 350hp   3873858: 427ci, 450/425hp
3872702: 427ci, 390hp

Carburetor: Holley R3247A #3886101: 427ci, 450/425hp
Holley R3367A #3884505: 327ci, 300hp, 350hp
Holley R3370A #3882835: 427ci, 390hp
Holley R3605A #3890499: 327ci, 300hp, 350hp, ar
Holley R3606A #3892341: 427ci, 390hp, ar

Distributor: 1111093: 427ci, 450/425hp, ig   1111153: 327ci, 300hp
1111141: 427ci, 390hp   1111156: 327ci, 350hp
1111142: 427ci, 390hp, ig   1111157: 327ci, 350hp, ig

Alternator: 1100693: 327ci, 427ci   1100696: 327ci, 427ci, ig
1100694: 327ci, 427ci, ac 1100750: 327ci, 427ci, ac

Ending Vehicle: Sep 65: 102031   Jan 66: 112587   May 66: 123016
Oct 65: 104384   Feb 66: 115283   Jun 66: 125469
Nov 65: 107186   Mar 66: 118091   Jul 66: 127720
Dec 65: 109892   Apr 66: 120664

Abbreviations: ac=air conditioning, ar=air injection reactor,
at=automatic transmission, ci=cubic inch, ep=early production,
hp=horsepower, ig=transistor ignition, lp=late production,
mt=manual transmission, ps=power steering, uu=uncertain usage.

1966 FACTS

• The 1966 Corvette's styling was similar to the previous model. There were differences in trim, including the addition of the Corvette script (elongated vertical style) to the hood, and a new, plated, square-mesh, cast grill. Also, roof vents which had been both functional and non-functional in previous mid-year Corvette coupes, were deleted completely.
• Seats were similar to 1965, except that 1966 seats had additional pleats in the upper and lower sections for better weight distribution at the seams.
• The knock-off wheel option continued in 1966, but with a dull-finish center cone instead of bright. The area between the fins was dark grey.
• The 427 cubic-inch engines were introduced in the 1966 model. All with 427 engines received special hoods. The high performance, solid-lifter 427 was initially listed at 450hp but, for reasons unclear, the rating (not the actual output) was reduced to 425hp shortly after introduction. Also, the 390hp engine was sometimes rated at 400hp.
• Backup lights became standard equipment in the 1966 model. They were incorporated into the existing rear inboard taillight housings.
• The fiberboard headliners of coupes and convertible hardtops (except early) were replaced with vinyl-covered foam. Headrests were available for the first time. Interior door pulls were bright metal.

1966 OPTIONS

RPO #	DESCRIPTION	QTY	RETAIL$
19437	Base Corvette Sport Coupe	9,958	$4,295.00
19467	Base Corvette Convertible	17,762	4,084.00
—	Genuine Leather Seats	2,002	79.00
A01	Soft Ray Tinted Glass, all windows	11,859	15.80
A02	Soft Ray Tinted Glass, windshield	9,270	10.55
A31	Power Windows	4,562	57.95
A82	Headrests	1,033	42.15
A85	Shoulder Belts	37	26.35
C07	Auxiliary Hardtop (for convertible)	8,463	231.75
C48	Heater and Defroster Deletion (credit)	54	-97.85
C60	Air Conditioning	3,520	412.90
F41	Special Front and Rear Suspension	2,705	36.90
G81	Positraction Rear Axle, all ratios	24,056	42.15
J50	Power Brakes	5,464	42.15
J56	Special Heavy Duty Brakes	382	342.30
K19	Air Injection Reactor	2,380	44.75
K66	Transistor Ignition System	7,146	73.75
L36	427ci, 390hp Engine	5,116	181.20
L72	427ci, 450/425hp Engine	5,258	312.85
L79	327ci, 350hp Engine	7,591	105.35
M20	4-Speed Manual Transmission	10,837	184.35
M21	4-Speed Man Trans, close ratio	13,903	184.35
M22	4-Speed Man Trans, close ratio, heavy duty	15	237.00
M35	Powerglide Automatic Transmission	2,401	194.85
N03	36 Gallon Fuel Tank (for coupe)	66	198.05
N11	Off Road Exhaust System	2,795	36.90
N14	Side Mount Exhaust System	3,617	131.65
N32	Teakwood Steering Wheel	3,941	47.40
N36	Telescopic Steering Column	3,670	42.15
N40	Power Steering	5,611	94.80
P48	Cast Aluminum Knock-Off Wheels (5)	1,194	316.00
P92	Whitewall Tires, 7.75x15, (rayon cord)	17,969	31.30
T01	Goldwall Tires, 7.75x15 (nylon cord)	5,557	46.55
U69	AM-FM Radio	26,363	199.10
V74	Traffic Hazard Lamp Switch	5,764	11.60

• A 327ci, 300hp engine, 3-speed manual transmission, vinyl interior trim, and soft top (convertible) were included in the base price.
• The 8,463 C07 quantity included 1,303 in lieu of soft tops at no extra cost.
• The 3,520 C60 quantity was split 2,138 coupe, 1,382 convertible.
• The 2,401 M35 quantity was split 2,381 with 300hp, 20 with 390hp .
• The K19 emission device was not limited to California use.

1966 COLORS

CODE	EXTERIOR	QTY	SOFT TOP	WHEELS	INTERIORS
900	Tuxedo Black	1,190	Bk-W-Bg	Black	Bk-R-Bb-WB-S-Si-G-B
972	Ermine White	2,120	Bk-W-Bg	Black	Bk-R-Bb-WB-S-Si-G-B
974	Rally Red	3,366	Bk-W-Bg	Black	Bk-R
976	Nassau Blue	6,100	Bk-W-Bg	Black	Bk-Bb-WB-B
978	Laguna Blue	2,054	Bk-W-Bg	Black	Bk-Bb-B
980	Trophy Blue	1,463	Bk-W-Bg	Black	Bk-Bb-B
982	Mosport Green	2,311	Bk-W-Bg	Black	Bk-G
984	Sunfire Yellow	2,339	Bk-W-Bg	Black	Bk
986	Silver Pearl	2,967	Bk-W-Bg	Black	Bk-Si
988	Milano Maroon	3,799	Bk-W-Bg	Black	Bk-S

• Suggested interiors shown. Other combinations were possible.
• In 1966, 11 Corvettes were painted non-standard colors, or primer.
Interior Codes: Std=Bk/V; 402=Bk/L; 407=R/V; 408=R/L; 414=Bb/V; 415=Bb/L; 418=B/V; 419=B/L; 420=S/V; 421=S/L; 426=Si/V; 427=Si/L; 430=G/V; 450=W+B/V.
Abbreviations: B=Blue, Bb=Bright Blue, Bg=Beige; Bk=Black, G=Green, L=Leather, R=Red, S=Saddle, Si=Silver, V=Vinyl, W=White, WB=White +Blue.

1967 CORVETTE

Production: 8,504 coupe, 14,436 convertible, 22,940 total.

1967 NUMBERS

Vehicle: 194377S100001 through 194377S122940
       • For convertibles, fourth digit is a 6.

Suffix:

HD: 327ci, 350hp, mt, ar	IT: 427ci, 430hp (L88), mt
HE: 327ci, 300hp, mt	IU: 427ci, 435hp, mt, ah
HH: 327ci, 300hp, mt, ar	JA: 427ci, 435hp, mt, ar
HO: 327ci, 300hp, at	JC: 427ci, 400hp, mt
HP: 327ci, 350hp, mt, ac, ps	JD: 427ci, 400hp, at
HR: 327ci, 300hp, at, ar	JE: 427ci, 435hp, mt
HT: 327ci, 350hp, mt	JF: 427ci, 400hp, mt, ar
IL: 427ci, 390hp, mt	JG: 427ci, 400hp, at, ar
IM: 427ci, 390hp, mt, ar	JH: 427ci, 435hp, mt, ar, ah
IQ: 427ci, 390hp, at	KH: 327ci, 350hp, mt, ar, ac, ps
IR: 427ci, 390hp, at, ar	

Block:

3892657: 327ci	3869942: 427ci, ep, uu
3904351: 427ci	3916321: 427ci, lp, uu

Head:

3890462: 327ci, 300hp, 350hp	3904392: 427ci, 430hp, 435hp, ah
3904390: 427ci, 390hp, 400hp,ep	3909802: 427ci, 390hp, 400hp, lp
3904391: 427ci, 435hp, ih, ep	3919840: 427ci, 435hp, ih, lp

Carburetor:
Holley R3418A: 427ci, 430hp (L88)
Holley R3659A: 427ci, 400hp, 435hp, fc, rc
Holley R3660A: 427ci, 400hp(cc,mt), 435hp(cc)
Holley R3810A: 327ci, 300hp, 350hp
Holley R3814A: 327ci, 300hp, 350hp, ar
Holley R3811A: 427ci, 390hp
Holley R3815A: 427ci, 390hp, ar
Holley R3888A: 427ci, 400hp, at, cc

Distributor:

1111117: 327ci, 300hp, at	1111141: 427ci, 390hp, ep
1111157: 327ci, 350hp, ig	1111240: 427ci, 430hp (L88)
1111194: 327ci, 300hp, mt	1111247: 427ci, 390hp, 400hp
1111196: 327ci, 350hp	1111248: 427ci, 390hp, 400hp, ig, ep
1111258: 427ci, 435hp, ig	1111294: 427ci, 390hp, 400hp, ig

Alternator:

1100693: 327ci, 427ci	1100696: 327ci, 427ci, ig
1100694: 327ci, 427ci, ac	1100750: 327ci, 427ci,ac,ig,uu

Ending Vehicle:

Sep 66: 102110	Jan 67: 109465	May 67: 119747
Oct 66: 102685	Feb 67: 112264	Jun 67: 122214
Nov 66: 104981	Mar 67: 115316	Jul 67: 122940
Dec 66: 107110	Apr 67: 117395	

Abbreviations: ac=air conditioning, ah=aluminum head, ar=air injection reactor, at=automatic transmission, cc=center carburetor, ci=cubic inch, ep=early production, fc=front carburetor, hp=horsepower, ig=transistor ignition, ih=iron head, lp=late production, mt=manual transmission, ps=power steering, rc=rear carburetor, uu=uncertain usage.

1967 FACTS

• Last of the 1963-67 "mid years," 1967's exterior was the least adorned due to removal of trim, including hood script emblems and fender flags. Functional fender vents were a new style for 1967 with five angled slots.
• Seat design was modified and the parking brake handle was redesigned and relocated from under the instrument panel to between the seats.
• Safety legislation required a modification of the knock-off wheel option. For 1967, it changed to a bolt-on, cast alloy style with a clip-on center cap to conceal the lug nuts. Rally wheels were no-cost standard equipment.

1967 OPTIONS

RPO #	DESCRIPTION	QTY	RETAIL $
19437	Base Corvette Sport Coupe	8,504	$4,388.75
19467	Base Corvette Convertible	14,436	4,240.75
—	Genuine Leather Seats	1,601	79.00
A01	Soft Ray Tinted Glass, all windows	11,331	15.80
A02	Soft Ray Tinted Glass, windshield	6,558	10.55
A31	Power Windows	4,036	57.95
A82	Headrests	1,762	42.15
A85	Shoulder Belts	1,426	26.35
C07	Auxiliary Hardtop (for convertible)	6,880	231.75
C08	Vinyl Covering (for auxiliary hardtop)	1,966	52.70
C48	Heater and Defroster Deletion (credit)	35	-97.85
C60	Air Conditioning	3,788	412.90
F41	Special Front and Rear Suspension	2,198	36.90
G81	Positraction Rear Axle, all ratios	20,308	42.15
J50	Power Brakes	4,766	42.15
J56	Special Heavy Duty Brakes	267	342.30
K19	Air Injection Reactor	2,573	44.75
K66	Transistor Ignition System	5,759	73.75
L36	427ci, 390hp Engine	3,832	200.15
L68	427ci, 400hp Engine	2,101	305.50
L71	427ci, 435hp Engine	3,754	437.10
L79	327ci, 350hp Engine	6,375	105.35
L88	427ci, 430hp Engine	20	947.90
L89	Aluminum Cylinder Heads for L71	16	368.65
M20	4-Speed Manual Transmission	9,157	184.35
M21	4-Speed Man Trans, close ratio	11,015	184.35
M22	4-Speed Man Trans, close ratio, heavy duty	20	237.00
M35	Powerglide Automatic Transmission	2,324	194.35
N03	36 Gallon Fuel Tank (for coupe)	2	198.05
N11	Off Road Exhaust System	2,326	36.90
N14	Side Mount Exhaust System	4,209	131.65
N36	Telescopic Steering Column	2,415	42.15
N40	Power Steering	5,747	94.80
N89	Cast Aluminum Bolt-On Wheels (5)	720	263.30
P92	Whitewall Tires, 7.75x15	13,445	31.35
QB1	Redline Tires, 7.75x15	4,230	46.65
U15	Speed Warning Indicator	2,108	10.55
U69	AM-FM Radio	22,193	172.75

• A 327ci, 300hp engine, 3-speed manual transmission, vinyl interior trim, and soft top (convertible) were included in the base price.
• The 6,880 C07 quantity included 895 in lieu of soft tops at no extra cost.
• The 3,788 C60 quantity was split 2,235 coupe, 1,553 convertible.
• The 2,324 M35 quantity was split 1,725 with 300hp engines, 392 with 390hp engines, and 207 with 400hp engines.

1967 COLORS

CODE	EXTERIOR	QTY	SOFT TOP	WHEELS	INTERIORS
900	Tuxedo Black	815	Bk-W-Tb	Silver	Bk-R-Bb-S-W-Tb-G
972	Ermine White	1,423	Bk-W-Tb	Silver	Bk-R-Bb-S-W-Tb-G
974	Rally Red	2,341	Bk-W-Tb	Silver	Bk-R-W
976	Marina Blue	3,840	Bk-W-Tb	Silver	Bk-Bb-W
977	Lynndale Blue	1,381	Bk-W-Tb	Silver	Bk-W-Tb
980	Elkhart Blue	1,096	Bk-W-Tb	Silver	Bk-Tb
983	Goodwood Green	4,293	Bk-W-Tb	Silver	Bk-S-W-G
984	Sunfire Yellow	2,325	Bk-W-Tb	Silver	Bk-W
986	Silver Pearl	1,952	Bk-W-Tb	Silver	Bk-Tb
988	Marlboro Maroon	3,464	Bk-W-Tb	Silver	Bk-W-S

• Suggested interiors shown. Other combinations were possible.
• In 1967, 10 Corvettes had non-standard paint, or primer.
Interiors: Std=Bk/V; 402=Bk/L; 407=R/V; 408=R/L; 414=Bb/V; 415=Bb/L; 418=Tb/V; 419=Tb/L; 420=S/V; 421=S/L; 430=G/V; 450=W+B/V; 455=W+Bk/V.
Abbreviations: Bb=Bright Blue, Bk=Black, G=Green, L=Leather, R=Red, S=Saddle, Tb=Teal Blue, V=Vinyl, W=White.

1968 CORVETTE

Production: 9,936 coupe, 18,630 convertible, 28,566 total.

1968 NUMBERS

Vehicle: 194378S400001 through 194378S428566
  • For convertibles, fourth digit is a 6.

Suffix:
HE: 327ci, 300hp, mt
HO: 327ci, 300hp, at
HP: 327ci, 350hp, mt, ac, ps
HT: 327ci, 350hp, mt
IL: 427ci, 390hp, mt
IM: 427ci, 400hp, mt

IO: 427ci, 400hp, at
IQ: 427ci, 390hp, at
IR: 427ci, 435hp, mt
IT: 427ci, 430hp (L88), mt, ah
IU: 427ci, 435hp, mt, ah

Block: 3914678: 327ci, 300hp, 350hp
3916321: 427ci, 390hp, 400hp, 430hp, 435hp
3935439: 427ci, 430hp, 435hp

Head: 3917215: 427ci, 390hp, 400hp   3919840: 427ci, 435hp, ih
3917291: 327ci, 300hp, 350hp   3919842: 427ci, 430hp, 435hp, ah
3917292: 327ci, 350hp

Carb: Rochester Q-jet #7028207: 327ci, 300hp, mt
Rochester Q-jet #7028208: 327ci, 300hp, at
Rochester Q-jet #7028209: 427ci, 390hp, mt
Rochester Q-jet #7028216: 427ci, 390hp, at
Rochester Q-jet #7028219: 327ci, 350hp, mt
Holley R3659A #3902353: 427ci, 400hp, 435hp, fc, rc
Holley R4054A #3925519: 427ci, 430hp (L88)
Holley R4055A #3925517: 427ci, 400hp(cc,mt), 435hp(cc), fd
Holley R4055-1A #3940929: 427ci, 400hp(cc,mt), 435hp(cc), sd
Holley R4056A #3902516: 427ci, 400hp, cc, at, fd
Holley R4056-1A #3940930: 427ci, 400hp, cc, at, sd

Distributor: 1111194: 327ci, 300hp   1111296: 427ci, 435hp,ig
1111293: 427ci, 390hp,400hp   1111438: 327ci, 350hp
1111294: 427ci, 390hp,400hp,ig 1111441: 327ci, 350hp,ig,fd
1111295: 427ci, 430hp,ig   1111475: 327ci, 350hp,ig,sd

Alternator: 1100693: 300hp, 350hp, 390hp, 400hp
1100696: 350hp, 390hp, 400hp, 430hp, 435hp, ig
1100750: All with ac

Ending Vehicle: Sep 67: 400905   Jan 68: 410386   May 68: 420928
Oct 67: 403410   Feb 68: 412647   Jun 68: 423978
Nov 67: 405682   Mar 68: 415000   Aug 68: 428566
Dec 67: 407922   Apr 68: 417676

Abbreviations: ac=air conditioning, ah=aluminum heads,
at=automatic transmission, cc=center carburetor, ci=cubic inch, fc=front
carburetor, fd=first design, hp=horsepower, ig=transistor ignition,
ih=iron head, mt=manual transmission, ps=power steering, rc=rear
carburetor, sd=second design.

1968 FACTS

• The 1968 Corvette exterior and interior were redesigned. Coupes
featured removable roof panels and rear window.
• Automatic transmissions changed for 1968 from the two-speed Power-
glide to the three-speed Turbo Hydra-Matic.
• Hidden headlights "poped up" into position, rather than rotated. The
mechanism was vacuum operated instead of electric as before.
• The battery moved to a compartment behind the seats.
• Windshield wipers were hidden under a vacuum-operated panel.
• Side vent windows were eliminated starting with the 1968 Corvette.

1968 OPTIONS

RPO #	DESCRIPTION	QTY	RETAIL$
19437	Base Corvette Sport Coupe	9,936	$4,663.00
19467	Base Corvette Convertible	18,630	4,320.00
—	Genuine Leather Seats	2,429	79.00
A01	Soft Ray Tinted Glass, all windows	17,635	15.80
A02	Soft Ray Tinted Glass, windshield	5,509	10.55
A31	Power Windows	7,065	57.95
A82	Headrests	3,197	42.15
A85	Custom Shoulder Belts (std with coupe)	350	26.35
C07	Auxiliary Hardtop (for convertible)	8,735	231.75
C08	Vinyl Covering (for auxiliary hardtop)	3,050	52.70
C50	Rear Window Defroster	693	31.60
C60	Air Conditioning	5,664	412.90
F41	Special Front and Rear Suspension	1,758	36.90
G81	Positraction Rear Axle, all ratios	27,008	46.35
J50	Power Brakes	9,559	42.15
J56	Special Heavy Duty Brakes	81	384.45
K66	Transistor Ignition System	5,457	73.75
L36	427ci, 390hp Engine	7,717	200.15
L68	427ci, 400hp Engine	1,932	305.50
L71	427ci, 435hp Engine	2,898	437.10
L79	327ci, 350hp Engine	9,440	105.35
L88	427ci, 430hp Engine	80	947.90
L89	Aluminum Cylinder Heads with L71	624	805.75
M20	4-Speed Manual Transmission	10,760	184.35
M21	4-Speed Man Trans, close ratio	12,337	184.35
M22	4-Speed Man Trans, close ratio, heavy duty	00	263.30
M40	Turbo Hydra-Matic Automatic Transmission	5,063	226.45
N11	Off Road Exhaust System	4,695	36.90
N36	Telescopic Steering Column	6,477	42.15
N40	Power Steering	12,364	94.80
P01	Bright Metal Wheel Cover	8,971	57.95
PT6	Red Stripe Tires, F70x15, nylon	11,686	31.30
PT7	White Stripe Tires, F70x15, nylon	9,692	31.30
UA6	Alarm System	388	26.35
U15	Speed Warning Indicator	3,453	10.55
U69	AM-FM Radio	24,609	172.75
U79	AM-FM Radio, stereo	3,311	278.10

• A 327ci, 300hp engine, 3-speed manual transmission, vinyl interior trim, and soft top (convertible) were included in the base price.
• The M40 Turbo Hydra-Matic transmission cost $226.45 when combined with the 327ci, 300hp engine, but was $237.00 when combined with the 427ci, 390hp or 400hp engines.

1968 COLORS

CODE	EXTERIOR	QTY	SOFT TOP	INTERIORS
900	Tuxedo Black	708	Bk-W-Bg	Bk-Db-Do-Gu-Mb-R-To
972	Polar White	1,868	Bk-W-Bg	Bk-Db-Do-Gu-Mb-R-To
974	Rally Red	2,918	Bk-W-Bg	Bk-R
976	LeMans Blue	4,722	Bk-W-Bg	Bk-Mb-Db
978	International Blue	2,473	Bk-W-Bg	Bk-Mb-Db
983	British Green	4,779	Bk-W-Bg	Bk
984	Safari Yellow	3,133	Bk-W-Bg	Bk
986	Silverstone Silver	3,435	Bk-W-Bg	Bk-Db-Gu
988	Cordovan Maroon	1,155	Bk-W-Bg	Bk
992	Corvette Bronze	3,374	Bk-W-Bg	Bk-Do-To

• Suggested interiors shown. Other combinations were possible.
• All 1968 wheels were painted silver.
• In 1968, 1 Corvette had non-standard (pink) paint.

Interior Codes: Std=Bk/V, 402=Bk/L, 407=R/V, 408=R/L, 411=Db/V, 414=Mb/V, 415=Mb/L, 425=Do/V, 426=Do/L, 435=To/V, 436=To/L, 442=Gu/V.

Abbreviations: Bg=Beige, Bk=Black, Db=Dark Blue, Do=Dark Orange, Gu=Gunmetal, L=Leather, Mb=Medium Blue, R=Red, To=Tobacco, V=Vinyl, W=White.

1969 CORVETTE
Production: 22,129 coupe, 16,633 convertible, 38,762 total.

1969 NUMBERS

Vehicle: 194379S700001 through 194379S738762
• For convertibles, fourth digit is a 6.

Suffix:
GC: 350ci, 350hp, mt, ig	LT: 427ci, 435hp, mt, hc
GD: 350ci, 350hp, mt, ac, ig	LU: 427ci, 435hp, mt, ah, hc
HW: 350ci, 350hp, mt	LV: 427ci, 430hp(L88), at
HX: 350ci, 350hp, mt, ac	LW: 427ci, 435hp, at, ah
HY: 350ci, 300hp, mt	LX: 427ci, 435hp, at
HZ: 350ci, 300hp, at	ME: 427ci, 430hp(ZL1), mt
LL: 427ci, 390hp, at	MG: 427ci, 430hp(ZL1), at
LM: 427ci, 390hp, mt	MH: 427ci, 390hp, mt, ig
LN: 427ci, 400hp, at	MI: 427ci, 390hp, at, ig
LO: 427ci, 430hp, mt	MJ: 427ci, 400hp, at, ig
LP: 427ci, 435hp, mt, ah	MK: 427ci, 400hp, mt, ig
LQ: 427ci, 400hp, mt	MR: 427ci, 430hp(L88), mt
LR: 427ci, 435hp, mt	MS: 427ci, uu

Block:
3932386, 3932388: 350ci, 300hp, 350hp
3935439: 427ci, 390hp, 400hp, 430hp, 435hp
3946052: 427ci, 430hp (ZL1)
3955270: 427ci, 390hp, 400hp, 430hp, 435hp
3956618: 350ci, 300hp, 350hp
3963512: 427ci, 390hp, 400hp, 430hp, 435hp, lp
3970010: 350ci, 300hp, 350hp, lp

Head:
3919840: 427ci, 435hp, ih	3931063: 427ci, 390hp, 400hp
3919842: 427ci, 435hp, ah	3946074: 427ci, 430hp, ah
3927186: 350ci, 300hp, 350hp	3947041: 350ci, 300hp
3927187: 350ci, 300hp	

Carb:
Rochester Q-jet #7029202: 350ci, 300hp, at
Rochester Q-jet #7029203: 350ci, 300hp, mt
Rochester Q-jet #7029204: 427ci, 390hp, at
Rochester Q-jet #7029207: 350ci, 350hp, mt
Rochester Q-jet #7029215: 427ci, 390hp, mt
Holley R3659A #3902353: 427ci, 400hp(fc,rc), 435hp(fc,rc)
Holley R4055-1A #3940929: 427ci, 400hp(cc,mt), 435hp(cc)
Holley R4056-1A #3940930: 427ci, 400hp, cc, at
Holley R4054A #3925519: 427ci, 430hp, fd
Holley R4296A #3955205: 427ci, 430hp, sd

Distributor:
1111490: 350ci, 300hp	1111926: 427ci, 390hp, 400hp
1111491: 350ci, 350hp, ig	1111928: 427ci, 435hp, ig
1111493: 350ci, 350hp	1111954: 427ci, 390hp, 400hp, ig
1111927: 427ci, 430hp, ig	

Alternator:
1100825: ac and/or ig	1100882: 427ci, 430hp,435hp,ig
1100833: 427ci, 390hp, 400hp	1100884: 350ci, 300hp, ac (uu)
1100859: 350ci, 300hp, 350hp	1100884: ig (uu)

Ending Vehicle:
Sep 68: 703041	Feb 69: 717571	Aug 69: 728107
Oct 68: 706272	Mar 69: 720543	Sep 69: 730963
Nov 68: 709159	Apr 69: 721315	Oct 69: 734067
Dec 68: 711742	Jun 69: 723374	Nov 69: 736798
Jan 69: 714695	Jul 69: 725875	Dec 69: 738762

Abbreviations: ac=air conditioning, ah=aluminum heads, at=automatic transmission, cc=center carburetor, ci=cubic inch, fd=first design, fc=front carburetor, hc=heavy-duty clutch, hp=horsepower, ig=transistor ignition, ih=iron head, lp=late production, mt=manual transmission, ps=power steering, rc=rear carburetor, sd=second design, uu=uncertain usage.

1969 OPTIONS

RPO #	DESCRIPTION	QTY	RETAIL $
19437	Base Corvette Sport Coupe	22,129	$4,781.00
19467	Base Corvette Convertible	16,633	4,438.00
—	Genuine Leather Seats	3,729	79.00
A01	Soft Ray Tinted Glass, all windows	31,270	16.90
A31	Power Windows	9,816	63.20
A82	Headrests	38,762	17.95
A85	Custom Shoulder Belts (std with coupe)	600	42.15
C07	Auxiliary Hardtop (for convertible)	7,878	252.80
C08	Vinyl Covering (for auxiliary hardtop)	3,266	57.95
C50	Rear Window Defroster	2,485	32.65
C60	Air Conditioning	11,859	428.70
F41	Special Front and Rear Suspension	1,661	36.90
G81	Positraction Rear Axle, all ratios	36,965	46.35
J50	Power Brakes	16,876	42.15
J56	Special Heavy Duty Brakes	115	384.45
K05	Engine Block Heater	824	10.55
K66	Transistor Ignition System	5,702	81.10
L36	427ci, 390hp Engine	10,531	221.20
L46	350ci, 350hp Engine	12,846	131.65
L68	427ci, 400hp Engine	2,072	326.55
L71	427ci, 435hp Engine	2,722	437.10
L88	427ci, 430hp Engine	116	1,032.15
L89	Aluminum Cylinder Heads with L71	390	832.05
MA6	Heavy Duty Clutch	102	79.00
M20	4-Speed Manual Transmission	16,507	184.80
M21	4-Speed Man Trans, close ratio	13,741	184.80
M22	4-Speed Man Trans, close ratio, heavy duty	101	290.40
M40	Turbo Hydra-Matic Automatic Transmission	8,161	221.80
N14	Side Mount Exhaust System	4,355	147.45
N37	Tilt-Telescopic Steering Column	10,325	84.30
N40	Power Steering	22,866	105.35
P02	Deluxe Wheel Covers	8,073	57.95
PT6	Red Stripe Tires, F70x15, nylon	5,210	31.30
PT7	White Stripe Tires, F70x15, nylon	21,379	31.30
PU9	White Letter Tires, F70x15, nylon	2,398	33.15
TJ2	Front Fender Louver Trim	11,962	21.10
UA6	Alarm System	12,436	26.35
U15	Speed Warning Indicator	3,561	11.60
U69	AM-FM Radio	33,871	172.75
U79	AM-FM Radio, stereo	4,114	278.10
ZL1	Special L88 (aluminum block)	2	4,718.35

• A 350ci, 300hp engine, 3-speed manual transmission, vinyl interior, and soft top (conv) or T-tops (cpe) were included in the base. A82 was a required RPO early, then part of base. M40 cost $290.40 with L71 or L88.

1969 COLORS

CODE	EXTERIOR	SOFT TOP	WHEELS	INTERIORS
900	Tuxedo Black	Bk-W-Bg	Silver	Bk-Bb-G-Gu-R-S
972	Can-Am White	Bk-W-Bg	Silver	Bk-Bb-G-Gu-R-S
974	Monza Red	Bk-W-Bg	Silver	Bk-R-S
976	LeMans Blue	Bk-W-Bg	Silver	Bk-Bb
980	Riverside Gold	Bk-W-Bg	Silver	Bk-S
983	Fathom Green	Bk-W-Bg	Silver	Bk-G-S
984	Daytona Yellow	Bk-W-Bg	Silver	Bk
986	Cortez Silver	Bk-W-Bg	Silver	Bk-Bb-G-Gu-R-S
988	Burgundy	Bk-W-Bg	Silver	Bk-S
990	Monaco Orange	Bk-W-Bg	Silver	Bk

• Suggested interiors shown. Other combinations were possible.

Interior Codes: ZQ4 or std=Bk/V, 402=Bk/L, 407=R/V, 408=R/L, 411=Bb/V, 412=Bb/L, 416=G/V, 417=G/L, 420=S/V, 421=S/L, 427=G/V, 428=G/L.

Abbreviations: Bb=Bright Blue, Bg=Beige, Bk=Black, G=Green, Gu=Gunmetal, L=Leather, R=Red, S=Saddle, V=Vinyl, W=White.

1970 CORVETTE

1970 NUMBERS

Vehicle: 194370S400001 through 194370S417316
  • For convertibles, fourth digit is a 6.

Suffix:
CGW: 454ci, 390hp, at
CRJ: 454ci, 390hp, at, ig
CRI: 454ci, 390hp, mt, ig
CTD: 350ci, 300hp, mt
CTG: 350ci, 300hp, at
CTH: 350ci, 350hp, mt
CTJ: 350ci, 350hp, mt, ac
CTK: 350ci, 370hp, mt, ig
CTL: 350ci, 300hp, mt

CTM: 350ci, 300hp, at
CTN: 350ci, 350hp, mt
CTO: 350ci, 350hp, mt, ac
CTP: 350ci, 350hp, mt, ig
CTQ: 350ci, 350hp, mt, ac, ig
CTR: 350ci, 370hp, mt, ig
CTU: 350ci, 370hp, mt, ig
CTV: 350ci, 370hp (ZR1), mt
CZU: 454ci, 390hp

  • Some early 1970 models may have 1969 engine codes.

Block: 3970010: 350ci, 300hp, 350hp, 370hp
   3963512: 454ci, 390hp

Head: 3927186: 350ci, 300hp, 350hp, 370hp   3964290: 454ci, 390hp
   3927187: 350ci, 350hp   3973414: 350ci, 370hp

Carburetor: Rochester Q-jet #7040202: 350ci, 300hp, at, fd
   Rochester Q-jet #7040203: 350ci, 300hp, mt, fd
   Rochester Q-jet #7040204: 454ci, 390hp, at
   Rochester Q-jet #7040205: 454ci, 390hp, mt
   Rochester Q-jet #7040207: 350ci, 350hp, mt
   Rochester Q-jet #7040212: 350ci, 300hp, at, sd
   Rochester Q-jet #7040213: 350ci, 300hp, mt, sd
   Rochester Q-jet #7040502: 350ci, 300hp, at, ec
   Rochester Q-jet #7040503: 350ci, 300hp, mt, ec, fd
   Rochester Q-jet #7040504: 454ci, 390hp, at, ec
   Rochester Q-jet #7040505: 454ci, 390hp, mt, ec
   Rochester Q-jet #7040507: 350ci, 350hp, mt, ec
   Rochester Q-jet #7040513: 350ci, 300hp, mt, ec, sd
   Holley R4489A #3972123: 350ci, 370hp, mt, ec
   Holley R4555A #3972121: 350ci, 370hp, mt

Distributor: 1111464: 454ci, 390hp   1111493: 350ci, 350hp, ep
   1111490: 350ci, 300hp, ep   1112020: 350ci, 300hp
   1111491: 350ci, 370hp, ig   1112021: 350ci, 350hp

Alternator: 1100884: 350ci, 370hp or ac(all)   1100901: 350ci, 300hp
   1100900: 350ci(350hp), 454ci(390hp)

Ending Vehicle: Jan 70: 402261   Apr 70: 408314   Jul 70: 417316
   Feb 70: 405183   May 70: 410652
   Mar 70: 407977   Jun 70: 413829

Abbreviations: ac=air conditioning, at=automatic transmission, ci=cubic inch, ec=evaporative emission control, ep=early production, fd=first design, hp=horsepower, ig=transistor ignition, mt=manual transmission, sd=second design.

1970 FACTS

• Body design for 1970 was updated with fender swells to reduce wheel-thrown debris damage, a problem with 1968-69 models. New fender louvers replaced the four vertical slots of the 1968-69 models.
• Big block displacement increased to 454ci. Small block stayed 350ci, but a new solid-lifter version, the LT1, debuted.
• Interiors in 1970 had subtle refinements, including redesigned seats for additional headroom and easier access to rear storage.

1970 OPTIONS

RPO #	DESCRIPTION	QTY	RETAIL $
19437	Base Corvette Sport Coupe	10,668	$5,192.00
19467	Base Corvette Convertible	6,648	4,849.00
—	Custom Interior Trim	3,191	158.00
A31	Power Windows	4,813	63.20
A85	Custom Shoulder Belts (std with coupe)	475	42.15
C07	Auxiliary Hardtop (for convertible)	2,556	273.85
C08	Vinyl Covering (for auxiliary hardtop)	832	63.20
C50	Rear Window Defroster	1,281	36.90
C60	Air Conditioning	6,659	447.65
G81	Optional Rear Axle Ratio	2,862	12.65
J50	Power Brakes	8,984	47.40
L46	350ci, 350hp Engine	4,910	158.00
LS5	454ci, 390hp Engine	4,473	289.65
LT1	350ci, 370hp Engine	1,287	447.60
M21	4-Speed Man Trans, close ratio	4,383	0.00
M22	4-Speed Man Trans, close ratio, heavy duty	25	95.00
M40	Turbo Hydra-Matic Automatic Transmission	5,102	0.00
NA9	California Emissions	1,758	36.90
N37	Tilt-Telescopic Steering Column	5,803	84.30
N40	Power Steering	11,907	105.35
P02	Deluxe Wheel Covers	3,467	57.95
PT7	White Stripe Tires, F70x15, nylon	6,589	31.30
PU9	White Letter Tires, F70x15, nylon	7,985	33.15
T60	Heavy Duty Battery (std with LS5)	165	15.80
UA6	Alarm System	6,727	31.60
U69	AM-FM Radio	14,529	172.75
U79	AM-FM Radio, stereo	2,462	278.10
ZR1	Special Purpose Engine Package	25	968.95

• A 350ci, 300hp engine, 4-speed wide ratio manual transmission, vinyl interior trim, soft top (conv) or T-tops (cpe) were included in the base price.
• The ZR1 included the LT1 engine, M22 transmission, heavy-duty power brakes, transistor ignition, special aluminum radiator, and special springs, shocks and front and rear stabilizer bars (ZH1s have appeared with and without rear stabilizers). RPOs A31, C50, C60, N40, P02, UA6, U69 and U79 were not available. ZR1's also had metal fan shrouds.
• A ZR2 package like ZR1, but with a 460hp (also listed as 465hp), 454ci engine, was planned and advertised for 1970, but not delivered to retail customers. Suffix was to be CZL for manual, CZN for automatic.
• Custom interior included leather seat trim, wood-grain accents and lower carpet trim on interior door panels, wood-grain accents on console, and special cut-pile carpeting,.
• Previously optional tinted glass, Positraction axle, and 4-speed wide ratio manual transmission were included in the 1970 base price.

1970 COLORS

CODE	EXTERIOR	SOFT TOP	WHEELS	INTERIORS
972	Classic White	Bk-W-Bg	Silver	B-Bk-Br-G-R-S
974	Monza Red	Bk-W-Bg	Silver	Bk-Br-R-S
975	Marlboro Maroon	Bk-W-Bg	Silver	Bk-Br-S
976	Mulsanne Blue	Bk-W-Bg	Silver	B-Bk
979	Bridgehampton Blue	Bk-W-Bg	Silver	B-Bk
982	Donnybrooke Green	Bk-W-Bg	Silver	Bk-Br-G-S
984	Daytona Yellow	Bk-W-Bg	Silver	Bk-G
986	Cortez Silver	Bk-W-Bg	Silver	B-Bk-Br-G-R-S
991	Ontario Orange	Bk-W-Bg	Silver	Bk-S
992	Laguna Gray	Bk-W-Bg	Silver	B-Bk-Br-G-R-S
993	Corvette Bronze	Bk-W-Bg	Silver	Bk

• Suggested interiors shown. Other combinations were possible.
Interior Codes: 400=Bk/V, 403=Bk/L, 407=R/V, 411=B/V, 414=Br/V, 418=S/V, 422=G/V, 424=S/L.
Abbreviations: B=Blue, Bk=Black, Bg=Beige, Br=Brown, G=Green, L=Leather, R=Red, S=Saddle, V=Vinyl, W=White.

1971 CORVETTE

Production: 14,680 coupe, 7,121 convertible, 21,801 total.

1971 NUMBERS

Vehicle: 194371S100001 through 194371S121801
• For convertibles, fourth digit is a 6.

Suffix:
CGT: 350ci, 270hp, at
CGY: 350ci, 330hp(ZR1), mt
CGZ: 350ci, 330hp(LT1), mt
CJK: 350ci, 270hp, at
CJL: 350ci, 270hp, mt

CPH: 454ci, 365hp, mt
CPJ: 454ci, 365hp, at
CPW: 454ci, 425hp, mt, ah
CPX: 454ci, 425hp, at, ah

Block: 3970010: 350ci, 270hp, 330hp
3963512: 454ci, 365hp, 425hp

Head: 3946074: 454ci, 425hp   3993820: 454ci, 365hp
3973487: 350ci, 270hp, 330hp   3994026: 454ci, 425hp (uu)

Carburetor: Rochester Q-jet #7041204: 454ci, 365hp, at
Rochester Q-jet #7041205: 454ci, 365hp, mt
Rochester Q-jet #7041212: 350ci, 270hp, at
Rochester Q-jet #7041213: 350ci, 270hp, mt
Holley R4801A #3989021: 350ci, 330hp, mt
Holley R4802A #3986195: 454ci, 425hp, mt
Holley R4803A #3986196: 454ci, 425hp, at

Distributor: 1112038: 350ci, 330hp, ig   1112053: 454ci, 425hp, at, ig
1112050: 350ci, 270hp   1112076: 454ci, 425hp, mt, ig
1112051: 454ci, 365hp

Alternator: 1100543: 454ci, 365hp, 425hp   1100544: All with ac
1100950: 350ci, 270hp, 330hp

Ending Vehicle:
Aug 70: 101212   Jan 71: 108230   May 71: 118223
Sep 70: 102226   Feb 71: 110886   Jun 71: 120686
Nov 70: 102675   Mar 71: 113626
Dec 70: 105269   Apr 71: 115983

Abbreviations: ac=air conditioning, ah=aluminum heads,
at=automatic transmission, ci=cubic inch, hp=horsepower, ig=transistor
ignition, mt=manual transmission, uu=uncertain usage.

1971 FACTS

• The 1971 Corvette was one of the least-changed in appearance. A labor
dispute in May 1969 caused 1969 production to run long, shortening
normal 1970 production by over four months. Chevrolet then treated 1971
Corvette production as an extension of 1970. Plus, GM directed its
divisions to reduce octane requirements in 1971 engines, an effort which
carried a higher priority than appearance changes.
• With the exception of RPO LS6, 1971 engines were detuned variants of
1970 engines. GM's intention in reducing octane requirements to 91
(research) in 1971 was to give oil companies phase-in time for the
unleaded fuels needed for catalytic converters still four years away.
• The 454ci LS6 engine with 425hp was designed to operate on low-lead
fuel, but a comparable engine was not available in 1970, so it won the
horsepower race for the two years despite it's lower octane appetite. It
featured aluminum heads and could be combined with an automatic
transmission, although not when combined with the ZR2 package.
• One visible clue to a 1971's outward appearance was amber parking light
lenses, although very early production had clear lenses.
• The 1971 Corvette was the last model to feature the fiber-optics light
monitoring system. It's thought the cost savings permitted inclusion of the
optional anti-theft alarm system as standard equipment the following year.

56

1971 OPTIONS

RPO #	DESCRIPTION	QTY	RETAIL $
19437	Base Corvette Sport Coupe	14,680	$5,496.00
19467	Base Corvette Convertible	7,121	5,259.00
—	Custom Interior Trim	2,602	158.00
A31	Power Windows	6,192	79.00
A85	Custom Shoulder Belts (std with coupe)	677	42.00
C07	Auxiliary Hardtop (for convertible)	2,619	274.00
C08	Vinyl Covering (for auxiliary hardtop)	832	63.00
C50	Rear Window Defroster	1,598	42.00
C60	Air Conditioning	11,481	459.00
—	Optional Rear Axle Ratio	2,395	13.00
J50	Power Brakes	13,558	47.00
LS5	454ci, 365hp Engine	5,097	295.00
LS6	454ci, 425hp Engine	188	1,221.00
LT1	350ci, 330hp Engine	1,949	483.00
M21	4-Speed Man Trans, close ratio	2,387	0.00
M22	4-Speed Man Trans, close ratio, heavy duty	130	100.00
M40	Turbo Hydra-Matic Automatic Transmission	10,060	0.00
N37	Tilt-Telescopic Steering Column	8,130	84.30
N40	Power Steering	17,904	115.90
P02	Deluxe Wheel Covers	3,007	63.00
PT7	White Stripe Tires, F70x15, nylon	6,711	28.00
PU9	White Letter Tires, F70x15, nylon	12,449	42.00
T60	Heavy Duty Battery (std with LS5, LS6)	1,455	15.80
UA6	Alarm System	8,501	31.60
U69	AM-FM Radio	18,078	178.00
U79	AM-FM Radio, stereo	3,431	283.00
ZR1	Special Purpose LT1 Engine Package	8	1,010.00
ZR2	Special Purpose LS6 Engine Package	12	1,747.00

• A 350ci, 270hp engine, 4-speed wide-ratio manual transmission, vinyl interior trim, and soft top (conv) or T-tops were included in the base price.
• The ZR1 included the LT1 engine, M22 transmission, heavy-duty power brakes, transistor ignition, special aluminum radiator, and special springs, shocks, and front and rear stabilizer bars (ZR1s have appeared with and without rear stabilizers). ZR1s also had metal fan shrouds. RPOs A31, C50, C60, N40, P02, UA6, U69 and U79 were not available with ZR1.
• The ZR2 package was similar to ZR1, except ZR2 included RPO LS6, the 454ci, 425hp engine.
• Custom interior included leather seat trim, wood-grain accents and lower carpet trim on interior door panels, wood-grain accents on console, and special cut-pile carpeting.
• M40 was no cost with the base 350ci, 270hp engine, but cost $100.35 with LS5 or LS6. It was not available with LT1, ZR1 or ZR2.

1971 COLORS

CODE	EXTERIOR	QTY	SOFTTOP	WHEELS	INTERIORS
905	Nevada Silver	1,177	Bk-W	Silver	Bk-Db-Dg-R
912	Sunflower Yellow	1,177	Bk-W	Silver	Bk-Dg-S
972	Classic White	1,875	Bk-W	Silver	Bk-Db-Dg-R-S
973	Mille Miglia Red	2,180	Bk-W	Silver	Bk-R
976	Mulsanne Blue	2,465	Bk-W	Silver	Bk-Db
979	Bridgehampton Blue	1,417	Bk-W	Silver	Bk-Db
983	Brands Hatch Green	3,445	Bk-W	Silver	Bk-Dg
987	Ontario Orange	2,269	Bk-W	Silver	Bk-Dg-S
988	Steel Cities Gray	1,591	Bk-W	Silver	Bk-S
989	War Bonnet Yellow	3,706	Bk-W	Silver	Bk-Dg-S

• Suggested interiors shown. Other combinations were possible.
• Exterior color quantity total is 499 short of total production.

Interior Codes: std=Bk/V, 402=Bk/L, 407=R/V, 412=Db/V, 417=S/V, 420=S/L, 423=Dg/V.

Abbreviations: Bk=Black, Db=Dark Blue, Dg=Dark Green, L=Leather, R=Red, S=Saddle, V=Vinyl, W=White.

1972 CORVETTE
Production: 20,496 coupe, 6,508 convertible, 27,004 total.

1972 NUMBERS

Vehicle: 1Z37K2S500001 through 1Z37K2S527004
- For convertibles, third digit is a 6.
- Fifth digit varies as follows: K=350ci, 200hp;
  L=350ci, 255hp; W=454ci, 270hp.

Suffix:
CDH: 350ci, 200hp, mt, ec   CPH: 454ci, 270hp, mt
CDJ: 350ci, 200hp, at, ec   CPJ: 454ci, 270hp, at, uu
CKW: 350ci, 200hp, mt   CRS: 350ci, 255hp, ar, at
CKX: 350ci, 200hp, at   CRT: 350ci, 255hp, mt, ar, uu
CKY: 350ci, 255hp, mt   CSR: 454ci, 270hp, mt, ar
CKZ: 350ci, 255hp(ZR1), mt   CSS: 454ci, 270hp, at, ar

Block: 3970010: 350ci, 200hp, 255hp   3999289: 454, 270hp
3970014: 350ci, 200hp, 255hp, lp

Head: 3973487: 350ci, 200hp, 255hp   3998993: 350ci, 200hp (uu)
3998916: 350ci, 255hp (uu)   3999241: 454ci, 270hp

Carburetor: Rochester Q-jet #7042202: 350ci, 200hp, at
Rochester Q-jet #7042203: 350ci, 200hp, mt
Rochester Q-jet #7042216: 454ci, 270hp, at
Rochester Q-jet #7042217: 454ci, 270hp, mt
Rochester Q-jet #7042902: 350ci, 200hp, at, ec
Rochester Q-jet #7042903: 350ci, 200hp, mt, ec
Holley R6239A #3999263: 350ci, 255hp

Distributor: 1112050: 350ci, 200hp   1112101: 350ci, 255hp
1112051: 454ci, 270hp

Alternator: 1100543: 454ci, 270hp   1100544: All with ac
1100950: 350ci, 200hp, 255hp

Ending Vehicle:
Aug 71: 501344   Dec 71: 510310   Apr 72: 519993
Sep 71: 503697   Jan 72: 512661   May 72: 522611
Oct 71: 506050   Feb 72: 515020   Jun 72: 525226
Nov 71: 508406   Mar 72: 517613   Jul 72: 527004

Abbreviations: ac=air conditioning, ar=air injection reactor, at=automatic transmission, ci=cubic inch, ec=emission control, hp=horsepower, lp=late production, mt=manual transmission, uu=uncertain usage.

1972 FACTS

• Appearance changes were again minimal for 1972, but this model's significance is more associated with its "end of an era" status than by new looks or features. The 1972 Corvette was the last to feature front and rear chrome bumpers, a bright egg-crate grill, side-fender grills (later models do have functional vents and some have vent trim). Also, the 1972 model was the last to feature the removable rear window available from 1968-72.
• The 1972 did not have the fiber-optics light-monitoring system used in 1968-1971 models, but the previously optional alarm (sounding horn type) was included in its base price.
• This was the last year for RPO ZR1 and RPO LT1, although the ZR1 code was used again in 1990, and LT1 designated a new base engine in 1992.
• This was the only year the 1970-1972 LT1 engine could be combined with air conditioning. The number built is believed to be 240. Previous restrictions were based on the possibility of air conditioning belts being spun off by higher engine rpm permitted by solid valve lifters. To discourage higher rpm, LT1s with air had the base engine's 5600 rpm tach instead of the 6500 rpm unit used with non-air LT1s.

1972 OPTIONS

RPO #	DESCRIPTION	QTY	RETAIL $
19437	Base Corvette Sport Coupe	20,496	$5,533.00
19467	Base Corvette Convertible	6,508	5,296.00
—	Custom Interior Trim	8,709	158.00
AV3	Three Point Seat Belts	17,693	—
A31	Power Windows	9,495	85.35
A85	Custom Shoulder Belts (std with coupe)	749	42.15
C07	Auxiliary Hardtop (for convertible)	2,646	273.85
C08	Vinyl Covering (for auxiliary hardtop)	811	158.00
C50	Rear Window Defroster	2,221	42.15
C60	Air Conditioning	17,011	464.50
—	Optional Rear Axle Ratio	1,986	12.65
J50	Power Brakes	18,770	47.40
K19	Air Injection Reactor	3,912	—
LS5	454ci, 270hp Engine (n/a California)	3,913	294.90
LT1	350ci, 255hp Engine	1,741	483.45
M21	4-Speed Manual Trans, close ratio	1,638	0.00
M40	Turbo Hydra-Matic Automatic Transmission	14,543	0.00
N37	Tilt-Telescopic Steering Column	12,992	84.30
N40	Power Steering	23,794	115.90
P02	Deluxe Wheel Covers	3,593	63.20
PT7	White Stripe Tires, F70x15, nylon	6,666	30.35
PU9	White Letter Tires, F70x15, nylon	16,623	43.65
T60	Heavy Duty Battery (std with LS5)	2,969	15.80
U69	AM-FM Radio	19,480	178.00
U79	AM-FM Radio, stereo	7,189	283.35
YF5	California Emission Test	1,967	15.80
ZR1	Special Purpose LT1 Engine Package	20	1,010.05

• A 350ci, 200hp engine, 4-speed wide-ratio manual transmission, vinyl interior trim, and soft top (convertible) or T-tops (coupe) were included in the base price.
• The ZR1 package included the LT1 engine, heavy-duty close-ratio 4-speed manual transmission, heavy-duty power brakes, transistor ignition, special aluminum radiator, and special springs, shocks, and front and rear stabilizer bars (ZR1s have appeared with and without rear stabilizers). 1972 ZR1s generally did not have fan shrouds. RPOs A31, C50, C60, N40, P02, U69 and U79 were not available with ZR1.
• M40 was no cost with the base 350ci, 200 hp engine, but cost $97 with LS5 (454ci, 270hp). It was not available with LT1 or ZR1.

1972 COLORS

CODE	EXTERIOR	QTY	SOFT TOP	INTERIORS
912	Sunflower Yellow	1,543	Bk-W	Bk-S
924	Pewter Silver	1,372	Bk-W	B-Bk-R-S
945	Bryar Blue	1,617	Bk-W	Bk
946	Elkhart Green	4,200	Bk-W	Bk-S
972	Classic White	2,763	Bk-W	B-Bk-R-S
973	Mille Miglia Red	2,478	Bk-W	Bk-R-S
979	Targa Blue	3,198	Bk-W	B-Bk
987	Ontario Orange	4,891	Bk-W	Bk-S
988	Steel Cities Gray	2,346	Bk-W	Bk-R-S
989	War Bonnet Yellow	2,550	Bk-W	Bk-S

• Suggested interiors shown. Additional combinations were possible.
• All 1972 wheels were painted silver.
• Paint quantities do not add to total production because additional units had non-standard paint, or primer only.
• Seat and shoulder belts matched interior colors except for the blue interior which received darker blue belts.

Interior Codes: 400=Bk/V, 404=Bk/L, 407=R/V, 412=B/V, 417=S/V, 421=S/L.

Abbreviations: B=Blue, Bk=Black, L=Leather, R=Red, S=Saddle, V=Vinyl, W=White.

1973 CORVETTE

Production: 25,521 coupe, 4,943 convertible, 30,464 total.

1973 NUMBERS

Vehicle: 1Z37J3S400001 through 1Z37J3S434464
- For convertibles, third digit is a 6.
- Fifth digit varies as follows: J=350ci, 190hp; T=350ci, 250hp; Z=454ci, 275hp.

Suffix:

CKZ: 350ci, 190hp, mt	CLR: 350ci, 250hp, mt
CLA: 350ci, 190hp, at	CLS: 350ci, 250hp, mt, ce
CLB: 350ci, 190hp, mt, ce	CWM: 454ci, 275hp, mt
CLC: 350ci, 190hp, at, ce	CWR: 454ci, 275hp, at
CLD: 350ci, 250hp, at	CWS: 454ci, 275hp, at, ce
CLH: 350ci, 250hp, at, ce	CWT: 454ci, 275hp, mt, ce

Block: 3970010: 350ci, 190hp, 250hp   3999289: 454ci, 275hp

Head: 353049: 454ci, 275hp   330545: 350ci, 250hp
3998993: 350ci, 190hp

Carburetor: Rochester Q-jet #7043200: 454ci, 275hp, at
Rochester Q-jet #7043201: 454ci, 275hp, mt
Rochester Q-jet #7043202: 350ci, 190hp, at
Rochester Q-jet #7043203: 350ci, 190hp, mt
Rochester Q-jet #7043212: 350ci, 250hp, at
Rochester Q-jet #7043213: 350ci, 250hp, mt

Distributor: 1112098: 350ci, 190hp   1112130: 350ci, 250hp
1112114: 454ci, 275hp   1112150: 350ci, 250hp

Alternator: 1100544: 350ci, 454ci, ac   1102353: 454ci
1100950: 350ci

Ending Vehicle:

Aug 72: 01138	Dec 72: 10679	Apr 73: 21933
Sep 72: 03539	Jan 73: 13600	May 73: 28892
Oct 72: 06054	Feb 73: 16301	Jun 73: 31731
Nov 72: 08696	Mar 73: 19253	Jul 73: 34464

- During May, 4,000 vehicle identification numbers were not used.

Abbreviations: ac=air conditioning, at=automatic transmission, ce=california emissions, ci=cubic inch, hp=horsepower, mt=manual transmission.

1973 FACTS

- In the 1973 model year, 4,000 serial numbers were never built. The last 1973 Corvette's serial number ends with 34,464, but production totaled 30,464. The unused VIN numbers were 24,001 through 28,000.
- Rear 1973 bumpers were essentially unchanged from 1972, but fronts were redesigned to meet federal 5-mph standards. The front body-color bumper system added thirty-five pounds of weight and could withstand 5-mph impacts without damage to lights or safety equipment.
- A new coolant recovery system routed high temperature overflow coolant into a holding reservoir for return to the radiator after cooling.
- Material was sprayed on several inner panels for sound deadening, and a new sound-absorbing pad was installed on the inner-hood surface.
- New chassis mounts were used in 1973 to better isolate road chatter and vibration. The mounts are rubber with steel sleeves. The rubber provides vertical cushioning while the steel maintains stability.
- The lifting windshield wiper panel was deleted from 1973 models, but a new hood with rear cold air induction was introduced.
- Doors have interior beams for improved side impact protection.
- Radial tires were first used with Corvettes in 1973.
- Rear windows weren't removable in 1973, but luggage space height increased two inches due to removal of the window storage shelf.

1973 OPTIONS

RPO #	DESCRIPTION	QTY	RETAIL $
1YZ37	Base Corvette Sport Coupe	25,521	$5,561.50
1YZ67	Base Corvette Convertible	4,943	5,398.50
—	Custom Interior Trim	13,434	154.00
A31	Power Windows	14,024	83.00
A85	Custom Shoulder Belts (std with coupe)	788	41.00
C07	Auxiliary Hardtop (for convertible)	1,328	267.00
C08	Vinyl Covering (for auxiliary hardtop)	323	62.00
C50	Rear Window Defroster	4,412	41.00
C60	Air Conditioning	21,578	452.00
—	Optional Rear Axle Ratio	1,791	12.00
J50	Power Brakes	24,168	46.00
LS4	454ci, 275hp Engine	4,412	250.00
L82	350ci, 250hp Engine	5,710	299.00
M21	4-Speed Manual Trans, close ratio	3,704	0.00
M40	Turbo Hydra-Matic Automatic Transmission	17,927	0.00
N37	Tilt-Telescopic Steering Column	17,949	82.00
N40	Power Steering	27,872	113.00
P02	Deluxe Wheel Covers	1,739	62.00
QRM	White Stripe Steel Belted Tires, GR70x15	19,903	32.00
QRZ	White Letter Steel Belted Tires, GR70x15	4,541	45.00
T60	Heavy Duty Battery (standard with LS4)	4,912	15.00
U58	AM-FM Radio, stereo	12,482	276.00
U69	AM-FM Radio	17,598	173.00
UF1	Map Light (on rearview mirror)	8,186	5.00
YF5	California Emission Test	3,008	15.00
YJ8	Cast Aluminum Wheels (4)	4	175.00
Z07	Off Road Suspension and Brake Package	45	369.00

• A 350ci, 190hp engine, 4-speed wide-ratio manual transmission, soft top (convertible) or T-tops (coupe), and vinyl interior trim were included in the base price.

• The Z07 package was available only with L82 or LS4 engines, and required J50 and M21. It included special front and rear suspension and heavy-duty power front and rear brakes. It was not available with C60.

• YJ8 cast aluminum wheels were offered, but sales records show only four sets sold. Early in production, Chevrolet rejected the wheels for porosity problems and recalled the wheels that had been released. Rumors place the number of wheels produced at 800 sets. Some wheels are definitely in private hands, but the actual number remaining is unknown.

• Custom interior included leather seat trim, wood-grain accents and lower carpet trim on interior door panels, wood-grain accents on console, and special cut-pile carpeting.

• M40 was no cost with base engine, but cost $97 with LS4 or L82.

1973 COLORS

CODE	EXTERIOR	SOFT TOP	WHEELS	INTERIORS
910	Classic White	Bk-W	Silver	Bk-Dr-Ds-Mb-Ms
914	Silver	Bk-W	Silver	Bk-Dr-Ds-Mb-Ms
922	Medium Blue	Bk-W	Silver	Bk-Mb-Ms
927	Dark Blue	Bk-W	Silver	Bk-Dr-Mb-Ms
945	Blue-Green	Bk-W	Silver	Bk-Dr-Ds-Ms
947	Elkhart Green	Bk-W	Silver	Bk-Ms
952	Yellow	Bk-W	Silver	Bk-Ds-Mb
953	Metallic Yellow	Bk-W	Silver	Bk-Mb
976	Mille Miglia Red	Bk-W	Silver	Bk-Dr-Ds-Mb-Ms
980	Orange	Bk-W	Silver	Bk-Ms

• Suggested interiors shown. Other combinations were possible.

Interior Codes: 400=Bk/V, 404=Bk/L, 413=Mb/V, 415=Ms/V, 416=Ms/L, 418=Ds/V, 422=Ds/L, 425=Dr/V.

Abbreviations: Bk=Black, Dr=Dark Red, Ds=Dark Saddle, L=Leather, Mb=Midnight Blue, Ms=Medium Saddle, V=Vinyl, W=White.

1974 CORVETTE

Production: 32,028 coupe, 5,474 convertible, 37,502 total.

1974 NUMBERS

Vehicle: 1Z37J4S400001 through 1Z37J4S437502
- For convertibles, third digit is a 6.
- Fifth digit varies as follows: J=350ci, 195hp; T=350ci, 250hp; Z=454ci, 270hp.

Suffix:
CKZ: 350ci, 195hp, mt	CLR: 350ci, 250hp, mt
CLA: 350ci, 195hp, at	CLS: 350ci, 250hp, mt, ce
CLB: 350ci, 195hp, mt, ce	CWM: 454ci, 270hp, mt
CLC: 350ci, 195hp, at, ce	CWR: 454ci, 270hp, at
CLD: 350ci, 250hp, at	CWS: 454ci, 270hp, at, ce
CLH: 350ci, 250hp, at, ce	CWT: 454ci, 270hp, mt, ce

Block: 3970010: 350ci, 195hp, 250hp
3999289: 454ci, 270hp

Head: 333882: 350ci, 195hp, 250hp
336781: 454ci, 270hp

Carburetor: Rochester Q-jet #7044221: 454ci, 270hp, mt
Rochester Q-jet #7044206: 350ci, 195hp, at
Rochester Q-jet #7044207: 350ci, 195hp, mt
Rochester Q-jet #7044210: 350ci, 250hp, at
Rochester Q-jet #7044211: 350ci, 250hp, mt
Rochester Q-jet #7044225: 454ci, 270hp, at
Rochester Q-jet #7044505: 454ci, 270hp, at, ce
Rochester Q-jet #7044506: 350ci, 250hp, at, ce
Rochester Q-jet #7044507: 350ci, 250hp, mt, ce

Distributor:
1112114: 454ci, 270hp	1112850: 350ci, 195hp, mt, ce
1112150: 350ci, 250hp	1112851: 350ci, 195hp, at, ce
1112247: 350ci, 195hp	1112853: 350ci, 250hp, at
1112544: 350ci, 195hp, mt, ce	

Alternator: 1100544: All with ac   1100950: All without ac

Ending Vehicle:
Aug 73: 01250	Jan 74: 16184	Jun 74: 33257
Sep 73: 04111	Feb 74: 19258	Jul 74: 33257
Oct 73: 07605	Mar 74: 22367	Aug 74: 33257
Nov 73: 10813	Apr 74: 25751	Sep 74: 37251
Dec 73: 12830	May 74: 29602	Oct 74: 37502

• A labor dispute closed the Corvette assembly plant in 1974 from about June 28, 1974 to September 2, 1974.

Abbreviations: ac=air conditioning, at=automatic transmission, ce=california emissions, ci=cubic inch, hp=horsepower, mt=manual transmission.

1974 FACTS

• The transition to "soft" bumpers was completed in 1974 with the new body-color rear bumpers. The urethane plastic skin had built-in recesses for the license plate and taillights, and a vertical center seam. The skin covered an aluminum impact bar mounted on two telescopic brackets.
• These were the last Corvettes without catalytic converters. Fuel requirement was 91-octane leaded or low-lead regular.
• Radiators were redesigned for more efficient cooling at low speeds.
• Shoulder belts on 1974 models were integrated with the lap belts. Also, the locking mechanism was changed from a pull-rate type to a swinging-weight type activated by the car's deceleration.
• The alarm activator moved from the rear panel to the driver-side fender.
• Magnets were added to power steering units to attract debris in the fluid.
• The inside rearview mirror increased in width to ten inches.

1974 OPTIONS

RPO #	DESCRIPTION	QTY	RETAIL $
1YZ37	Base Corvette Sport Coupe	32,028	$6,001.50
1YZ67	Base Corvette Convertible	5,474	5,765.50
—	Custom Interior Trim	19,959	154.00
A31	Power Windows	23,940	86.00
A85	Custom Shoulder Belts (std with coupe)	618	41.00
C07	Auxiliary Hardtop (for convertible)	2,612	267.00
C08	Vinyl-Covered Auxiliary Hardtop	367	329.00
C50	Rear Window Defroster	9,322	43.00
C60	Air Conditioning	29,397	467.00
FE7	Gymkhana Suspension	1,905	7.00
—	Optional Rear Axle Ratios	1,219	12.00
J50	Power Brakes	33,306	49.00
LS4	454ci, 270hp Engine	3,494	250.00
L82	350ci, 250hp Engine	6,690	299.00
M21	4-Speed Manual Trans, close ratio	3,494	0.00
M40	Turbo Hydra-Matic Automatic Transmission	25,146	0.00
N37	Tilt-Telescopic Steering Column	27,700	82.00
N41	Power Steering	35,944	117.00
QRM	White Stripe Steel Belted Tires, GR70x15	9,140	32.00
QRZ	White Letter Steel Belted Tires, GR70x15	24,102	45.00
U05	Dual Horns	5,258	4.00
U58	AM-FM Radio, stereo	19,581	276.00
U69	AM-FM Radio	17,374	173.00
UA1	Heavy Duty Battery (std with LS4)	9,169	15.00
UF1	Map Light (on rearview mirror)	16,101	5.00
YF5	California Emission Test	—	20.00
Z07	Off Road Suspension and Brake Package	47	400.00

• A 350ci, 195hp engine, 4-speed wide-ratio manual transmission, soft top (conv) or T-tops (cpe), and vinyl interior were included in the base price.
• YJ8 cast aluminum wheels appeared on early 1974 option lists, but Chevrolet records indicate none were sold.
• Custom interior included leather seat trim, wood-grain accents and lower carpet trim on interior door panels, wood grain accents on console, and special cut-pile carpeting.
• M40 was no cost with the base 350ci, 195hp engine, but cost $103 ($97 early in production) with LS4 or L82. It was not available with Z07.
• The Z07 package was available only with L82 and LS4 engines, and required M21. It included special front and rear suspension and heavy-duty front and rear power brakes.
• The FE7 gymkhana suspension included stiffer front sway bar and stiffer springs. It was included with Z07. There were no order restrictions.
• This was the last year for 454ci "big block" engines in Corvettes.

1974 COLORS

CODE	EXTERIOR	SOFT TOP	WHEELS	INTERIORS
910	Classic White	Bk-W	Silver	Bk-Db-Dr-N-S-Si
914	Silver Mist	Bk-W	Silver	Bk-Db-Dr-S-Si
917	Corvette Gray	Bk-W	Silver	Bk-Db-Dr-N-S-Si
922	Corvette Med Blue	Bk-W	Silver	Bk-Db-Si
948	Dark Green	Bk-W	Silver	Bk-N-S-Si
956	Bright Yellow	Bk-W	Silver	Bk-N-S-Si
968	Dark Brown	Bk-W	Silver	Bk-N-S-Si
974	Medium Red	Bk-W	Silver	Bk-Dr-N-S-Si
976	Mille Miglia Red	Bk-W	Silver	Bk-Dr-N-S-Si
980	Corvette Orange	Bk-W	Silver	Bk-N-S-Si

• Suggested interiors shown. Other combinations were possible.

Interior Codes: 400=Bk/V, 404=Bk/L, 406=Si/V, 407=Si/L, 408=N/V, 413=Db/V, 415=S/V, 416=S/L, 425=Dr/V.

Abbreviations: Bk=Black, Db=Dark Blue, Dr=Dark Red, L=Leather, N=Neutral, S=Saddle, Si=Silver, V=Vinyl W=White.

1975 CORVETTE
Production: 33,836 coupe, 4,629 convertible, 38,465 total

1975 NUMBERS

Vehicle: 1Z37J5S400001 through 1Z37J5S438465
- For convertibles, third digit is a 6.
- Fifth digit varies as follows: J=350ci, 165hp
  T=350ci, 205hp

Suffix:

CHA: 350ci, 165hp, mt	CRK: 350ci, 165hp, at
CHB: 350ci, 165hp, at	CRL: 350ci, 205hp, mt
CHC: 350ci, 205hp, mt	CRM: 350ci, 205hp, at
CHR: 350ci, 205hp, at, ce	CUA: 350ci, 165hp, mt
CHU: 350ci, 165hp, mt	CUB: 350ci, 165hp, mt
CHZ: 350ci, 165hp, at, ce	CUD: 350ci, 205hp, mt
CKC: 350ci, 205hp, at,	CUT: 350ci, 205hp, mt
CRJ: 350ci, 165hp, mt	

Block: 3970010: 350ci, 165hp, 205hp

Head: 333882: 350ci, 165hp, 205hp

Carburetor: Rochester Q-jet #7045210: 350ci, 205hp, at
Rochester Q-jet #7045211: 350ci, 205hp, mt
Rochester Q-jet #7045222: 350ci, 165hp, at
Rochester Q-jet #7045223: 350ci, 165hp, mt

Distributor: 1112880: 350ci, 165hp, ce   1112888: 350ci, 165hp
1112883: 350ci, 205hp   1112979: 350ci, 205hp, sd

Alternator: 1100544: With ac   1102474: With ac, lp
1100950: Without ac   1102484: Without ac, lp

Ending Vehicle:

Oct 74: 02385	Feb 75: 17112	Jun 75: 33474
Nov 74: 06180	Mar 75: 20856	Jul 75: 38465
Dec 74: 09190	Apr 75: 25228	
Jan 75: 13159	May 75: 29379	

Abbreviations: ac=air conditioning, at=automatic transmission, ce=california emissions, ci=cubic inch, hp=horsepower, lp=late production, mt=manual transmission.

1975 FACTS

- The 1975 convertible was for a time the "last," but convertible production resumed in 1986. The last 1975 convertible was built in late July, 1975.
- Catalytic converters first appeared in Corvettes with the 1975 model. Dual exhausts were routed to a single converter, then split for dual exit.
- Soft bumpers were redesigned structurally for 1975, and external appearance varied slightly from the previous year. The front bumper had an inner honeycomb core and simulated "pads" on the exterior. The rear bumper had inner shock absorbers for impact. The rear bumper skin was one-piece, unlike the two-piece 1974 unit. Simulated pads like those of the front were also added to the rear.
- High Energy Ignition (HEI) appeared first in Corvettes in 1975 models. Quite different from the transistor ignitions previously available, HEI included the Corvette's first no-points distributor. The HEI system's new type of distributor required the tachometer to be electronically driven.
- Optional engine choice for 1975 (one) was the lowest since 1955. And it was the first year since 1964 that only one displacement was offered.
- Hood emblems designating the L82 engine first appeared in 1975, but some 1975 L82 models didn't have the emblems.
- Kilometer-per-hour subfaces appeared on Corvette's speedometers first in 1975; it was also the first year with a headlight-warning buzzer.

1975 OPTIONS

RPO #	DESCRIPTION	QTY	RETAIL $
1YZ37	Base Corvette Sport Coupe	33,836	$6,810.10
1YZ67	Base Corvette Convertible	4,629	6,550.10
—	Custom Interior Trim	—	154.00
A31	Power Windows	28,745	93.00
A85	Custom Shoulder Belts (std with coupe)	646	41.00
C07	Auxiliary Hardtop (for convertible)	2,407	267.00
C08	Vinyl Covered Auxiliary Hardtop (conv)	279	350.00
C50	Rear Window Defroster	13,760	46.00
C60	Air Conditioning	31,914	490.00
FE7	Gymkhana Suspension	3,194	7.00
—	Optional Rear Axle Ratios	1,969	12.00
J50	Power Brakes	35,842	50.00
L82	350ci, 205hp Engine	2,372	336.00
M21	4-Speed Manual Trans, close ratio	1,057	0.00
M40	Turbo Hydra-Matic Automatic Transmission	28,473	0.00
N37	Tilt-Telescopic Steering Column	31,830	82.00
N41	Power Steering	37,591	129.00
QRM	White Stripe Steel Belted Tires, GR70x15	5,233	35.00
QRZ	White Letter Steel Belted Tires, GR70x15	30,407	48.00
U05	Dual Horns	22,011	4.00
U58	AM-FM Radio, stereo	24,701	284.00
U69	AM-FM Radio	12,902	178.00
UA1	Heavy Duty Battery	16,778	15.00
UF1	Map Light (on rearview mirror)	21,676	5.00
YF5	California Emission Test	3,037	20.00
Z07	Off Road Suspension and Brake Package	144	400.00

• A 350ci, 165hp engine, 4-speed wide-ratio manual transmission, soft top (conv) or T-tops (cpe), and vinyl interior were included in the base price.
• Custom interior included leather seat trim, wood-grain accents and lower carpet trim on inner door panels, wood-grain accents on console, and special cut-pile carpeting.
• The Z07 package was available only with L82 engines and required M21 transmission. It included special front and rear suspension and heavy-duty front and rear power brakes..
• The FE7 gymkhana suspension included stiffer front sway bar and stiffer springs. It was included with Z07. There were no engine or transmission order restrictions with FE7.
• M40 was no cost with the base 350ci, 165hp engine, but cost $120.00 with optional L82 engine. M21 was no cost but required optional L82.

1975 COLORS

CODE	EXTERIOR	QTY	SOFT TOP	INTERIORS
10	Classic White	8,007	Bk-W	Bk-Db-Dr-Ms-N-Si
13	Silver	4,710	Bk-W	Bk-Db-Dr-Ms-Si
22	Bright Blue	2,869	Bk-W	Bk-Db-Si
27	Steel Blue	1,268	Bk-W	Bk-Db-Si
42	Bright Green	1,664	Bk-W	Bk-Ms-N-Si
56	Bright Yellow	2,883	Bk-W	Bk-Ms-N
67	Medium Saddle	3,403	Bk-W	Bk-Ms-N
70	Orange Flame	3,030	Bk-W	Bk-Ms-N
74	Dark Red	3,342	Bk-W	Bk-Dr-Ms-N-Si
76	Mille Miglia Red	3,355	Bk-W	Bk-Dr-Ms-N-Si

• Suggested interiors shown. Additional combinations were possible.
• Paint quantities do not add to total production because additional units had non-standard paint, or primer only.
• All 1975 wheels were painted silver.
• Steel Blue exterior was available for approximately three months.

Interior Codes: 19V=Bk/V, 192=Bk/L, 14V=Si/V, 142=Si/L, 26V=Db/V, 262=Db/L, 60V=N/V, 65V=Ms/V, 652=Ms/L, 73V=Dr/V, 732=Dr/L.

Abbreviations: Bk=Black, Db=Dark Blue, Dr=Dark Red, L=Leather, Ms=Medium Saddle, N=Neutral, Si=Saddle, V=Vinyl, W=White.

1976 CORVETTE
Production: 46,558 coupes

1976 NUMBERS

Vehicle: 1Z37L6S400001 through 1Z37L6S446558
        • Fifth digit varies as follows: L=350ci, 180hp
                                    X=350ci, 210hp

Suffix: CHC: 350ci, 210hp, mt   CKX: 350ci, 180hp, at
          CKC: 350ci, 210hp, at   CLS: 350ci, 180hp, at, ce
          CKW: 350ci, 180hp, mt

Block: 3970010: 350ci, 180hp, 210hp

Head: 333882: 350ci, 180hp, 210hp

Carburetor: Rochester Q-jet #17056206: 350ci, 180hp, at
                 Rochester Q-jet #17056207: 350ci, 180hp, mt
                 Rochester Q-jet #17056210: 350ci, 210hp, at
                 Rochester Q-jet #17056211: 350ci, 210hp, mt
                 Rochester Q-jet #17056226: 350ci, 210hp, at, ac
                 Rochester Q-jet #17056506: 350ci, 180hp, at, ce
                 Rochester Q-jet #17056507: 350ci, 180hp, mt, ce

Distributor: 1103200: 350ci, 210hp,mt   1112905: 350ci, 180hp, at, ce
               1112888: 350ci, 180hp   1112979: 350ci, 210hp, at

Alternator: 1102474: All with ac
             1102484: All without ac

Ending Vehicle: Aug 75: 01602   Jan 76: 20568   Jun 76: 40830
                      Sep 75: 05693   Feb 76: 24370   Jul 76: 44767
                      Oct 75: 09982   Mar 76: 28760   Aug 76: 46558
                      Nov 75: 13481   Apr 76: 32805
                      Dec 75: 16696   May 76: 36656

Abbreviations: ac=air conditioning, at=automatic transmission, ce=california emissions, ci=cubic inch, hp=horsepower, mt=manual transmission.

1976 FACTS

• The carburetor air induction system was revised in 1976. Previously, air was drawn in at the rear of the hood, producing a howl audible from within the car. The air source point was moved forward, so that air was pulled in over the radiator. The 1976 hood is unique to the year.

• The aluminum wheels announced for 1973 arrived as a bona fide option with the 1976 model. These were made by Kelsey Hayes in Mexico and the wheels are identified on their inside surfaces as to source and build location. The YJ8 option included four wheels and a conventional steel spare, in contrast to the five-wheel sets provided with the knock-off and bolt-on aluminum wheel options of 1963-1967.

• Engineers put a partial steel underbelly in the forward section of Corvettes starting with the 1976 model for added rigidity and to better isolate the cockpit from the heat generated by engines calibrated to run hotter. The hotter engines were intentional, one way to increase efficiency and partially offset emissions-related power losses.

• Vents on the rear deck (just rear of the back window) were deleted.

• A new "sport" steering wheel for 1976 Corvettes was the same unit used for Chevrolet Vegas.

• GM's "freedom" battery, a new sealed and maintenance-free unit, was included with all 1976 models.

• A significant number of late-build 1976 Corvettes received parts normally associated with 1977 production, especially interior components.

• Two styles of rear bumbers were used. The first had smaller, recessed "Corvette" letters. The second style had larger letters, not recessed.

1976 OPTIONS

RPO #	DESCRIPTION	QTY	RETAIL $
1YZ37	Base Corvette Sport Coupe	46,558	$7,604.85
—	Custom Interior Trim	—	164.00
A31	Power Windows	38,700	107.00
C49	Rear Window Defogger	24,960	78.00
C60	Air Conditioning	40,787	523.00
FE7	Gymkhana Suspension	5,368	35.00
—	Optional Rear Axle Ratios	1,371	13.00
J50	Power Brakes	46,558	59.00
L82	350ci, 210hp Engine	5,720	481.00
M21	4-Speed Manual Trans, close ratio	2,088	0.00
M40	Turbo Hydra-Matic Automatic Transmission	36,625	0.00
N37	Tilt-Telescopic Steering Column	41,797	95.00
N41	Power Steering	46,385	151.00
QRM	White Stripe Steel Belted Tires, GR70x15	3,992	37.00
QRZ	White Letter Steel Belted Tires, GR70x15	39,923	51.00
U58	AM-FM Radio, stereo	34,272	281.00
U69	AM-FM Radio	11,083	187.00
UA1	Heavy Duty Battery	25,909	16.00
UF1	Map Light (on rearview mirror)	35,361	10.00
YF5	California Emission Test	3,527	50.00
YJ8	Aluminum Wheels (4)	6,253	299.00

• A 350ci, 180hp engine, 4-speed wide-ratio manual transmission, T-Tops, and vinyl interior trim were included in the base price.
• Custom interior included leather seat trim, wood-grain accents and lower carpet trim on inner door panels, wood grain accents on console, and special cut-pile carpeting.
• The FE7 gymkhana suspension included stiffer front sway bar and stiffer springs. There were no engine or transmission order restrictions with FE7.
• M40 was no cost with the base 350ci, 180hp engine, but cost $134.00 with optional L82 engine. M21 was no cost but required optional L82.
• The only engine-transmission combination available in California was the base 350ci, 180hp engine with M40 automatic transmission.
• Listed as separate options initially, power brakes (J50) and power steering (N41) were included in an increased base price during 1976. All 1976 Corvettes had power brakes; all but 173 had power steering.
• RPO C49 used glass heating elements instead of forced air and the terminology changed from "defroster" to "defogger."

1976 COLORS

CODE	EXTERIOR	QTY	WHEELS	INTERIORS
10	Classic White	10,674	Silver	Bk-Bg-Bu-Db-F-Sg-W
13	Silver	6,934	Silver	Bk-Bg-Bu-F-Sg-W
22	Bright Blue	3,268	Silver	Bk-Sg
33	Dark Green	2,038	Silver	Bk-Bu-Sg-W
37	Mahogany	4,182	Silver	Bk-Bu-F-Sg-W
56	Bright Yellow	3,389	Silver	Bk-Db
64	Buckskin	2,954	Silver	Bk-Bu-Db-F-W
69	Dark Brown	4,447	Silver	Bk-Bu-Db-W
70	Orange Flame	4,073	Silver	Bk-Bu-Db
72	Red	4,590	Silver	Bk-Bu-F-Sg-W

• Suggested interiors shown. Additional combinations were possible.
• Paint quantities do not add to total production because additional units had non-standard paint, and primer only.
• Early Chevrolet order guides show an exterior code 39 for Dark Green Metallic. This code was changed to code 33, but production records indicate one code 39 Dark Green Metallic 1976 Corvette built.

Interior Codes: 112=W/L, 15V=W/V, 152=Sg/L, 19V=Bk/V, 192=Bk/L, 322=Bg/L, 64V=Bu/V, 642=Bu/L, 692=Db/L, 71V=F/V, 712=F/L.

Abbreviations: Bg=Blue-Green, Bk=Black, Bu=Buckskin, Db=Dark Brown, F=Firethorn, L=Leather, Sg=Smoked Grey, V=Vinyl, W=White.

1977 CORVETTE
Production: 49,213 coupes

1977 NUMBERS

Vehicle: 1Z37L7S400001 through 1Z37L7S449213
- Fifth digit varies as follows: L=350ci, 180hp
X=350ci, 210hp

Suffix:
CHD: 350ci, 180hp, at, ce	CLB: 350ci, 180hp, at, ha
CKD: 350ci, 180hp, at, ha	CLC: 350ci, 180hp, at, ce
CKZ: 350ci, 180hp, mt	CLD: 350ci, 210hp, mt
CLA: 350ci, 180hp, at	CLF: 350ci, 210hp, at

Block: 3970010: 350ci, 180hp, 210hp

Head: 333882: 350ci, 180hp, 210hp

Carburetor: Rochester Q-jet #17057202: 350ci, 180hp, at
Rochester Q-jet #17057203: 350ci, 180hp, mt
Rochester Q-jet #17057204: 350ci, 180hp, at, ac
Rochester Q-jet #17057210: 350ci, 210hp, at
Rochester Q-jet #17057211: 350ci, 210hp, mt
Rochester Q-jet #17057228: 350ci, 210hp, at, ac
Rochester Q-jet #17057502: 350ci, 180hp, at, ce
Rochester Q-jet #17057504: 350ci, 180hp, at, ac, ce
Rochester Q-jet #17057510: 350ci, 210hp, at, uu
Rochester Q-jet #17057582: 350ci, 180hp, at, ha
Rochester Q-jet #17057584: 350ci, 180hp, at, ac, ha

Distributor: 1103246: 350ci, 180hp   1103256: 350ci, 210hp
1103248: 350ci, 180hp, at, ce

Alternator: 1102474: ac, ep   1102908: ac or rd
1102484: All without ac   1102909: ac or rd

Ending Vehicle:
Aug 76: 02287	Jan 77: 21118	May 77: 37029
Sep 76: 06337	Feb 77: 24662	Jun 77: 41233
Nov 76: 14216	Mar 77: 29041	Jul 77: 45179
Dec 76: 17551	Apr 77: 33057	Aug 77: 49213

Abbreviations: ac=air conditioning, at=automatic transmission, ce=california emissions, ci=cubic inch, ep=early production, ha=high altitude, hp=horsepower, mt=manual transmission, rd=rear defogger.

1977 FACTS

• A new console held heater and air conditioning controls and accepted standard Delco radios due to its increased depth. A new steering column positioned the steering wheel two inches closer to the instrument panel to provide more of an "arms out" driving position and easier entry and exit. 1977 models without RPO N37 had 1976 style steering wheels.
• The V54 rack was designed to hold the T-top panels, permitting use of the full luggage compartment when panels were removed.
• Early 1977 option listings contained CC1 glass roof panels, but these were never available during 1977 due to a marketing exclusivity dispute between Chevrolet and the panel vendor. Chevrolet released its own glass panels in 1978; the vendor sold their panels in the aftermarket under the trade name "Moon Roofs."
• Effective with #1Z37X7S427373, the alarm activator was moved from the driver-side fender to the driver-side door lock.
• New option K30 speed control required automatic transmission.
• Leather seats were standard for the first time in 1977, but a cloth-leather combination could be substituted at no cost.
• The headlight dimmer and windshield wiper/washer controls were located on steering column stalks in 1977 models.

1977 OPTIONS

RPO #	DESCRIPTION	QTY	RETAIL $
1YZ37	Base Corvette Sport Coupe	49,213	$8,647.65
A31	Power Windows	44,341	116.00
B32	Color Keyed Floor Mats	36,763	22.00
C49	Rear Window Defogger	30,411	84.00
C60	Air Conditioning	45,249	553.00
D35	Sport Mirrors	20,206	36.00
FE7	Gymkhana Suspension	7,269	38.00
G95	Optional Rear Axle Ratios	972	14.00
K30	Speed Control	29,161	88.00
L82	350ci, 210hp Engine	6,148	495.00
M21	4-Speed Manual Trans, close ratio	2,060	0.00
M40	Turbo Hydra-Matic Automatic Transmission	41,231	0.00
NA6	High Altitude Emission Equipment	—	22.00
N37	Tilt-Telescopic Steering Column	46,487	165.00
QRZ	White Letter Steel Belted Tires, GR70x15	46,227	57.00
UA1	Heavy Duty Battery	32,882	17.00
U58	AM-FM Radio, stereo	18,483	281.00
U69	AM-FM Radio	4,700	187.00
UM2	AM-FM Radio, stereo with 8-track tape	24,603	414.00
V54	Luggage and Roof Panel Rack	—	73.00
YF5	California Emission Certification	—	70.00
YJ8	Aluminum Wheels (4)	12,646	321.00
ZN1	Trailer Package	289	83.00
ZX2	Convenience Group	40,872	22.00

• A 350ci, 180hp engine, 4-speed wide-ratio manual transmission, T tops, and leather interior trim were included in the base price.
• RPO ZX2 convenience group included dome light delay, headlight warning buzzer, underhood light, low fuel warning light, interior courtesy lights and right side visor mirror.
• RPO FE7 suspension included stiffer front sway bar and stiffer springs. There were no engine or transmission order restrictions with FE7.
• RPO M40 was no cost with the base 350ci, 180hp engine, but cost $146 with optional L82 engine. M21 was no cost but required optional L82.
• The only engine-transmission combination available in California was the base 350ci, 180hp engine with M40 automatic transmission.
• RPO NA6 high altitude emission equipment was required for +4000ft; available only with the base 350ci, 180hp engine and M40 transmission.

1977 COLORS

CODE	EXTERIOR	QTY	WHEELS	INTERIORS
10	Classic White	9,408	Silver	B-Bk-Br-Bu-R-Sg-W
13	Silver	5,518	Silver	B-Bk-R-Sg-W
19	Black	6,070	Silver	Bk-Bu-R-Sg-W
26	Corvette Light Blue	5,967	Silver	Bk-Sg-W
28	Corvette Dark Blue	4,065	Silver	B-Bk-Bu-Sg-W
41	Corvette Chartreuse	1	Silver	Bk
52	Corvette Yellow	71	Silver	Bk-Br
56	Corvette Bright Yellow	1,942	Silver	Bk-Br
66	Corvette Orange	4,012	Silver	Bk-Br-Bu
80	Corvette Tan	4,588	Silver	Bk-Br-Bu-R-W
72	Medium Red	4,057	Silver	Bk-Bu-R-Sg-W
83	Corvette Dark Red	3,434	Silver	Bk-Bu-Sg

• Suggested interiors shown. Additional combinations were possible.
• Paint quantities do not add up to total production because additional units had non-standard paint, or primer only.

Interior Codes: 112=W/L, 15C=Sg/C, 152=Sg/L, 19C-Bk/C, 192=Bk/L, 27C=B/C, 272=B/L, 64C=Bu/C, 642=Bu/L, 69C=Br/C, 692=Br/L, 72C=R/C, 722=R/L.
• Cloth codes actually designate cloth-leather combinations.

Abbreviations: B=Blue, Bk=Black, Bu=Buckskin, Br=Brown, C=Cloth, L=Leather, R=Red, Sg=Smoked Grey, W=White.

1978 CORVETTE

Production: 40,274 coupe, 6,502 coupe (pace car), 46,776 total

1978 NUMBERS

Vehicle: 1Z87L8S400001 through 1Z87L8S440274
1Z87L8S900001 through 1Z87L8S906502 (pace car)
• Fifth digit varies as follows: L=350ci, 175hp,185hp
4=350ci, 220hp

Suffix:
CHW: 350ci, 185hp, mt
CLM: 350ci, 185hp, at
CLR: 350ci, 175hp, ce, at
CLS: 350ci, 175hp, ha, at

CMR: 350ci, 220hp, mt
CMS: 350ci, 220hp, at
CUT: 350ci, 185hp, at

Block: 3970010: All   376450, 460703: uncertain usage

Head: 462624: All

Carburetor: Rochester Q-jet #17058202: 350ci, 185hp, at
Rochester Q-jet #17058203: 350ci, 185hp, mt
Rochester Q-jet #17058204: 350ci, 185hp, at, ac, fd
Rochester Q-jet #17058206: 350ci, 185hp, at, ac, sd
Rochester Q-jet #17058210: 350ci, 220hp, at
Rochester Q-jet #17058211: 350ci, 220hp, mt
Rochester Q-jet #17058228: 350ci, 220hp, at, ac
Rochester Q-jet #17058502: 350ci, 175hp, at, ce
Rochester Q-jet #17058504: 350ci, 175hp, at, ac, ce
Rochester Q-jet #17058582: 350ci, 175hp, at, ha
Rochester Q-jet #17058584: 350ci, 175hp, at, ac, ha

Distributor: 1103285: 350ci, 175hp, ce   1103337: 350ci, 185hp, mt
1103291: 350ci, 220hp   1103353: 350ci, 185hp, at

Alternator: 1102474: 350ci, ac or rd, ep   1102908: 350ci, ac or rd, lp
1102484: 350ci

Abbreviations: at=automatic transmission, ce=california emissions, ci=cubic inch, ep=early production, fd=first design, ha=high altitude, hp=horsepower, lp=late production, mt=manual transmission, rd=rear defogger, sd=second design.

1978 FACTS

• Chevrolet marked the Corvette's twenty-fifth year by introducing the most extensively redesigned Corvette since the 1968 model. New "fastback' rear end styling featured a large rear window, but not a hatchback. The change created significantly more luggage space behind the seats.
• The 1978 interior was redesigned significantly. The speedometer and tachometer were redone in a more square, vertical mode. A glove box was added. Inner door panels were completely new and featured screwed-on arm rests instead of the molded-in style common to Corvettes since 1965.
• "25th Anniversary" emblems appeared exclusively on 1978 models.
• Wider 60-series tires became available as a 1978 Corvette option and required fender trimming at the Corvette assembly plant for clearance.
• The Corvette was honored as the pace car for the 1978 Indy 500 race. To commemorate the event, Chevrolet built limited edition Corvettes with their own vehicle identification number sequence. Initially, they were to have two-tone silver paint with red striping, special Goodyear tires with "Corvette" sidewall letters, and a build quantity of 300. The special tires were eliminated and the quantity became at least one for each Chevrolet dealer. The final build quantity released by Chevrolet was 6,502; however, other quantities have been published and some question remains.
• The "Silver Anniversary" paint option consisted of two-tone silver, lighter silver upper surface and darker silver lower surface, divided by silver striping. Sport mirrors and aluminum wheels were required.

1978 OPTIONS

RPO#	DESCRIPTION	QTY	RETAIL $
1YZ87	Base Corvette Sport Coupe	40,274	$9,351.89
1YZ87/78	Limited Edition Corvette (pace car)	6,502	13,653.21
A31	Power Windows	36,931	130.00
AU3	Power Door Locks	12,187	120.00
B2Z	Silver Anniversary Paint	15,283	399.00
CC1	Removable Glass Roof Panels	972	349.00
C49	Rear Window Defogger	30,912	95.00
C60	Air Conditioning	37,638	605.00
D35	Sport Mirrors	38,405	40.00
FE7	Gymkhana Suspension	12,590	41.00
G95	Optional Rear Axle Ratio	382	15.00
K30	Cruise Control	31,608	99.00
L82	350ci, 220hp Engine	12,739	525.00
M21	4-Speed Manual Trans, close ratio	3,385	0.00
MX1	Automatic Transmission	38,614	0.00
NA6	High Altitude Emission Equipment	—	33..00
N37	Tilt-Telescopic Steering Column	37,858	175.00
QBS	White Letter SBR Tires, P255/60R15	18,296	216.32
QGR	White Letter SBR Tires, P225/70R15	26,203	51.00
UA1	Heavy Duty Battery	28,243	18.00
UM2	AM-FM Radio, stereo with 8-track tape	20,899	419.00
UP6	AM-FM Radio, stereo with CB	7,138	638.00
U58	AM-FM Radio, stereo	10,189	286.00
U69	AM-FM Radio	2,057	199.00
U75	Power Antenna	23,069	40.00
U81	Dual Rear Speakers	12,340	49.00
YF5	California Emission Certification	—	75.00
YJ8	Aluminum Wheels (4)	28,008	340.00
ZN1	Trailer Package	972	89.00
ZX2	Convenience Group	37,222	84.00

• A 350ci, 185hp engine, 4-speed wide-ratio manual transmission, T-tops, and leather interior trim were included in the base price.
• ZX2 included dome light delay, headlight warning buzzer, underhood light, low fuel warning light, interior courtesy lights, floor mats, intermittent wipers, and right side visor mirror.
• Pace car replica included A31, AU3, CC1, C49, C60, D35, N37, QBS, UA1, UM2, U75, U81, YJ8 (rod accent), and ZX2. Other options available at normal prices except UP6 substitution for UM2 at $170.00.
• Manual transmission and/or L82 not available California or high altitude.

1978 COLORS

CODE	EXTERIOR	QTY	WHEELS	INTERIORS
10	Classic White	4,150	Silver	Bk-Db-Dbr-Lb-O-M-R
13	Silver	3,232	Silver	Bk-Db-M-R
13/07	Silver Anniversary	15,283	Silver	Bk-O-R
19	Black	11,075	Silver	Bk-Lb-M-O-R
26	Corvette Light Blue	1,960	Silver	Db
52	Corvette Yellow	1,243	Silver	Bk-Dbr-O
59	Corvette Light Beige	1,686	Silver	Bk-Db-Dbr-Lb-M
72	Corvette Red	2,074	Silver	Bk-Lb-O-R
82	Corvette Mahogany	2,121	Silver	Bk-Dbr-Lb-M-O
83	Corvette Dark Blue	2,084	Silver	Db-Lb-O
89	Corvette Dark Brown	1,991	Silver	Dbr-Lb-O

• Suggested interiors shown. Additional combinations were possible.
• The 11,075 quantity for code 19 black included 6,502 Pace Cars.
• Paint quantities exceed actual units sold. Sixteen units had primer only; additional excess units may be due to pilot builds not sold.

Interior Codes: 12C=O/C, 122=O/L, 15C=Sv/C, 152=Sv/L, 19C=Bk/C, 192=Bk/L, 29C=Db/C, 292=Db/L, 59C=Lb/C, 592=Lb/L, 69C=Dbr/C, 692=Dbr/L, 72C=R/C, 722=R/L, 76C=M/C, 762=M/L.

Abbreviations: Bk=Black, C=Cloth, Db=Dark Blue, Dbr=Dark Brown, L=Leather, Lb=Light Beige, M=Mahogany, O=Oyster, R=Red, Sv=Silver.

1979 CORVETTE
Production: 53,807 coupes

1979 NUMBERS

Vehicle: 1Z8789S400001 through 1Z8789S453807
  • Fifth digit varies as follows: 8=350ci, 195hp
  4=350ci, 225hp

Suffix: ZAA: 350ci, 195hp, mt, ep   ZAH: 350ci, 195hp, at
  ZAB: 350ci, 195hp, at, ep   ZAJ: 350ci, 195hp, at, ce
  ZAC: 350ci, 195hp, at, ce, ep ZBA: 350ci, 225hp, mt
  ZAD: 350ci, 195hp, at, ha   ZBB: 350ci, 225hp, at
  ZAF: 350ci, 195hp, mt

Block: 3970010: All   14016379: All (late production)

Head: 462624: All

Carb: Rochester Q-jet #17059202, 17059217: 350ci, 195hp, at
  Rochester Q-jet #17059203: 350ci, 195hp, mt
  Rochester Q-jet #17059210: 350ci, 225hp, at
  Rochester Q-jet #17059211: 350ci, 225hp, mt
  Rochester Q-jet #17059216: 350ci, 195hp, at, ac
  Rochester Q-jet #17059228: 350ci, 225hp, at, ac
  Rochester Q-jet #17059502: 350ci, 195hp, at, ce
  Rochester Q-jet #17059504, 17059507: 350ci, 195hp, at, ac, ce
  Rochester Q-jet #17059582: 350ci, 195hp, at, ha
  Rochester Q-jet #17059584: 350ci, 195hp, at, ac, ha

Distributor: 1103285: 350ci, 195hp, ce   1103302: 350ci, 195hp
  1103291: 350ci, 225hp   1103353: 350ci, 195hp

Alternator: 1101041, 1102394, 1102484: 350ci
  1102474, 1102908: 350ci, ac

Abbreviations: ac=air conditioning, at=automatic transmission, ce=california emissions, ci=cubic inch, ep=early production, ha=high altitude, hp=horsepower, mt=manual transmission.

1979 FACTS

• The new "high back" seat style introduced in the 1978 pace car replicas were made standard equipment in 1979. Extensive use of plastic resulted in weight reduction of about twelve pounds per seat. The new seats had better side bolster support, and the backs folded at a higher point to permit easier rear storage access. Inertia locking mechanisms restrained the backs in sudden deceleration, negating the need for manual locks. Driver and passenger seats had an additional inch of forward travel.

• The 1979 fuel filler pipe was redesigned to make it more difficult to modify for leaded-fuel access.

• Output of both the base L48 and optional L82 engines increased by 5hp due to a new "open flow" muffler design. Also, adding the L82's low restriction, dual-snorkel air intake to the base engine added another 5hp. The base L48 was rated at 195hp, the optional L82 at 225hp.

• The 85-mph speedometers associated with 1980 production were used for several late-build 1979s.

• In 1979, an AM-FM radio became standard equipment, and an illuminated visor-mirror combination became available for the passenger side.

• The front and rear spoilers developed for the 1978 pace car became 1979 options. They were functional, decreasing drag by about 15% and increasing fuel economy by about a half-mile per gallon.

• Tungsten-halogen headlight beams were phased into 1979 production early in the production year for increased visibility. These replaced only the high-beam units.

1979 OPTIONS

RPO #	DESCRIPTION	QTY	RETAIL $
1YZ87	Base Corvette Sport Coupe	53,807	$10,220.23
A31	Power Windows	20,631	141.00
AU3	Power Door Locks	9,054	131.00
CC1	Removable Glass Roof Panels	14,480	365.00
C49	Rear Window Defogger	41,587	102.00
C60	Air Conditioning	47,136	635.00
D35	Sport Mirrors	48,211	45.00
D80	Spoilers, front and rear	6,853	265.00
FE7	Gymkhana Suspension	12,321	49.00
F51	Heavy Duty Shock Absorbers	2,164	33.00
G95	Optional Rear Axle Ratio	428	19.00
K30	Cruise Control	34,445	113.00
L82	350ci, 225hp Engine	14,516	565.00
MM4	4-Speed Manual Trans, close ratio	4,062	0.00
MX1	Automatic Transmission	41,454	0.00
NA6	High Altitude Emission Equipment	—	35.00
N37	Tilt-Telescopic Steering Column	47,463	190.00
N90	Aluminum Wheels (4)	33,741	380.00
QBS	White Letter SBR Tires, P255/60R15	17,920	226.20
QGR	White Letter SBR Tires, P225/70R15	29,603	54.00
U58	AM-FM Radio, stereo	9,256	90.00
UM2	AM-FM Radio, stereo with 8-track	21,435	220.00
UN3	AM-FM Radio, stereo with cassette	12,110	234.00
UP6	AM-FM Radio, stereo with CB	4,483	439.00
U75	Power Antenna	35,730	52.00
U81	Dual Rear Speakers	37,754	52.00
UA1	Heavy Duty Battery	3,405	21.00
YF5	California Emission Certification	—	83.00
ZN1	Trailer Package	1,001	98.00
ZQ2	Power Windows and Door Locks	28,465	272.00
ZX2	Convenience Group	41,530	94.00

• A 350ci, 195hp engine, 4-speed manual transmission, T-tops, and leather or cloth/leather interior trim were included in the base price.

• The Corvette's base price and some options increased several times during 1979. Base price climbed from $10,220.23 to $12,313.23 by year end. The largest single increase was $706.00 effective 5-7-79, due to air conditioning, power windows and tilt-telescopic steering column made standard equipment.

• RPO ZX2 included dome and courtesy light delay, headlight warning buzzer, underhood light, low fuel warning light, floor mats, intermittent wipers, and right side visor mirror.

• Manual transmission and/or L82 not available California or high altitude.

1979 COLORS

CODE	EXTERIOR	QTY	WHEELS	INTERIORS
10	Classic White	8,629	Silver	Bk-Db-Dg-Lb-O-R
13	Silver	7,331	Silver	Bk-Db-Dg-O-R
19	Black	10,465	Silver	Bk-Lb-O-R
28	Corvette Light Blue	3,203	Silver	Bk-Db-O
52	Corvette Yellow	2,357	Silver	Bk-Lb-O
58	Corvette Dark Green	2,426	Silver	Bk-Dg-Lb-O
59	Corvette Light Beige	2,951	Silver	Bk-Db-Dg-Lb-R
72	Corvette Red	6,707	Silver	Bk-Lb-O-R
82	Corvette Dark Brown	4,053	Silver	Bk-Lb-O
83	Corvette Dark Blue	5,670	Silver	Bk-Db-Lb-O-R

• Suggested interiors shown. Additional combinations were possible.
• Code 82 Corvette Dark Brown may also be coded 67.
• Fifteen 1979 Corvettes had primer only.

Interior Codes: 12C=O/C, 122=O/L, 192=Bk/L, 29C=Db/C, 292=Db/L, 49C=Dg/C, 492=Dg/L, 59C=Lb/C, 592=Lb/L, 722=R/L.

Abbreviations: Bk=Black, C=Cloth, Db=Dark Blue, Dg=Dark Green, L=Leather, Lb=Light Beige, O=Oyster, R=Red.

1980 CORVETTE
Production: 40,614 coupes

1980 NUMBERS

Vehicle: 1Z878AS400001 through 1Z878AS440614
　　　　• Fifth digit varies as follows: 8=350ci,190hp　H=305ci,180hp
　　　　　　　　　　　　　　　　　　　6=350ci, 230hp

Suffix: ZAK: 350ci, 190hp, at　　ZBD: 350ci, 230hp, uu
　　　　ZAM: 350ci, 190hp, mt　　ZCA: 305ci, 180hp, at, ce
　　　　ZBC: 350ci, 230hp, at

Block: 14010207: 350ci, 190hp, 230hp, lp　　4715111: 305ci, 180hp
　　　　3970010: 350ci, 190hp, 230hp

Head: 462624: 350ci, 190hp, 230hp　　14014416: 305ci, 180hp

Carb: Rochester Q-jet #17080204: 350ci, 190hp, at
　　　　Rochester Q-jet #17080207: 350ci, 190hp, mt
　　　　Rochester Q-jet #17080228: 350ci, 230hp, at
　　　　Rochester Q-jet #17080504, 17080517: 305ci, 180hp, at, ce

Distributor: 1103287: 350ci, 190hp, mt　1103368: 305ci, 180hp, at, ce
　　　　　　1103352: 350ci, 190hp　　1103435: 350ci, 230hp, at
　　　　　　1103353: 350ci, 190hp, at

Alternator: 1101041, 1101075, 1101085, 1101088, 1103122

Abbreviations: at=automatic transmission, ce=california emissions, ci=cubic inch, hp=horsepower, lp=late production, mt=manual transmission, uu=uncertain usage.

1980 FACTS

• For the first time since 1974, two engine displacements were available in Corvettes, but not optional. Because of tightened California emission restrictions, Chevrolet did not certify its 350 cubic-inch engines there in 1980. California Corvette buyers were required to purchase a 305ci engine, the RPO LG4, with a $50 credit. This was a standard passenger car engine, built at Chevrolet's Tonawanda, New York, engine plant. In Corvettes, it could be combined only with automatic transmissions.
• The 4-speed manual transmission was not available with the optional L82 engine, with the possible exception of a few early production builds.
• The 1980 model featured new front and rear bumper "caps" with integral spoilers. Radiator air flow increased by nearly fifty-percent. The integrated spoilers improved the drag coefficient from .503 to .443 compared to the 1979 model equipped with optional, non-integrated spoilers.
• The crossed flag emblems for 1980 were a new, more elongated design.
• The speedometers for 1980 Corvettes read to a maximum of 85 mph, a new federal requirement. These were phased in during 1979 production.
• The three behind-seat storage compartments were changed to two in the 1980 model. The battery remained in its own compartment behind the driver, but the center and passenger-side compartments were combined with one access door.
• After several years of weight increases, the Corvette was lighter in 1980 as engineers trimmed weight by using lower density roof panels, reducing the thickness of hood and outer doors, and using aluminum for the differential housing and crossmember. For the base L48 engine, the L82's aluminum intake manifold became standard.
• The California RPO LG4 305ci engine included stainless-steel tubular exhaust headers with an oxygen sensor in a "closed loop" system. Despite its lower displacement and more restrictive emissions equipment, the Corvette application of this engine developed 180hp, just 10hp less than the 350ci, L48 base engine for other states.

1980 OPTIONS

RPO#	DESCRIPTION	QTY	RETAIL $
1YZ87	Base Corvette Sport Coupe	40,614	$13,140.24
AU3	Power Door Locks	32,692	140.00
CC1	Removable Glass Roof Panels	19,695	391.00
C49	Rear Window Defogger	36,589	109.00
FE7	Gymkhana Suspension	9,907	55.00
F51	Heavy Duty Shock Absorbers	1,695	35.00
K30	Cruise Control	30,821	123.00
LG4	305ci, 180hp Engine (required in California)	3,221	-50.00
L82	350ci, 230hp Engine	5,069	595.00
MM4	4-Speed Manual Transmission	5,726	0.00
MX1	Automatic Transmission	34,838	0.00
N90	Aluminum Wheels (4)	34,128	407.00
QGB	White Letter SBR Tires, P225/70R15	26,208	62.00
QXH	White Letter SBR Tires, P255/60R15	13,140	426.16
UA1	Heavy Duty Battery	1,337	22.00
U58	AM-FM Radio, stereo	6,138	46.00
UM2	AM-FM Radio, stereo with 8-track	15,708	155.00
UN3	AM-FM Radio, stereo with cassette	15,148	168.00
UP6	AM-FM Radio, stereo with CB	2,434	391.00
U75	Power Antenna	32,863	56.00
UL5	Radio Delete	201	-126.00
U81	Dual Rear Speakers	36,650	52.00
V54	Roof Panel Carrier	3,755	125.00
YF5	California Emission Certification	3,221	250.00
ZN1	Trailer Package	796	105.00

• A 350ci, 190hp, 350ci (180hp, 305ci in California for $50 credit), 4-speed manual transmission or automatic transmission, T-tops, and leather/vinyl or cloth/vinyl interior trim were included in the base price.
• The Corvette's base price increased four times during 1980, increasing from $13,140.24 to $14,345.24. Option prices were not affected.
• RPO A31 power windows, RPO C60 air conditioning, and RPO N37 tilt-telescopic steering column, all optional for part of 1979, were included in the 1980's base price.
• RPO C49 rear window defogger included UA1 heavy-duty battery.
• RPO LG4 305ci, 180hp engine was required for California and not available elsewhere. It was not available with manual transmission.
• RPO V54 roof panel carrier mounted to the rear deck for external transport of removable roof panels. It was new for 1980.
• RPO ZN1 trailer package included heavy-duty radiator, not available as a separate option, and RPO FE7 gymkhana suspension.

1980 COLORS

CODE	EXTERIOR	QTY	WHEELS	INTERIORS
10	White	7,780	Silver	Bk-Cl-Db-Ds-O-R
13	Silver	4,341	Silver	Bk-Cl-Db-O-R
19	Black	7,250	Silver	Bk-Ds-O-R
28	Dark Blue	4,135	Silver	Bk-Db-Ds-O-R
47	Dark Brown	2,300	Silver	Bk-Ds-O
52	Yellow	2,077	Silver	Bk-O
58	Dark Green	844	Silver	Bk-Ds-O
59	Frost Beige	3,070	Silver	Bk-Cl-Db-Ds-R
76	Dark Claret	3,451	Silver	Bk-Cl-Ds-O
83	Red	5,714	Silver	Bk-Ds-O-R

• Suggested interiors shown. Additional combinations were possible.
• Paint quantites exceed actual units sold. Records show no primer only, but additional special colors coded "spec" were used.
• Code 492 for green leather interior was released, but cancelled early.
Interior Codes: 12C=O/C, 122=O/L, 192=Bk/L, 29C=Db/C, 292=Db/L, 59C=Ds/C, 592=Ds/L, 722=R/L, 79C=CL/C, 792=CL/L.
Abbreviations: Bk=Black, C=Cloth, CL=Claret, Db=Dark Blue, Ds=Doeskin, L=Leather, O=Oyster, R=Red.

1981 CORVETTE
Production: 40,606 coupes

1981 NUMBERS

Vehicle: 1G1AY8764BS400001 thru 1G1AY8764BS431611 (St Louis)
1G1AY8764B5100001 thru 1G1AY8764B5108995 (B-Green)
• Ninth digit is a check code and varies.

Suffix: ZDA: 350ci, 190hp, mt   ZDC: 350ci, 190hp, mt, ce
ZDB: 350ci, 190hp, at, ce   ZDD: 350ci, 190hp, at

Block: 14010207: All

Head: 462624: All

Carburetor: Rochester Q-jet #17081217: 350ci, 190hp, mt
Rochester Q-jet #17081218: 350ci, 190hp, at, ce
Rochester Q-jet #17081228: 350ci, 190hp, at

Distributor: 1103443: All

Alternator: 1101075, 1101085, 1103088, 1103091, 1103103

Abbreviations: at=automatic transmission, ce=california emissions, ci=cubic inch, hp=horsepower, mt=manual transmission.

1981 FACTS

• The 1981 Corvette was the first model year to be built simultaneously in two locations. The first Corvette was completed at the new Bowling Green, Kentucky, assembly line on June 1, 1981. The last Corvette to be built at St. Louis was completed on August 1, 1981.
• Although there were no engine options for 1981, the base 350ci, 190hp L81 engine was certified for sale in California, and was available in all states including California with both 4-speed manual and automatic transmissions.
• Exterior styling carried over from 1980, but emblems did change slightly.
• The tubular stainless steel exhaust manifolds, used for 1980 Corvettes sold in California with the LG4 305ci engine, were standard with the 1981 base engine.
• Chevrolet's "computer command control" used on 1980 Corvettes sold in California became standard equipment on all 1981 Corvettes. The system automatically adjusted ignition timing and air-fuel mixture.
• Chevrolet introduced a fiberglass-reinforced monoleaf rear spring for 1981 Corvettes equipped with automatic transmissions and standard suspensions. The plastic spring weighed eight pounds compared to forty-four pounds for the steel unit it replaced.
• The anti-theft alarm system was improved in 1981 by the addition of an ignition interrupt to prevent engine start.
• All 1981 valve covers were magnesium for weight reduction.
• For improved fuel economy, 1981 Corvettes with automatic transmissions had torque converter clutches for second and third gears.
• A detail change to the 1981 Corvette interior was the color-keying of the headlamp and windshield wiper switch bezels to the interior color. In 1980, they were black regardless of interior color.
• The 1981 Corvette was the last model to have a manual transmission available until well into the 1984 production year.
• The St. Louis Corvette assembly plant continued to use lacquer paints through the end of 1981 production in that facility. Meanwhile in Bowling Green, a new paint process was developed which used enamel basecoats followed by clear topcoats.
• A power driver seat became available in Corvettes for the first time in 1981 as RPO A42. It was not available for the passenger side.

1981 OPTIONS

RPO#	DESCRIPTION	QTY	RETAIL $
1YY87	Base Corvette Sport Coupe	40,606	$16,258.52
AU3	Power Door Locks	36,322	145.00
A42	Power Driver Seat	29,200	183.00
CC1	Removable Glass Roof Panels	29,095	414.00
C49	Rear Window Defogger	36,893	119.00
DG7	Electric Sport Mirrors	13,567	117.00
D84	Two-Tone Paint	5,352	399.00
FE7	Gymkhana Suspension	7,803	57.00
F51	Heavy Duty Shock Absorbers	1,128	37.00
G92	Performance Axle Ratio	2,400	20.00
K35	Cruise Control	32,522	155.00
MM4	4-Speed Manual Transmission	5,757	0.00
N90	Aluminum Wheels (4)	36,485	428.00
QGR	White Letter SBR Tires, P225/70R15	21,939	72.00
QXH	White Letter SBR Tires, P255/60R15	18,004	491.92
UL5	Radio Delete	315	-118.00
UM4	AM-FM Radio, etr stereo with 8-track	8,262	386.00
UM5	AM-FM Radio, etr stereo with 8-track/CB	792	712.00
UM6	AM-FM Radio, etr stereo with cassette	22,892	423.00
UN5	AM-FM Radio, etr stereo with cassette/CB	2,349	750.00
U58	AM-FM Radio, stereo	5,145	95.00
U75	Power Antenna	32,903	55.00
V54	Roof Panel Carrier	3,303	135.00
YF5	California Emission Certification	4,951	46.00
ZN1	Trailer Package	916	110.00

• A 350ci, 190hp engine, 4-speed manual transmission or automatic transmission, T-tops, and leather/vinyl or cloth/vinyl interior trim were included in the base price.

• There were no optional Corvette engines in 1981.

• All optional radios except U58 were new style Delcos with electronic tuned receivers (etr). Available with 8-track, 8-track plus citizens band, cassette, or cassette with citizens band, the radios featured digital station tuning readout and had built-in clocks. If a 1981 Corvette had one of these radios, the standard quartz instrument panel clock was replaced with an oil temperature gauge.

1981 COLORS

CODE	EXTERIOR	QTY	WHEELS	INTERIORS
06	Mahogany Metallic	1,092	Silver	Cm-Dr
10	White	6,387	Silver	Ch-Cm-Db-Dr-Mr-Sg
13	Silver Metallic	2,590	Silver	Ch-Db-Mr-Sg
19	Black	4,712	Silver	Ch-Cm-Dr-Mr-Sg
24	Bright Blue Metallic	1	Silver	Ch-Cm-Db-Sg
28	Dark Blue Metallic	2,522	Silver	Cm-Db-Mr-Sg
52	Yellow	1,031	Silver	Ch-Cm
59	Beige	3,842	Silver	Cm-Db-Dr-Mr
75	Red	4,310	Silver	Ch-Cm-Mr-Sg
79	Maroon Metallic	1,618	Silver	Ch-Cm-Mr-Sg
84	Charcoal Metallic	3,485	Silver	Ch-Cm-Mr-Sg
33/38	Silver/Dark Blue	—	Silver	Db-Sg
33/39	Silver/Charcoal	—	Silver	Ch-Sg
50/74	Beige/Dark Bronze	—	Silver	Cm
80/98	Autumn Red/Dark Claret	—	Silver	Dr-Sg

• Suggested interiors shown. Other combinations were possible.

• Color quantities shown are for St. Louis production and should not be relied upon as exact because the total is 21 less than actual production. All two-tone combinations were painted at the new Bowling Green facility and precise paint quantity records are not currently available.

• **Interior Codes:** 152=Sg/L, 19C=Ch/C, 192=Ch/L, 29C=Db/C, 292=Db/L, 64C=Cm/C, 642=Cm/L, 67C=Dr/C, 672=Dr/L, 752=Mr/L.

• **Abbreviations:** C=Cloth, Ch=Charcoal, Cm=Camel, Db=Dark Blue, Dr=Dark Red, L=Leather, Mr=Medium Red, Sg=Silver Gray.

1982 CORVETTE

Production: 18,648 coupe, 6,759 collector coupe, 25,407 total

1982 NUMBERS

Vehicle: 1G1AY8786C5100001 thru 1G1AY8786C5125408
- Sixth digit is a zero for the Collector Edition
- Ninth digit is a check code and varies

Note: Vin tag ending 00017 was lost and not built.

Suffix: ZBA: 350ci, 200hp, at   ZBN: 350ci, 200hp, at, ce
ZBC: 350ci, 200hp, at, ce, ep

Block: 14010207: All

Head: 462624: All

Throttle Body Injection: 17082052: Rear Unit   17082053: Front Unit

Distributor: 1103479: All

Alternator: 1101071, 1101075, 1103091, 1103103

Abbreviations: at=automatic transmission, ce=california emissions, ci=cubic inch, ep=early production, hp=horsepower.

1982 FACTS

- The 1982 Corvette was the last of a generation. Its basic body shape dated to 1968 and its chassis to 1963. To honor the 1982 model's special status, Chevrolet offered a "Collector Edition." It differed from base models in several ways. In addition to a higher level of standard features optional on base models, the Collector Edition had a lifting rear hatchback glass, special wheels styled similarly to the 1967 "bolt on" optional wheels, unique silver-beige paint, unique silver-beige leather interior and special cloisonne emblems.
- The Collector Edition Hatchback Coupe carried a special code (zero in the sixth digit) in its vehicle identification number, but didn't have a separate serial sequence. At $22,537.59, it was the first Corvette with a base price exceeding $20,000.00.
- A manual transmission was not available in 1982 Corvettes.
- The automatic transmission in 1982 Corvettes was a new four-speed unit with a torque converter clutch operating in the top three gears. It used a higher first gear ratio (3.07:1) for improved acceleration.
- Hoods of 1982 models had solenoid-operated doors to direct fresh air directly into the air cleaner during full throttle.
- Chevrolet introduced "cross fire injection" on the 1982 Corvette. This wasn't fuel injection of the type available in 1957-1965 Corvettes; rather, it combined two "injectors" with Chevrolet's Computer Command Control system to achieve better economy, driveability and performance through more precise metering of the fuel. The Computer Command Control itself was refined in 1982 so that it was capable of making eighty adjustments per second compared to ten the previous year.
- The new fuel metering system used in 1982 included a positive fuel cutoff to prevent engine run-on (dieseling).
- The charcoal air filtering element of the 1981 model was replaced with a paper element in the cross-fire-injection 1982.
- The exhaust system of 1982 models was redesigned with a smaller and lighter catalytic converter. The exhaust pipes leading into the converter were redesigned to deliver hotter exhaust gases to the converter to increase its efficiency.
- All 1982 Corvettes were built in the new Corvette plant in Bowling Green, Kentucky. Production was initiated in 1981 when 8,995 models were built.
- The 1982 Corvette was the last model with optional radio packages that included an 8-track tape (RPO UM4), and Citizens Band (RPO UN5).

1982 OPTIONS

RPO #	DESCRIPTION	QTY	RETAIL $
1YY87	Base Corvette Sport Coupe	18,648	$18,290.07
1YY07	Corvette Collector Edition Hatchback	6,759	22,537.59
AG9	Power Driver Seat	22,585	197.00
AU3	Power Door Locks	23,936	155.00
CC1	Removable Glass Roof Panels	14,763	443.00
C49	Rear Window Defogger	16,886	129.00
DG7	Electric Sport Mirrors	20,301	125.00
D84	Two-Tone Paint	4,871	428.00
FE7	Gymkhana Suspension	5,457	61.00
K35	Cruise Control	24,313	165.00
N90	Aluminum Wheels	16,844	458.00
QGR	White Letter SBR Tires, P225/70R15	5,932	80.00
QXH	White Letter SBR Tires, P255/60R15	19,070	542.52
UL5	Radio Delete	150	-124.00
UM4	AM-FM Radio, etr stereo with 8-track	923	386.00
UM6	AM-FM Radio, etr stereo with cassette	20,355	423.00
UN5	AM-FM Radio, etr stereo with cassette/CB	1,987	755.00
U58	AM/FM Radio, stereo	1,533	101.00
U75	Power Antenna	15,557	60.00
V08	Heavy Duty Cooling	6,006	57.00
V54	Roof Panel Carrier	1,992	144.00
YF5	California Emission Certification	4,951	46.00

• A 350ci, 200hp engine, automatic transmission, T-tops, and leather/vinyl or cloth/vinyl interior trim were included in the base price.
• There were no optional Corvette engines in 1982.
• Manual transmissions were not available.
• Corvette Collector Edition Hatchback Coupe included RPOs CC1, C49, QXH, U75, special silver-beige paint, graduated hood and side body decals, commemorative aluminum wheels, frameless glass hatchback with manual remote release, accent pinstriping, multi-tone silver-beige leather seats and door trim, leather wrapped steering wheel and horn cap, cloisonne exterior and interior emblems, and luxury carpeting. If UN5 radio was selected, it cost $695 instead of $755.

1982 COLORS

CODE	EXTERIOR	QTY	WHEELS	INTERIORS
10	White	2,975	Silver	Ch-Cm-Db-Dr-Sgn-Sgy
13	Silver	711	Silver	Ch-Db-Dr-Sgy
19	Black	2,357	Silver	Ch-Cm-Dr-Sgn-Sgy
24	Silver Blue	1,124	Silver	Ch-Cm-Sgy
26	Dark Blue	562	Silver	Cm-Db-Sgy
31	Bright Blue	567	Silver	Ch-Cm-Db-Sgy
39	Charcoal	1,093	Silver	Ch-Dr-Sgy
40	Silver Green	723	Silver	Ch-Sgn
56	Gold	648	Silver	Ch-Cm
59	Silver Beige	6,759	Silver	Sb
70	Red	2,155	Silver	Ch-Cm-Dr-Sgy
99	Dark Claret	853	Silver	Cm-Dr-Sgy
10/13	White/Silver	664	Silver	Ch-Sgy
13/39	Silver/Charcoal	1,239	Silver	Ch-Dr-Sgy
13/99	Silver/Dark Claret	1,301	Silver	Dr-Sgy
24/26	Silver Blue/Dark Blue	1,667	Silver	Db-Sgy

• Suggested interiors shown. Other combinations were possible.
• Nine 1982 Corvettes had primer only.
• Exterior code 59 Silver-Beige, and interior code 592 silver-beige leather were exclusive to the Collector Edition Hatchback.

Interior Codes: 132=Sgy/L, 182=Ch/L, 22C=Db/C, 222=Db/L, 402=Sgn/L, 592=Sb/L, 64C=Cm/C, 642=Cm/L, 74C=Dr/C, 742=Dr/L.

Abbreviations: C=Cloth, Ch=Charcoal, Cm=Camel, Db=Dark Blue, Dr=Dark Red, L=Leather, Sb=Silver Beige, Sgn=Silver Green, Sgy=Silver Gray.

1984 CORVETTE
Production: 51,547 coupes

1984 NUMBERS

Vehicle: 1G1AY0782E5100001 thru 1G1AY0782E5151547
   • Ninth digit is a check code and varies.

Suffix: ZFC: 350ci, 205hp, at
   ZFD: 350ci, 205hp, mt
   ZFF: 350ci, 205hp, at, ce
   ZFH: 350ci, 205hp, ex
   ZFJ: 350ci, 205hp, mt, ex

   ZFK: 350ci, 205hp, at
   ZFL: 350ci, 205hp, mt
   ZFM: 350ci, 205hp, at, ce
   ZFN: 350ci, 205hp, mt, ce
   ZFR: 350ci, 205hp, mt, ce

Block: 14010207: All

Head: 462624: All

Abbreviations: at=automatic transmission, ce=california emissions, ci=cubic inch, ex=export, hp=horsepower, mt=manual transmission.

1984 FACTS

• The 1984 Corvette was a complete redesign in almost every aspect. Handling considerations dominated and the result was praised by the motoring press as the world's best cornering automobile.

• The 1984 Corvette was introduced in March 1983. Because it met all 1984 federal requirements, Chevrolet decided to skip the 1983 model designation. The result was a very long production run and the second highest model year volume in the Corvette's history. 1983 Corvettes were built, serial numbered, and tested by both Chevrolet and the motoring press at the "long lead" preview at Riverside Raceway in December 1982. But 1983 Corvettes were not released for public sale.

• Design criteria specified that the 1984 Corvette have more ground clearance and more interior room, but less overall height. In order to achieve it, engineers routed the exhaust system through the center tunnel.

• A "4+3", 4-speed manual transmission, built by Doug Nash, had overdrives in the top three gears for improved fuel economy. Not available early.

• All 1984 Corvettes were designed with one-piece, lift-off roof panels and rear hatch windows. At the time, the rear window glass was the largest compound glass ever installed in an American automobile. The front windshield was raked at the greatest angle, 64%.

• Brakes remained disc at all four wheels, but components were new and included aluminum calipers supplied by Girlock of Australia.

• Electronic instrumentation was standard and included digital readouts for engine monitoring and liquid crystal graphic displays for speed and engine revolutions. Analog instrumentation was not available.

• The 1984 Corvette was designed with a pad protruding from the passenger side of the dash. This was part of a passive restraint system conceived when it was assumed the federal regulation would require such restraints. The Reagan Administration dropped the restraint proposals, but the Corvette's pad remained.

• The 1984 Corvette was designed without fiberglass seams on exposed panels to eliminate factory finishing. The exterior seams were under the rub strip extending around the entire body.

• The radiator was a new design using aluminum for the cooling fins and plastic for the reservoirs. A thermostatically controlled electric fan operates only when needed and only under 35mph.

• Chevrolet built specially modified 1984 Corvettes for the export markets of European, Middle East, Japanese, and Latin American countries. Changes included different license plate provisions, leaded fuel capability, and electrical, glass, lighting and mirror modifications.

• Single transverse plastic leaf springs were used front and rear.

1984 OPTIONS

RPO #	DESCRIPTION	QTY	RETAIL $
1YY07	Base Corvette Sport Coupe	51,547	$21,800.00
AG9	Power Driver Seat	48,702	210.00
AQ9	Sport Seats, cloth	4,003	625.00
AR9	Base Seats, leather	40,568	400.00
AU3	Power Door Locks	49,545	165.00
CC3	Removable Transparent Roof Panel	15,767	595.00
D84	Two-Tone Paint	8,755	428.00
FG3	Delco-Bilstein Shock Absorbers	3,729	189.00
G92	Performance Axle Ratio	410	22.00
KC4	Engine Oil Cooler	4,295	158.00
K34	Cruise Control	49,832	185.00
MM4	4-Speed Manual Transmission	6,443	0.00
QZD	P255/50VR16 Tires/16" Wheels	51,547	561.20
UL5	Radio Delete	104	-331.00
UM6	AM-FM Stereo Cassette	6,689	153.00
UN8	AM-FM Stereo, Citizens Band	178	215.00
UU8	Stereo System, Delco-Bose	43,607	895.00
V01	Heavy-Duty Radiator	12,008	57.00
YF5	California Emission Requirements	6,833	75.00
Z51	Performance Handling Package	25,995	600.20
Z6A	Rear Window+Side Mirror Defoggers	47,680	160.00

• A 350ci, 205hp engine, 4-speed automatic transmission, removable body-color roof panel, and cloth seats were included in the base price.
• Optional leather seats were the same design as the base cloth style. Sport seats were available in cloth (different material than base) and featured inflatable lumbar support and power-adjusted side bolsters.
• The RPO QZD 16-inch tire and wheel package, initially intended to be included as part of the Z51 option, and as a separate option for base models, was required for all 1984 Corvettes sold. The scheduled standard 15-inch alloy wheels and P215/65R15 tires were not used.
• RPO Z51 included heavy-duty front and rear springs, shock absorbers, stabilizer bars and bushings, fast steering ratio, engine oil cooler, extra radiator fan (pusher), P255/50VR16 tires and directional alloy wheels, 16x8.5-inch front, 16x9.5-inch rear.

1984 COLORS

CODE	EXTERIOR	QTY	WHEELS	INTERIORS
10	White	6,417	Alloy	Ca-Br-Gr-Mb-Mg-S
16	Bright Silver Metallic	3,109	Alloy	Gr-Mg
18	Medium Gray Metallic	3,147	Alloy	Gr-Mg
19	Black	7,906	Alloy	Ca-Gr-Mg-S
20	Light Blue Metallic	1,196	Alloy	Mb
23	Medium Blue Metallic	1,822	Alloy	Mb
53	Gold Metallic	2,430	Alloy	S
63	Light Bronze Metallic	2,452	Alloy	Br
66	Dark Bronze Metallic	1,371	Alloy	Br
72	Bright Red	12,942	Alloy	Gr-S
16/18	Silver/Medium Gray	3,629	Alloy	Gr-Mg
20/23	Light Blue/Medium Blue	1,433	Alloy	Mb
63/66	Light Bronze/Dark Bronze	3,693	Alloy	Br

• Additional codes: 70 and 33 for Bright Red, 41 for Black, 40 for White.
• Suggested interiors shown. Other combinations were possible.
• Interior colors sold in 1984 were 13,752 graphite, 12,768 carmine, 8,019 bronze, 6,685 saddle, 6,541 gray, 3,782 blue.
• All wheels were alloy with similar exterior appearance. Base models had all 16x8.5-inch. Z51 models had 16x8.5-inch front, 16x9.5-inch rear.

Interior Codes: 12C=Gr/C, 12V=Gr/Sc, 122=Gr/L, 15C=Mg/C, 15V=Mg/Sc, 152=Mg/L, 28C=Mb/C, 28V=Mb/Sc, 62C=S/C, 62V=S/Sc, 622=S/L, 65C=Br/C, 65V=Br/Sc, 652=Br/L, 742=Ca/L.

Abbreviations: Ca=Carmine, Br=Bronze, C=Cloth, Gr=Graphite, L=Leather, Mb=Medium Blue, Mg=Medium Gray, S=Saddle, Sc=Sport Seat Cloth.

1985 CORVETTE
Production: 39,729 coupes

1985 NUMBERS

Vehicle: 1G1YY0787F5100001 thru 1G1YY0787F5139729
  • Ninth digit is a check code and varies.

Suffix: ZDF: 350ci, 230hp, at   ZJJ: 350ci, 230hp, at, oc
ZJB: 350ci, 230hp, mt   ZJK: 350ci, 230hp, mt, oc
ZJC: Export

Block: 14010207: All

Head: 462624: All

Abbreviations: at=automatic transmission, ci=cubic inch, hp=horsepower, mt=manual transmission, oc=engine oil cooler.

1985 FACTS

• The 1982 and 1984 Corvette engines had "Cross Fire Injection," but genuine fuel injection returned to the Corvette in 1985 for the first time in two decades. The 1985 tuned-port injection, built by Bosch, was standard equipment and featured a mass airflow sensor, aluminum-tube tuned intake runners, a mold-cast plenum, and an air cleaner mounted forward of the radiator support. This new L98 engine delivered a horsepower increase from 205hp to 230hp, a torque increase from 290 lb.-ft. to 330, and a real-world fuel economy increase of about 11%.
• The overdrive selection switch for 4-speed manual transmissions was moved during 1985 production from the console to the gear shift knob.
• Suspension rates were lowered in 1985, a result of harsh ride criticism. Springs for the base suspension were softer by 26% in front, 25% in the rear. Springs for RPO Z51 were 16% softer in front and 25% softer in the rear. To compensate for the spring change, larger-diameter stabilizer bars were included with Z51-equipped models.
• In its January 1985 "ten best" issue, *Car and Driver* magazine pronounced the Corvette to be America's fastest production car at an even 150mph top speed. Corvette also took top honors in top-gear acceleration and tied for best (with Porsche) in roadholding as measured by G-force skidpad adhesion.
• The bore of the brake master cylinder was increased in 1985, and the booster itself was plastic, the first such application in an American car. The new plastic booster was 30% lighter and less subject to corrosion.
• Manual transmission 1985s came with a new, heavy-duty 8.5-inch ring differential. Rear axle gearing for manuals was 3.07:1. Standard gearing for automatic transmissions was 2.73:1, but the 3.07:1 could be ordered as RPO G92.
• Wheel balance weights changed in 1985 from the outside-rim, clip-on style, to an inner-surface adhesive type. The change was mainly for aesthetics, but Chevrolet also believed a better balance resulted because of the adhesive weight's proximity to the wheel's depth center.
• A full length oil pan gasket reinforcement was added to the 1985 Corvette engine to improve gasket compression seal.
• The 1985 Corvette distributor was modified to prevent distributor spark ignition of exterior fuel vapors.
• Electronic instrumentation continued much as the previous year, but displays were revised and improved with cleaner graphics, less color on the speedometer and tachometer, and larger digits for the center-cluster liquid crystal displays.
• A map strap was added to the 1985's driver-side sun visor.
• Electronic air conditioning was announced as a late 1985 option, but introduction was delayed into the 1986 model year.

1985 OPTIONS

RPO #	DESCRIPTION	QTY	RETAIL $
1YY07	Base Corvette Sport Coupe	39,729	$24,403.00
AG9	Power Driver Seat	37,856	215.00
AQ9	Sport Seats, leather	—	1,025.00
AR9	Base Seats, leather	—	400.00
—	Sport Seats, cloth	5,661	625.00
AU3	Power Door Locks	38,294	170.00
CC3	Removable Transparent Roof Panel	28,143	595.00
D84	Two-Tone Paint	6,033	428.00
FG3	Delco-Bilstein Shock Absorbers	9,333	189.00
G92	Performance Axle Ratio	5,447	22.00
K34	Cruise Control	38,369	185.00
MM4	4-Speed Manual Transmission	9,576	0.00
NN5	California Emission Requirements	6,583	99.00
UL5	Radio Delete	172	-256.00
UN8	AM-FM Stereo, Citizens Band	16	215.00
UU8	Stereo System, Delco-Bose	35,998	895.00
V08	Heavy-Duty Cooling	17,539	225.00
Z51	Performance Handling Package	14,802	470.00
Z6A	Rear Window+Side Mirror Defoggers	37,720	160.00

• A 350ci, 230hp engine, 4-speed automatic transmission, removable body-color roof panel, and cloth seats were included in the base price.
• The optional sport seat, available only in cloth for 1984, became available in leather after the start of 1985 production. The total number of leather seats sold was 30,955, but the individual quantities of base leather seats and sport leather seats is not currently available.
• RPO Z51 included FG3 Delco-Bilstein shock absorbers, V08 heavy-duty cooling, extra radiator fan (pusher), heavy-duty front and rear springs, stabilizers and bushings, fast steering ratio and 16x9.5-inch wheels. FG3 and V08 were available separately with non-Z51 models.
• The RPO CC3 removable transparent roof panel was given stronger sun screening for 1985.

1985 COLORS

CODE	EXTERIOR	QTY	WHEELS	INTERIORS
13	Silver Metallic	1,752	Alloy	Gr-Mg
18	Medium Gray Metallic	2,519	Alloy	Gr-Mg
20	Light Blue Metallic	1,021	Alloy	Mb
23	Medium Blue Metallic	2,041	Alloy	Mb
40	White	4,455	Alloy	Ca-Gr-S-Mb-Mg
41	Black	7,603	Alloy	Ca-Gr-S-Mg
53	Gold Metallic	1,411	Alloy	S
63	Light Bronze Metallic	1,440	Alloy	Br
66	Dark Bronze Metallic	1,030	Alloy	Br
81	Bright Red	10,424	Alloy	Ca-Gr-S-Mg
13/18	Silver/Gray	2,170	Alloy	Gr-Mg
20/23	Light Blue/Medium Blue	1,470	Alloy	Mb
63/66	Light Bronze/Dark Bronze	2,393	Alloy	Br

• Suggested interiors shown. Other combinations were possible.
• Code 33 also used for Bright Red. Exterior colors for 1985 were the same as 1984, except Silver and Bright Red were brighter hues.
• Interior colors sold in 1985 were 11,927 graphite, 8,272 carmine, 5,195 medium gray, 5,176 bronze, 4,715 saddle, 4,443 medium blue.
• All wheels were alloy with similar exterior appearance. Standard wheels were 16x8.5-inch front and rear; the RPO Z51 package had 16x9.5-inch wheels front and rear.

Interior Codes: 12C=Gr/C, 12V=Gr/Sc, 122=Gr/L, 15C=Mg/C, 15V=Mg/Sc, 152=Mg/L, 28C=Mb/C, 28V=Mb/Sc, 282=Mb/L, 62C=S/C, 62V=S/Sc, 622=S/L, 65C=Br/C, 65V=Br/Sc, 652=Br/L, 742=Ca/L.

Abbreviations: Ca=Carmine, Br=Bronze, C=Cloth, Gr=Graphite, L=Leather, Mb=Medium Blue, Mg=Medium Gray, S=Saddle, Sc=Sport Seat Cloth.

1986 CORVETTE

Production: 27,794 coupe, 7,315 convertible, 35,109 total

1986 NUMBERS

Vehicle: 1G1YY0789G5100001 thru 1G1YY0789G5127794 (coupe)
1G1YY6789G5900001 thru 1G1YY6789G5907315 (conv)
• Ninth digit is a check code and varies.

Suffix: DKF: 350ci, 230hp, ih, at, oc   ZJS: 350ci, 235hp, ah, at, oc
DKC: 350ci, 230hp, ih, at   ZJH: 350ci, 235hp, ah, at
DKH: 350ci, 230hp, ih, at, ex   ZKD: 350ci, 235hp, ah, at, ex
DKD: 350ci, 230hp, ih, mt, oc   ZJW: 350ci, 235hp, ah, mt, oc
DKB: 350ci, 230hp, ih, mt   ZKA: 350ci, 235hp, ah, mt

Block: 14088548: All

Head: 462624: 350ci, 230hp, ih   14101128: 350ci, 235hp, ah

Abbreviations: ah=aluminum heads, at=automatic transmission, ci=cubic inch, ex=export, hp=horsepower, ih=iron heads, mt=manual transmission, oc=engine oil cooler.

1986 FACTS

• A Corvette convertible model was introduced in interim 1986, the first Chevrolet-built Corvette convertible since the 1975 model. The 1986 Corvette was the pace car for the 1986 Indianapolis 500. All 1986 Corvette convertibles sold were designated as pace car replicas and all included decal packages for dealer or customer installation.
• An anti-lock brake system (ABS) became standard with 1986 Corvettes. An adaptation of Bosch's system, Corvette's ABS had rotational sensors at each wheel to feed data to a computerized electronic control unit (ECU). Brake line pressure was automatically distributed for optimum braking without wheel lock and loss of steering control.
• Cracking around the head attachment bosses required an introduction delay for design revisions to 1986's aluminum cylinder heads. The heads were ready in time for convertible production and all 1986 convertibles and late production coupes had aluminum heads. Engines fitted with aluminum heads were rated at 235hp, an increase of 5hp.
• Center high mount stoplights were added to 1986 Corvettes to conform to federal requirements. The coupe's was mounted above the rear window; the convertible's was in a less-conspicuous rear facia location.
• A new vehicle anti-theft system (VATS) required a special ignition key with an embedded pellet. Lock cylinder contacts measured the pellet's electrical resistance (there were fifteen variations) before allowing start.
• Caster was changed in 1986 from four degrees to six degrees to improve on-center road feel and to decrease wander.
• Fifty "Malcolm Konner Commemorative Edition" 1986 Corvettes were built in a special arrangement honoring the New Jersey Chevrolet dealership's founder, Malcolm Konner. Each Corvette had special two-tone paint schemes, Silver Beige over Black, coded "spec." Window stickers reflected 4001ZA as the RPO, and a $500 cost for MALCOLM KONNER SP. EDIT. PAI. All were coupes, twenty with manual transmissions, thirty with automatics. All had graphite leather interiors. One was retrofitted with a Callaway twin-turbo engine.
• The angle of the 1986 digital instrument display was changed to improve daytime viewing by reducing glare.
• A new upshift indicator light for manual and automatic transmission 1986 models was intended to improve fuel economy.
• "Low coolant" and "anti-lock" instrument displays were added.
• Wheel design was revised slightly for 1986, with the wheel center section natural finish instead of black as in 1984 and 1985.

1986 OPTIONS

RPO#	DESCRIPTION	QTY	RETAIL $
1YY07	Base Corvette Sport Coupe	27,794	$27,027.00
1YY67	Base Corvette Convertible	7,315	32,032.00
AG9	Power Driver Seat	33,983	225.00
AQ9	Sport Seats, leather	13,372	1,025.00
AR9	Base Seats, leather	—	400.00
AU3	Power Door Locks	34,215	175.00
B4P	Radiator Boost Fan	8,216	75.00
B4Z	Custom Feature Package	4,832	195.00
C2L	Dual Removable Roof Panels (coupe)	6,242	895.00
24S	Removable Roof Panel, blue tint (coupe)	12,021	595.00
64S	Removable Roof Panel, bronze tint (coupe)	7,819	595.00
C68	Electronic Air Conditioning Control	16,646	150.00
D84	Two-Tone Paint (coupe)	3,897	428.00
FG3	Delco-Bilstein Shock Absorbers	5,521	189.00
G92	Performance Axle Ratio, 3.07:1	4,879	22.00
KC4	Engine Oil Cooler	7,394	110.00
K34	Cruise Control	34,197	185.00
MM4	4-Speed Manual Transmission	6,835	0.00
NN5	California Emission Requirements	5,697	99.00
UL5	Radio Delete	166	256.00
UM6	AM-FM Stereo Cassette	2,039	122.00
UU8	Stereo System, Delco-Bose	32,478	895.00
V01	Heavy-Duty Radiator	10,423	40.00
Z51	Performance Handling Package (coupe)	12,821	470.00
Z6A	Rear Window+Side Mirror Defog (coupe)	21,837	165.00
4001ZA	Malcolm Konner Special Edition Paint (coupe)	50	500.00

• A 350ci, 230hp (iron cylinder heads) or 235hp (aluminum cylinder heads) engine, 4-speed automatic transmission, removable body-color roof panel (coupe) or soft top (conv), and cloth seats were included in the base price.
• RPO B4Z custom feature package included rear window defogger, outside remote heated mirrors, and inside rearview mirror with map light.
• RPO Z51 included B4P, FG3, KC4, V01, 16x9.5-inch wheels, heavy-duty suspension, and fast steering ratio. Limited to coupes.

1986 COLORS

CODE	EXTERIOR	QTY	SOFT TOP	INTERIORS
13	Silver Metallic	1,209	Bk-W	Gr-Mg
18	Medium Gray Metallic	1,603	Bk-W	Gr-Mg-R
20	Medium Blue Metallic	128	Bk-W	B-Gr
35	Yellow	1,464	Bk-W	Gr
40	White	4,176	Bk-S-W	B-Br-Gr-Mg-R-S
41	Black	5,464	Bk-S-W	Gr-Mg-R-S
53	Gold Metallic	777	Bk-S	Gr-S
59	Silver Beige Metallic	1,383	Bk	Br-Gr
66	Copper Metallic	4	Bk-S	Gr-S
69	Medium Brown Metallic	488	S	Br-S
74	Dark Red Metallic	5,002	Bk-S-W	Gr-S
81	Bright Red	9,466	Bk-S-W	Gr-R-S
13/18	Silver/Gray	1,049	none	Gr-Mg-R
18/41	Gray/Black	1,138	none	Gr-Mg
40/13	White/Silver	693	none	Gr-Mg
59/69	Silver Beige/Medium Brown	1,014	none	Br
spec	Silver Beige/Black	50	none	Gr

• Suggested interiors shown. Other combinations were possible.
• Restrictions applied to some soft top and interior color combinations.
• The code "spec" was used for fifty "Malcolm Konner Commemorative Edition" Corvettes with unique Silver Beige over Black two-tone paint.

Interior Codes: 12C=Gr/C, 122=Gr/L, 15C=Mg/C, 152=Mg/L, 21C=B/C, 212=B/L, 62C=S/C, 622=S/L, 65C=Br/C, 652=Br/L, 732=R/L.

Abbreviations: B=Blue, Bk=Black, Br=Bronze, C=Cloth, Gr=Graphite, L=Leather, Mg=Medium Gray, R=Red, S=Saddle, W=White.

1987 CORVETTE

Production: 20,007 coupe, 10,625 convertible, 30,632 total

1987 NUMBERS

Vehicle: 1G1YY2182H5100001 thru 1G1YY2182H5130632
- For convertibles, sixth digit is a 3.
- Ninth digit is a check code and varies.

Suffix: ZJN: 350ci, 240hp, at   ZLA: 350ci, 240hp, at, oc
ZLC: 350ci, 240hp, mt, oc   ZLB: Export

• For Callaway twin-turbo, Chevrolet engine coding was replaced as follows: First two digits for year, next three digits for Callaway sequence, last four digits to match last four digits of vehicle identification number.

Block: 14093638: All

Head: 14101128: All

Abbreviations: at=automatic transmission, ci=cubic inch, hp=horsepower, mt=manual transmission, oc=engine oil cooler.

1987 FACTS

• Friction reduction from roller valve lifters (new for 1987) resulted in a power increase to 240hp, up 5hp from 1986's aluminum-head engines.
• Center sections and radial slots of 1987 wheels were painted argent gray. 1986 wheel centers were not painted. Centers and radial slots for 1984 and 1985 were painted black.
• Convertibles and early coupes had outside mirror air deflectors.
• Chevrolet planned an RPO UJ6 low tire pressure indicator option, but the $325 option was on constraint during 1987 due to false signalling problems. However, Chevrolet records show forty-six units sold.
• The RPO Z51 package was refined to include structural enhancements developed for the convertible, and a finned power steering fluid cooler.
• A new RPO Z52 "sport" handling package combined elements of Z51 with the softer suspension of base models. RPO Z52 included the radiator boost fan, Bilstein shock absorbers, engine oil cooler, heavy-duty radiator, 16x9.5-inch wheels, faster 13:1 steering ratio, larger front stabilizer bar (except early production), and the convertible-inspired structural improvements for coupes. Z52 was available with coupes or convertibles, automatic or manual transmissions.
• The overdrive-engage light was moved from the center-dash area (1984-86) to an easier-to-view location within the 1987 tach display.
• The Callaway Twin-Turbo engine package introduced in 1987 was not a factory-installed option, but could be ordered through participating Chevrolet dealers as RPO B2K. Fully assembled Corvettes were shipped from the Bowling Green Corvette plant to Callaway Engineering in Old Lyme, Connecticut, for engine and other modifications. The 1987 Callaway had ratings of 345hp and 465 lb.-ft torque, and reached a top speed of 177.9 mph with .60 overdrive gearing. The first four 1987 Callaways used replacement LF5 (truck) shortblocks, but subsequent cars had reworked production Corvette engines. All 1987 Callaways had manual transmissions and none were certified for California sale. Of 184 twin-turbos built in 1987, 121 were coupes, 63 were convertibles.
• Electronic air conditioning control (RPO C68) became an available option for coupes and convertibles in 1987; in 1986, it was coupe-only.
• New 1987 convenience options included an illuminated vanity mirror (D74) for the driver's visor, and a passenger-side power seat base (AC1). Twin remote heated mirrors became available for convertibles as RPO DL8. The heated mirrors were included with the heated rear window in the RPO Z6A defogger option for coupes.

1987 OPTIONS

RPO #	DESCRIPTION	QTY	RETAIL $
1YY07	Base Corvette Sport Coupe	20,007	$27,999.00
1YY67	Base Corvette Convertible	10,625	33,172.00
AC1	Power Passenger Seat	17,124	240.00
AC3	Power Driver Seat	29,561	240.00
AQ9	Sport Seats, leather	14,119	1,025.00
AR9	Base Seats, leather	14,579	400.00
AU3	Power Door Locks	29,748	190.00
B2K	Callaway Twin Turbo (not GM installed)	184	19,995.00
B4P	Radiator Boost Fan	7,291	75.00
C2L	Dual Removable Roof Panels (coupe)	5,017	915.00
24S	Removable Roof Panel, blue tint (coupe)	8,883	615.00
64S	Removable Roof Panel, bronze tint (coupe)	5,766	615.00
C68	Electronic Air Conditioning Control	20,875	150.00
DL8	Twin Remote Heated Mirrors (convertible)	6,840	35.00
D74	Illuminated Driver Vanity Mirror	14,992	58.00
D84	Two-Tone Paint (for coupe)	1,361	428.00
FG3	Delco-Bilstein Shock Absorbers	1,957	189.00
G92	Performance Axle Ratio, 3.07:1	7,285	22.00
KC4	Engine Oil Cooler	6,679	110.00
K34	Cruise Control	29,594	185.00
MM4	4-Speed Manual Transmission	4,229	0.00
NN5	California Emission Requirements	5,423	99.00
UL5	Radio Delete	247	-256.00
UM6	AM-FM Stereo Cassette	2,182	132.00
UU8	Stereo System, Delco-Bose	27,721	905.00
V01	Heavy-Duty Radiator	7,871	40.00
Z51	Performance Handling Package (coupe)	1,596	795.00
Z52	Sport Handling Package	12,662	470.00
Z6A	Rear Window+Side Mirror Defog (coupe)	19,043	165.00

• A 350ci, 240hp engine, 4-speed automatic transmission, removable body-color roof panel (coupe) or soft top (convertible), and cloth seats were included in the base price.
• RPO Z51 included B4P, FG3, KC4, V01, 16x9.5-inch wheels, heavy-duty suspension, fast steering ratio. Coupes and manual transmissions only.
• RPO B2K generated a specific equipment build with standard engines at the Corvette assembly plant. The cars were then sent to Callaway's Connecticut shop for installation of Callaway-modified twin-turbo engines.

1987 COLORS

CODE	EXTERIOR	QTY	SOFT TOP	INTERIORS
13	Silver Metallic	767	Bk-W	Gr-Mg
18	Medium Gray Metallic	1,035	Bk-W	Gr-Mg-R
20	Medium Blue Metallic	2,677	Bk-W	B-Gr
35	Yellow	1,051	Bk-W	Gr
40	White	3,097	Bk-S-W	B-Br-Gr-Mg-R-S
41	Black	5,101	Bk-S-W	Gr-Mg-R-S
53	Gold Metallic	397	Bk-S	Gr-S
59	Silver Beige Metallic	950	Bk	Br-Gr
66	Copper Metallic	87	Bk-S	Gr-S
69	Medium Brown Metallic	245	S	Br-S
74	Dark Red Metallic	5,578	Bk-S-W	Gr-S
81	Bright Red	8,285	Bk-S-W	Gr-R-S
13/18	Silver/Gray	403	none	Gr-Mg-R
18/41	Gray/Black	316	none	Gr-Mg
40/13	White/Silver	195	none	Gr-Mg
59/69	Silver Beige/Medium Brown	447	none	Br

• Suggested interiors shown. Other combinations were possible.
• Restrictions applied to some soft top and interior color combinations.
Interior Codes: 12C=Gr/C, 122=Gr/L, 15C=Mg/C, 152=Mg/L, 21C=B/C, 212=B/L, 62C=S/C, 622=S/L, 65C=Br/C, 652=Br/L, 732=R/L.
Abbreviations: B=Blue, Bk=Black, Br=Bronze, C=Cloth, Gr=Graphite, L=Leather, Mg=Medium Gray, R=Red, S=Saddle, W=White.

1988 CORVETTE

Production: 15,382 coupe, 7,407 convertible, 22,789 total

1988 NUMBERS

Vehicle: 1G1YY2182J5100001 thru 1G1YY2182J5122789
- For convertibles, sixth digit is a 3.
- Ninth digit is a check code and varies.

Suffix: ZMA: 350ci, 240/245hp, at   ZMC: 350ci, 240/245hp, mt, oc
ZMD: 350ci, 240/245hp, at, oc

• For Callaway twin-turbo, Chevrolet engine coding was replaced as follows: First two digits for year, next three digits for Callaway sequence, last four digits to match last four digits of vehicle identification number.

Block: 14093638: All

Head: 10088113: All

Abbreviations: at=automatic transmission, ci=cubic inch, hp=horsepower, mt=manual transmission, oc=engine oil cooler.

1988 FACTS

• Refinements for 1988 included carpeted door sills, solution-dyed carpet, improved "flow through" ventilation for coupes, and a lower, rearward relocation of the parking brake handle.
• Engine power remained at 240hp for 1988 models except for coupes with 3.07:1 axle ratios which had 245hp. The 5hp increase came from less restrictive mufflers which were deemed too loud for convertibles and 2.59:1 axle coupes.
• A thirty-fifth anniversary edition 1988 Corvette package was available for coupes only. It featured a two-tone exterior of white with black roof bow, white leather seats, steering wheel, special interior and exterior accents, a console-mounted anniversary plaque, special emblems and other distinguishing features. Sales totaled 2,050 units.
• Chevrolet built fifty-six street-legal Corvettes for the 1988 SCCA Corvette Challenge race series. Engines, stock but matched for power output, were built at the Flint engine plant, sealed and shipped to Bowling Green for standard assembly. The cars weren't built in sequence because the Corvette plant built in color batches. Fifty cars were sent to Protofab in Wixom, Michigan for installation of roll cages and other gear. During the season, most engines were exchanged by Chevrolet for new, sealed engines with more evenly calibrated power output.
• New six-slot 16x8.5 wheels were standard with P255/50ZR16 tires.
• RPO Z51 and RPO Z52 content changed slightly for 1988. Both had newly styled 17x9.5-inch wheels with twelve cooling slots, and P275/40ZR17 tires. Z51 had higher spring rates and finned power steering cooler as before, but in 1988 it also received larger front brake rotors and calipers. RPO Z51 was limited to manual transmission coupes. RPO Z52 was not restricted.
• All 1988 Corvettes had new dual-piston front brakes and parking brakes which activated the rear pads instead of activating small, separate parking drum brakes as in all previous disc-brake Corvettes.
• Ratings for the 1988 RPO B2K Callaway Twin Turbo were 382hp and 562 lb.-ft torque. Automatic transmissions (reworked truck Turbo Hydra-Matic 400s) were available for $6,500. Either Z51 or Z52 suspensions could be specified. Later production with Z52 had Z51's larger front brakes, mufflers, longer air dams, and steering coolers because RPO B2K triggered these through Special Equipment Option (SEO) Z5G. Engines were reworked by Callaway at its Old Lyme, Connecticut shop.
• All 1988s had an improved hood support rod and a more efficient, higher capacity air conditioning compressor manufactured by Nippondenso.

1988 OPTIONS

RPO#	DESCRIPTION	QTY	RETAIL $
1YY07	Corvette Sport Coupe	15,382	$29,489.00
1YY67	Base Corvette Convertible	7,407	34,820.00
AC1	Power Passenger Seat	18,779	240.00
AC3	Power Driver Seat	22,084	240.00
AQ9	Sport Seats, leather	12,724	1,025.00
AR9	Base Seats, leather	9,043	400.00
B2K	Callaway Twin Turbo (not GM installed)	124	25,895.00
B4P	Radiator Boost Fan	19,035	75.00
C2L	Dual Removable Roof Panels (coupe)	5,091	915.00
24S	Removable Roof Panel, blue tint (coupe)	8,332	615.00
64S	Removable Roof Panel, bronze tint (coupe)	3,337	615.00
C68	Electronic Air Conditioning Control	19,372	150.00
DL8	Twin Remote Heated Mirrors (convertible)	6,582	35.00
D74	Illuminated Driver Vanity Mirror	14,249	58.00
FG3	Delco-Bilstein Shock Absorbers	18,437	189.00
G92	Performance Axle Ratio, 3.07:1	4,497	22.00
KC4	Engine Oil Cooler	18,877	110.00
MM4	4-Speed Manual Transmission	4,282	0.00
NN5	California Emission Requirements	3,882	99.00
UL5	Radio Delete	179	-297.00
UU8	Stereo System, Delco-Bose	20,304	773.00
V01	Heavy-Duty Radiator	19,271	40.00
Z01	35th Special Edition Package (coupe)	2,050	4,795.00
Z51	Performance Handling Package (coupe)	1,309	1,295.00
Z52	Sport Handling Package	16,017	970.00
Z6A	Rear Window+Side Mirror Defog (coupe)	14,648	165.00

• A 350ci, 240/245hp engine, 4-speed automatic transmission, removable body-color roof panel (coupe) or soft top (convertible), and cloth seats were included in the base price.
• RPO Z51 included B4P, FG3, KC4, V01, heavy-duty suspension, 17x9.5 wheels, and fast steering ratio. Limited to manual transmission coupes.
• RPO Z52 included B4P, FG3 and KC4, 17x9.5 wheels, and fast steering.
• RPO Z01 included AQ9, AC3, 24S, C68, D74, Z52 and Z6A. Not available with convertibles.
• RPO B2K generated a specific equipment build with standard engines at the Corvette assembly plant. The cars were then sent to Callaway's Connecticut shop for installation of Callaway-modified twin-turbo engines.

1988 COLORS

CODE	EXTERIOR	QTY	SOFT TOP	INTERIORS
13	Silver Metallic	385	Bk-W	Bk-G-R-S
20	Medium Blue Metallic	1148	Bk-W	B-Bk
28	Dark Blue Metallic	1,675	Bk-S-W	Bk-S
35	Yellow	578	Bk-W	Bk-S
40	White	3,620	Bk-S-W	B-Bk-G-R-S
41	Black	3,420	Bk-S-W	Bk-G-R-S
74	Dark Red Metallic	2,878	Bk-S-W	Bk-S
81	Bright Red	5,340	Bk-S-W	Bk-G-R-S
90	Gray Metallic	644	Bk-W	Bk-G
96	Charcoal Metallic	1,046	Bk-S-W	G-S
40/41	White/Black	2,050	none	W

• Suggested interiors shown. Other combinations were possible.
• Restrictions applied to some soft top and interior color combinations.
• Two-tone combinations of gray/charcoal and white/silver were indicated in early dealer order guides, but were dropped prior to 1988 production.
• Five code 66 dark orange exteriors were built for pilot production.

Interior Codes: 113=W/L, 19C=Bk/C, 192=Bk/L, 212=B/L, 60C=S/C, 602=S/L, 732=R/L, 902=G/L.

Abbreviations: B=Blue, Bk=Black, C=Cloth, G-Gray, L=Leather, R=Red, S=Saddle, W=White.

1989 CORVETTE

Production: 16,663 coupe, 9,749 convertible, 26,412 total

1989 NUMBERS

Vehicle: 1G1YY2186K5100001 thru 1G1YY2186K5126328
  • For convertibles, sixth digit is a 3.
  • Ninth digit is a check code and varies.

Suffix: ZRA: 350ci, 240/245hp, mt, oc   ZRC: 350ci, 240/245hp, at, oc
ZRB: 350ci, 240/245hp, at

• Production totals included 84 ZR-1s built, but not sold to the public.
• For Callaway twin-turbo, Chevrolet engine coding was replaced as follows: First two digits for year, next three digits for Callaway sequence, last four digits to match last four digits of vehicle identification number.

Block: 14093638: All

Head: 10088113: All

Abbreviations: at=automatic transmission, ci=cubic inch, hp=horsepower, mt=manual transmission, oc=engine oil cooler.

1989 FACTS

• The RPO MN6 manual transmission no-cost option for 1989 was a new 6-speed designed jointly by ZF (Zahnradfabrik Friedrichshafen) and Chevrolet and built by ZF in Germany. A computer-aided gear selection (CAGS) feature bypassed second and third gears (and locked out fifth and sixth) for improved fuel economy in specific non-performance conditions.
• The Corvette Challenge race series terminated at the end of the 1989 season. For 1989, Corvette's Bowling Green assembly plant built sixty Challenge cars with standard engines. Meanwhile, CPC Flint Engine built special, higher horsepower engines which were shipped to the Milford Proving Grounds for storage, then to Specialized Vehicles Inc. (SVI), Troy, Michigan, where they were equalized for power and sealed. Bowling Green sent thirty cars to Powell Development America, Wixom, Michigan, where the roll cages and safety equipment were installed and the engines from SVI were switched with the original engines. At season's end, Chevrolet returned the original numbers-matching engines to each racer.
• The RPO Z51 performance handing package option continued in 1989, available only in coupes with manual transmissions. A new suspension option, RPO FX3, permitted three variations of suspension control regulated by a console switch. It could be ordered only with RPO Z51. The RPO Z52 sport suspension (1987-1988) was not a 1989 option. However, though all 1989 Corvettes with FX3 were Z51s, these had Z52 springs and stabilizers for a wider range of suspension control. The only exceptions were the sixty Corvettes built for the Challenge race series which had FX3 suspensions with Z51 springs and stabilizers.
• The standard six-slot, 16x8.5-inch wheel introduced in 1988 was discontinued for 1989. The twelve-slot, 17x9.5-inch style included with 1988's Z51 and Z52 options became 1989's standard equipment wheel.
• On April 19, 1989, Chevrolet advised dealers that the ZR-1 would be a 1990 model, not a late-release 1989. The reason cited was "insufficient availability of engines caused by additional development." Eighty-four (84) 1989 ZR-1 Corvettes were built for evaluation, testing, media preview and photography, but none were released for public sale.
• Seats were restyled, but the three choices of cloth, optional leather, or optional sport leather continued. Due to weight and fuel economy factors, Chevrolet intentionally limited sales of the sport leather seats by making them available exclusively with Z51-optioned models during 1989.
• The manual top mechanism was simplified for 1989 convertibles.

1989 OPTIONS

RPO#	DESCRIPTION	QTY	RETAIL $
1YY07	Base Corvette Sport Coupe	16,663	$31,545.00
1YY67	Base Corvette Convertible	9,749	36,785.00
AC1	Power Passenger Seat	20,578	240.00
AC3	Power Driver Seat	25,606	240.00
AQ9	Sport Seats, leather	1,777	1,025.00
AR9	Base Seats, leather	23,364	400.00
B2K	Callaway Twin-Turbo (not GM installed)	69	25,895.00
B4P	Radiator Boost Fan	20,281	75.00
CC2	Auxiliary Hardtop (convertible)	1,573	1,995.00
C2L	Dual Removable Roof Panels (coupe)	5,274	915.00
24S	Removable Roof Panel, blue tint (coupe)	8,748	615.00
64S	Removable Roof Panel, bronze tint (coupe)	4,042	615.00
C68	Electronic Air Conditioning Control	24,675	150.00
D74	Illuminated Driver Vanity Mirror	17,414	58.00
FX3	Selective Ride and Handling, electronic	1,573	1,695.00
G92	Performance Axle Ratio	10,211	22.00
K05	Engine Block Heater	2,182	20.00
KC4	Engine Oil Cooler	20,162	110.00
MN6	6-Speed Manual Transmission	4,113	0.00
NN5	California Emission Requirements	4,501	100.00
UJ6	Low Tire Pressure Warning Indicator	6,976	325.00
UU8	Stereo System, Delco-Bose	24,145	773.00
V01	Heavy Duty Radiator	20,888	40.00
V56	Luggage Rack (convertible)	616	140.00
Z51	Performance Handling Package (coupe)	2,224	575.00

• A 350ci, 240/245hp engine, 4-speed automatic transmission, removable body-color roof panel (coupe) or soft top (convertible), and cloth seats were included in the base price.
• RPO Z51 included B4P, KC4 , V01, heavy-duty suspension, and fast steering ratio. Limited to manual transmission coupes..
• New convertible options for late 1989 introduction included an RPO V56 rear luggage rack, and RPO CC2 removable hardtop.
• RPO AQ9 leather sport seats and RPO FX3 selective ride and handling were available only when ordered with RPO Z51.
• RPO B2K generated a specific equipment build with standard engines at the Corvette assembly plant. The cars were then sent to Callaway's Connecticut shop for installation of Callaway-modified twin-turbo engines.

1989 COLORS

CODE	EXTERIOR	QTY	SOFT TOP	INTERIORS
10	White	5,426	Bk-S-W	B-Bk-G-R-S
20	Medium Blue Metallic	1,428	Bk-W	B-Bk
28	Dark Blue Metallic	1,931	Bk-S-W	Bk-S
41	Black	4,855	Bk-S-W	B-Bk-G-R-S
68	Dark Red Metallic	3,409	Bk-S-W	Bk-S
81	Bright Red	7,663	Bk-S-W	Bk-G-R-S
90	Gray Metallic	225	Bk-W	Bk-G
96	Charcoal Metallic	1,440	Bk-S-W	Bk-G-S

• Only interior-exterior combinations shown were considered acceptable.
• Restrictions applied to some soft top and interior color combinations.
• Code 90 Gray was cancelled in November, 1988.
• Though not listed on 1989 exterior color availability charts, Chevrolet records indicate six code 35 Yellow, and twenty-seven code 31 Arctic Pearl 1989 Corvettes were built.
• Interior colors sold in 1989 were 9,909 black, 7,139 red, 4,785 saddle, 3,096 gray, 1,483 blue.

Interior Codes: 19C=Bk/C, 192=Bk/L, 212=B/L, 60C=S/C, 602=S/L, 732=R/L, 902=G/L.

Abbreviations: B=Blue, Bk=Black, C=Cloth, G=Gray, L=Leather, R=Red, S=Saddle, W=White.

1990 CORVETTE
Production: 16,016 coupe, 7,630 convertible, 23,646 total

1990 NUMBERS

Vehicle: 1G1YY2380L5100001 thru 1G1YY2380L5120597
1G1YZ23J6L5800001 thru 1G1YZ23J6L5803049 (ZR1)
    • For convertibles, sixth digit is a 3.
    • Ninth digit is a check code and varies.

Suffix: ZSA: 350ci, 245/250hp, at   ZSD: 350ci, 375hp, ac
     ZSB: 350ci, 245/250hp, mt, oc   ZSH: 350ci, 375hp, ea
     ZSC: 350ci, 245/250hp, at, oc

• For Callaway twin-turbo, Chevrolet engine coding was replaced as follows: First two digits for year, next three digits for Callaway sequence, last four digits to match last four digits of vehicle identification number.

Block: 10090511: 350ci, 375hp   14093638: 350ci, 245/250hp

Head: 10088113: 350ci, 245/250hp
     10106178: 350ci, 375hp (rh)   10106179: 350ci, 375hp (lh)

Abbreviations: ac=air conditioning, at=automatic transmission, ci=cubic inch, ea=electronic air conditioning control, hp=horsepower, lh=left hand, mt=manual transmission, oc=engine oil cooler, rh=right hand.

1990 FACTS

• The ZR-1 (RPO ZR1) arrived as a 1990 model after much anticipation. At the heart of the ZR-1 was the 375hp LT5 engine. It was designed with the same V-8 configuration and 4.4-inch bore spacing as the standard L98 Corvette engine, but was an otherwise new design with four overhead camshafts and 32 valves. LT5 engines were manufactured and assembled by Mercury Marine in Stillwater, Oklahoma, then shipped to the Corvette Bowling Green assembly plant for ZR-1 vehicle assembly.
• For a limited time during 1990, dealers could order Corvettes destined for the new World Challenge race series. Merchandising code R9G triggered deviations from normal build, such as heavy-duty springs with FX3. Owners could buy race engines from Chevrolet or build their own, and all race modifications were the owner's responsibility. Twenty-three 1990 R9G Corvettes were built.
• An air intake speed density control system, camshaft revision, and compression ratio increase added 5hp to base-engines, up from 240hp to 245hp (except coupes with 3.07:1 or 3.33:1 axle ratios which increased from 245hp to 250hp because of their less-restrictive exhaust systems).
• 1990 Corvettes had improved ABS and improved yaw control.
• An engine oil life monitor calculated useful oil life based on engine temperatures and revolutions. An instrument panel display alerted the driver when an oil change was recommended.
• The RPO V01 radiator and B4P boost fan were not optional in 1990, both made unnecessary by 1990's more efficient, sloped-back radiator design.
• Two premium 200-watt Delco-Bose stereo systems were available, the top unit featuring a compact disc player. To discourage theft, the CD required electronic security code input after battery disconnect.
• The instrument panel for 1990 was redesigned as a "hybrid," combining a digital speedometer with analog tachometer and secondary gauges. A supplemental inflatable restraint system (SIR) with airbag was added to the driver side, a glovebox to the passenger side.
• The "ABS Active" light was removed from the driver information center.
• Seat designs were the same for 1990 as the previous year, except the backs would latch in the forward position.
• Chevrolet service departments returned LT5 engines to Mercury Marine for certain repairs. Customers had the choice of a replacement engine, or return of their original engine if repairable.

1990 OPTIONS

RPO #	DESCRIPTION	QTY	RETAIL $
1YY07	Base Corvette Sport Coupe	16,016	$31,979.00
1YY67	Base Corvette Convertible	7,630	37,264.00
AC1	Power Passenger Seat	20,419	270.00
AC3	Power Driver Seat	23,109	270.00
AQ9	Sport Seats, leather	11,457	1,050.00
AR9	Base Seats, leather	11,649	425.00
B2K	Callaway Twin-Turbo (not GM installed)	58	26,895.00
CC2	Auxiliary Hardtop (convertible)	2,371	1,995.00
C2L	Dual Removable Roof Panels (coupe)	6,422	915.00
24S	Removable Roof Panel, blue tint (coupe)	7,852	615.00
64S	Removable Roof Panel, bronze tint (coupe)	4,340	615.00
C68	Electronic Air Conditioning Control	22,497	180.00
FX3	Selective Ride and Handling, electronic	7,576	1,695.00
G92	Performance Axle Ratio	9,362	22.00
K05	Engine Block Heater	1,585	20.00
KC4	Engine Oil Cooler	16,220	110.00
MN6	6-Speed Manual Transmission	8,100	0.00
NN5	California Emission Requirements	4,035	100.00
UJ6	Low Tire Pressure Warning Indicator	8,432	325.00
UU8	Stereo System, Delco-Bose	6,401	823.00
U1F	Stereo System with CD, Delco-Bose	15,716	1,219.00
V56	Luggage Rack (convertible)	1,284	140.00
Z51	Performance Handling Package (coupe)	5,446	460.00
ZR1	Special Performance Package (coupe)	3,049	27,016.00

• A 350ci, 245/250hp engine, 4-speed automatic transmission, removable body-color roof panel (coupe) or soft top (convertible), and cloth seats were included in the base price.
• RPO Z51 included KC4, heavy-duty suspension and brakes. Available with coupe and manual transmission only.
• RPO ZR1 included unique bodywork (doors, rear quarters, rockers, rear facia, and rear upper panel) to accept Goodyear Z-rated P315/35ZR17 tires on 11-inch wide rear rims. RPOs AC1, AC3, AQ9, FX3, LT5 (32-valve engine, exclusive to the ZR-1), U1F, UJ6 and a specially laminated "solar" windshield were included. RPO MN6 manual transmission was required. Available in coupe body style only.
• RPO K05 engine block heater was not available with RPO ZR1.

1990 COLORS

CODE	EXTERIOR	QTY	SOFT TOP	INTERIORS
10	White	4,872	Bk-S-W	B-Bk-G-R-S
25	Steel Blue Metallic	813	Bk-W	B-Bk
41	Black	4,759	Bk-W	B-Bk-G-R
42	Turquoise Metallic	589	Bk-S	Bk-S
53	Competition Yellow	278	Bk-S-W	Bk-G-S
68	Dark Red Metallic	2,353	Bk-S-W	Bk-S
80	Quasar Blue Metallic	474	Bk-S	Bk-S
81	Bright Red	6,956	Bk-S-W	Bk-G-R-S
91	Polo Green Metallic	1,674	Bk-S	Bk-S
96	Charcoal Metallic	878	Bk-S	Bk-G

• Only interior-exterior combinations shown were considered acceptable.
• Restrictions applied to some soft top and interior color combinations.
• Codes 42, 53 and 80 were not available early.
• Code 53 Competition Yellow exterior was discontinued 5-11-90 due to pigment photosensitivity which caused the paint to temporarily darken after sunlight exposure.
• Interior colors sold in 1990 were 10,076 black, 6,467 red, 3,565 saddle, 2,802 gray, 736 blue.

Interior Codes: 19C=Bk/C, 193=Bk/L, 223=B/L, 60C=S/C, 603=S/L, 733=R/L, 903=G/L.

Abbreviations: B=Blue, Bk=Black, C=Cloth, G=Gray, L=Leather, R=Red, S=Saddle, W=White.

1991 CORVETTE

Production: 14,967 coupe, 5,672 convertible, 20,639 total

1991 NUMBERS

Vehicle: 1G1YY2386M5100001 thru 1G1YY2386M5118595
1G1YZ23J6M5800001 thru 1G1YZ23J6M5802044 (ZR-1)
 • For convertibles, sixth digit is a 3.
 • Ninth digit is a check code and varies.

Suffix: ZTA: 350ci, 245/250hp, at   ZTC: 350ci, 245/250hp, at, oc
ZTB: 350ci, 245/250hp, mt, oc   ZTK: 350ci, 375hp

• For Callaway twin-turbo, Chevrolet engine coding was replaced as follows: First two digits for year, next three digits for Callaway sequence, last four digits to match last four digits of vehicle identification number.

Block: 10153558: 350ci, 375hp   14093638: 350ci, 245/250hp

Head: 10088113: 350ci, 245/250hp
10174389: 350ci, 375hp (lh)   10174390: 350ci, 375hp (rh)

Abbreviations: at=automatic transmission, ci=cubic inch, hp=horsepower, lh=left hand, mt=manual transmission, oc=engine oil cooler, rh=right hand.

1991 FACTS

• All 1991 Corvettes had restyled rear exteriors which are similar in appearance to the 1990 ZR-1 because both had convex rear facias with four rectangular tail lamps. Both standard models and ZR-1s also featured new front designs with wraparound parking-cornering-fog lamps, new side panel louvers, and wider body-side moldings in body color.
• Despite similar appearance, the 1991 ZR-1 still received unique doors and rear body panels to accept 11-inch wide rear wheels. The high-mount center stop lamp for 1991 ZR-1s continued to be roof-mounted. For all other than ZR-1, the lamp was integrated into the new rear facia.
• Base wheels were same size as 1990 (17x9.5), but a new design.
• Finned power steering coolers were included with all 1991 models.
• A new option, RPO Z07, essentially combined the previously available Z51 performance handling package with FX3 selective ride/handling. But there were differences. In 1990, if FX3 and Z51 were combined, some base suspension components were used to provide an adjustable suspension range from soft to firm. The new RPO Z07 option used all heavy duty suspension parts so the ride adjusted from firm to very firm. Intended for aggressive driving or competition, Z07 was limited to coupes
• The World Challenge race series continued in 1991, but Bowling Green did not build specific Corvettes for the series. All race modifications were the owners' responsibility.
• Callaway Twin-Turbo conversions ended with the 1991 model year. Callaway built the 500th twin-turbo on 9-26-91 and subsequent builds were specially badged and optioned (extra $600) as "Callaway 500."
• A power wire for cellular phones or other 12-volt devices was added.
• A power delay feature was added to all models which permitted the stereo system and power windows to operate after the ignition was switched to "off" or "lock." Power was cut after the driver door was opened, or after fifteen minutes, whichever occurred first.
• A sensor utilizing an oil pan float was added to all models. The words "low oil" appeared on the driver information center to signal a low oil condition.
• Mufflers were revised for 1991 with larger section sizes and better control tuning of exhaust note. The mufflers had lower back pressure for improved performance, but power ratings were not changed.
• The AM band for radios was expanded to receive more frequencies.
• The ZR-1 "valet" power access system continued, but was revised to default to normal power on each ignition cycle. The full power light was relocated next to the valet key.

1991 OPTIONS

RPO #	DESCRIPTION	QTY	RETAIL $
1YY07	Base Corvette Sport Coupe	14,967	$32,455.00
1YY67	Base Corvette Convertible	5,672	38,770.00
AR9	Base Seats, leather	—	425.00
AQ9	Sport Seats, leather	10,650	1,050.00
AC1	Power Passenger Seat	17,267	290.00
AC3	Power Driver Seat	19,937	290.00
B2K	Callaway Twin-Turbo (not GM installed)	62	33,000.00
CC2	Auxiliary Hardtop (convertible)	1,230	1,995.00
C2L	Dual Removable Roof Panels (coupe)	5,031	915.00
24S	Removable Roof Panel, blue tint (coupe)	6,991	615.00
64S	Removable Roof Panel, bronze tint (coupe)	3,036	615.00
C68	Electronic Air Conditioning Control	19,233	180.00
FX3	Selective Ride and Handling, electronic	6,894	1,695.00
G92	Performance Axle Ratio	—	22.00
KC4	Engine Oil Cooler	7,525	110.00
MN6	6-Speed Manual Transmission	5,875	0.00
NN5	California Emission Requirements	3,050	100.00
UJ6	Low Tire Pressure Warning Indicator	5,175	325.00
UU8	Stereo System, Delco-Bose	3,786	823.00
U1F	Stereo System with CD, Delco-Bose	15,345	1,219.00
V56	Luggage Rack (convertible)	886	140.00
Z07	Adjustable Suspension Package (coupe)	733	2,155.00
ZR1	Special Performance Package (coupe)	2,044	31,683.00

• A 350ci, 245/250hp engine, 4-speed automatic transmission, removable body-color roof panel (coupe) or soft top (convertible), and cloth seats were included in the base price.

• RPO Z07 included KC4, FX3, heavy-duty springs, shocks, stabilizers and bushings, and heavy-duty brakes. Available manual transmission only.

• RPO ZR1 included unique bodywork (doors, rear quarters, rear facia, and rear upper panel) to accept Goodyear Z-rated P315/35ZR17 tires on 11-inch wide rear rims. RPOs AC1, AC3, AQ9, C68, FX3, LT5 (32-valve engine exclusive to the ZR-1), U1F, UJ6, and a specially laminated "solar" windshield were included. RPO MN6 manual transmission was required. Available in coupe body style only.

• The RPO K05 engine block heater was available with base engines and sold for Canada export only.

1991 COLORS

CODE	EXTERIOR	QTY	SOFT TOP	INTERIORS
10	White	4,305	Bk-S-W	B-Bk-G-R-S
25	Steel Blue Metallic	835	B-Bk-W	B-Bk
35	Yellow	650	Bk-S-W	Bk-G-S
41	Black	3909	Bk-S-W	B-Bk-G-S-R
42	Turquoise Metallic	1,621	B-Bk	Bk-S
75	Dark Red Metallic	1,311	Bk-S-W	Bk-S
80	Quasar Blue Metallic	1,038	Bk-S	Bk-S
81	Bright Red	5,318	Bk-S-W	Bk-G-R-S
91	Polo Green Metallic	1,230	Bk-S	Bk-S
96	Charcoal Metallic	417	Bk-W	Bk-G-S

• Only interior-exterior combinations shown were considered acceptable.

• Restrictions applied to some soft top and interior color combinations.

• Dark Red Metallic (also called Brilliant Red) paint code 75 was the same color as 1990's code 68.

• The blue soft top was not available early in production.

• Interior colors sold in 1991 were 10,376 black, 4,481 red, 3,084 saddle, 1,889 gray, 809 blue.

Interior Codes: 19C=Bk/C, 193=Bk/L, 223=B/L, 60C=S/C, 603=S/L, 733=R/L, 903=G/L.

Abbreviations: B=Blue, Bk=Black, C=Cloth, G=Gray, L=Leather, R=Red, S=Saddle, W=White.

1992 CORVETTE

Production: 14,604 coupe, 5,875 convertible, 20,479 total

1992 NUMBERS

Vehicle: 1G1YY23P6N5100001 thru 1G1YY23P6N5119977
1G1YZ23J6N5800001 thru 1G1YZ23J6N5800502 (ZR-1)
• For convertibles, sixth digit is a 3.
• Ninth digit is a check code and varies.

Suffix: ZAA: 350ci, 375hp   ZUB: 350ci, 300hp, mt
ZAC: 350ci, 300hp, at

Block: 10153558: 350ci, 375hp   10125327: 350ci, 300hp

Head: 10128374: 350ci, 300hp
10174389: 350ci, 375hp (lh)   10174390: 350ci, 375hp (rh)

Abbreviations: at=automatic transmission, ci=cubic inch, hp=horsepower, lh=left hand, mt=manual transmission, rh=right hand.

1992 FACTS

• Exterior appearance for 1992 was little changed. For the ZR-1, "ZR-1" emblems were added above the side fender vents. Two rectangular exhaust outlets were used for ZR-1s and for standard models.
• Instrument face plates and buttons were changed to all-black, replacing 1990-1991's gray-black. The digital speedometer was relocated above the fuel gauge. Gauge graphics were refined for better legibility.
• The base engine for 1992 was the LT1, a new generation small block. In 1992 Corvettes, the engine developed 300hp (net) at 5000 rpm. Torque was 330 lb.-ft at 4000 rpm. Redline was 5700 rpm, 700 higher than the L98. There was an automatic fuel cutoff at 5850 rpm. Power increases were attributed to computer-controlled ignition timing, a low-restriction exhaust system employing two catalytic converters and two oxygen sensors (one converter and one oxygen sensor for each cylinder bank), higher compression ratio, new camshaft profile, free-flow cylinder heads, and a new multiport fuel injection (MFI) system. At 452 pounds, the 1992 LT1 outweighed the 1991 L98 base engine by twenty-one pounds, due partly to replacement of stainless steel exhaust manifolds with cast iron.
• Corvette's new LT1 engine employed reverse flow cooling, a Chevrolet first. Rather than route coolant from the pump through the block to the heads, the LT1 routed coolant to the heads first. This permitted higher bore temperatures and reduced ring friction, and helped cooling around the valve seats and spark plug bosses.
• Synthetic oil was recommended for the LT1. An engine oil cooler was no longer available, thought unnecessary when synthetic oil was used.
• Traction control was standard for all 1992 Corvettes. Called Acceleration Slip Regulation (ASR), it was created by Bosch and developed with Corvette engineers. It engaged with the ignition, but could be turned off by an instrument panel switch. ASR used engine spark retard, throttle close down, and brake intervention to limit wheel spin when accelerating. When on and active, a slight accelerator pedal pushback could be felt.
• New Goodyear GS-C tires were introduced as standard equipment on all 1992 Corvettes and were exclusive to Corvettes worldwide for 1992. The GS-C tread design was directional and asymmetrical.
• Improvements in weather sealing were achieved with improved weatherstrip seals. Road noise reduction came from additional insulation in doors and improved insulation over the transmission tunnel.
• The power delay feature was modified so that the passenger door also cut power, in addition to the driver door or fifteen minute time period.
• The 1-millionth Corvette, a 1992 white convertible, was built July 2, 1992.
• The Corvette Americana Hall of Fame and Americana Museum, created by Dr. Allen Schery, opened July 31, 1992, in Cooperstown, New York.

1992 OPTIONS

RPO #	DESCRIPTION	QTY	RETAIL $
1YY07	Base Corvette Sport Coupe	14,604	$33,635.00
1YY67	Base Corvette Convertible	5,875	40,145.00
AR9	Base Seats, leather	10,565	475.00
AR9	Base Seats, white leather	752	555.00
AQ9	Sport Seats, leather	7,973	1,100.00
AQ9	Sport Seats, white leather	709	1,180.00
AC1	Power Passenger Seat	16,179	305.00
AC3	Power Driver Seat	19,378	305.00
CC2	Auxiliary Hardtop (convertible)	915	1,995.00
C2L	Dual Removable Roof Panels (coupe)	3,739	950.00
24S	Removable Roof Panel, blue tint (coupe)	6,424	650.00
64S	Removable Roof Panel, bronze tint (coupe)	3,005	650.00
C68	Electronic Air Conditioning Control	18,460	205.00
FX3	Selective Ride and Handling, electronic	5,840	1,695.00
G92	Performance Axle Ratio	2,283	50.00
MN6	6-Speed Manual Transmission	5,487	0.00
NN5	California Emission Requirements	3,092	100.00
UJ6	Low Tire Pressure Warning Indicator	3,416	325.00
UU8	Stereo System, Delco-Bose	3,241	823.00
U1F	Stereo System with CD, Delco-Bose	15,199	1,219.00
V56	Luggage Rack (for convertible)	845	140.00
Z07	Adjustable Suspension Package (coupe)	738	2,045.00
ZR1	Special Performance Package (coupe)	502	31,683.00

• A 350ci, 300hp engine, 4-speed automatic transmission, removable body-color roof panel (coupe) or soft top (convertible), and black cloth seats were included in the base price.
• RPO Z07 included RPO FX3, heavy-duty suspension and heavy-duty brakes. Available with manual and automatic transmission.
• RPO ZR1 included unique bodywork (doors, rear quarters, rear facia, and rear upper panel) to accept Goodyear Z-rated P315/35ZR17 tires on 11-inch wide rear rims. RPOs AC1, AC3, AQ9, C68, FX3, UJ6, LT5 (32-valve engine exclusive to the ZR-1), U1F, UJ6, and a specially laminated "solar" windshield were included. (Note: During the model year, RPO AC1 was deleted from the ZR1 package and the price reduced by $305.00)
• The RPO K05 engine block heater was available with base engines and sold for Canada export only.

1992 COLORS

CODE	EXTERIOR	QTY	SOFT TOP	INTERIORS
10	White	4,101	B-Bg-Bk-W	Bk-Lb-Lg-R-W
35	Yellow	678	Bg-Bk-W	Bk-Lb-Lg-W
41	Black	3,209	Bg-Bk-W	Bk-Lb-Lg-R-W
43	Bright Aqua Metallic	1,953	Bg-Bk-W	Bk-Lb-Lg-W
45	Polo Green II Metallic	1,995	Bg-Bk-W	Bk-Lb-W
73	Black Rose Metallic	1,886	Bg-Bk-W	Bk-Lb-Lg-W
75	Dark Red Metallic	1,148	Bg-Bk-W	Bk-Lb-Lg-W
80	Quasar Blue Metallic	1,043	Bg-Bk-W	Bk-Lb-Lg-W
81	Bright Red	4,466	Bg-Bk-W	Bk-Lb-Lg-R-W

• Only interior-exterior combinations shown were considered acceptable.
• Restrictions applied to some soft top and interior color combinations.
• White interiors were not available with coupes early in production.
• Base cloth seats were available only in black
• Three colors were new for 1992: Bright Aqua Metallic (43), Polo Green II Metallic (45), and Black Rose Metallic (73).
• Interior colors sold in 1992 were 9,186 black, 3,763 light beige, 3,235 red, 2,834 light gray, 1,461 white.

Interior Codes: 103=W/L, 143=Lg/L, 19C=Bk/C, 193=Bk/L, 643=Lb/L, 733=R/L.

Abbreviations: B=Blue, Bg=Beige, Bk=Black, C=Cloth, L=Leather, Lb=Light Beige, Lg=Light Gray, R=Red, W=White.

1993 CORVETTE

1993 NUMBERS

Vehicle: 1G1YY23PXP5100001 thru 1G1YY23PXP5121142
1G1YZ23J3P5800001 thru 1G1YZ23J3P5800448 (ZR1)
• For convertibles, sixth digit is a 3.
• Ninth digit is a check code and varies.

Suffix: ZVA: 350ci, 300hp, at   ZVC: 350ci, 405hp
ZVB: 350ci, 300hp, mt

Block: 10125327: 350ci, 300hp   10199001: 350ci, 405hp

Head: 10174389: 350ci, 405hp, lh   10174390: 350ci, 405hp, rh
10205245: 350ci, 300hp

Abbreviations: at=automatic transmission, ci=cubic inch, hp=horsepower, lh=left hand, mt=manual transmission, pl=possible late use, rh=right hand.

1993 FACTS

• Exterior appearance continued virtually unchanged for 1993, but a 40th Anniversary Package (RPO Z25) was optional with all models. The package included a Ruby Red metallic exterior, Ruby Red leather sport seats, power driver seat, special wheel center trim and emblems.

• All leather seats in 1993 Corvettes had "40th" anniversary embroidery in the headrest area. The base black cloth seats did not.

• Horsepower for the base LT1 engine remained 300, but three changes made the engine quieter. First, the heat shield design changed from a single-piece stamping to a two-piece sandwich type that was self-damping. Second, new thermoset polyester valve covers with "isolated" mounts replaced 1992's magnesium covers. Third, the LT1 camshaft exhaust lobe profile was modified to reduce the exhaust valve closing velocity. Also, a shortening of the inlet duration permitted more duration for the exhaust so there was no increase in overlap area. Emissions and idle quality weren't adversly affected. A side benefit of closing the inlet valve sooner was an increase in torque from 330 to 340 lb.-ft at 3600 rpm.

• Horsepower increased for the optional ZR1's LT5 engine from 375 to 405hp, a result of modifications to the cylinder heads and valvetrain. Other changes included four-bolt main bearings, a Mobil 1 synthetic oil requirement, platinum-tipped spark plugs, and an electrical, linear exhaust gas recirculation (EGR) system for improved emission control.

• The 1993 Corvette was the first auto sold by GM to feature a passive keyless entry (PKE) system. Working by proximity, a battery-operated key-fob transmitter sent a unique code picked up by a receiver in the Corvette through one of two antennas (in coupes, antennas were in the driver door and rear deck; in convertibles, antennas were in both doors). The transmitter required no specific action by the owner; approaching the vehicle with the transmitter would unlock the doors, turn on the interior light, and disarm the theft-deterrent. Leaving an unlocked vehicle with the transmitter would lock the doors and arm the theft-deterrent. The PKE could be turned off completely and transmitters were programmable for locking and unlocking just the driver door, or both driver and passenger doors. Transmitters for convertibles had a single button for programming and driver/passenger door unlocking; transmitters for coupes had an extra button for rear hatch release.

• Front wheels for base cars were decreased from 9.5x17 to 8.5x17 and the front tire size from P275/40ZR17 to P255/45ZR17. Rear tire size was increased from P275/40ZR17 to P285/40ZR17. For RPO Z07, 9.5x17 wheels and P275/40ZR17 tires were used front and rear.

• Although the same in design as the previous model, 1993's wheels had a different surface appearance due to a change in finish machining.

1993 OPTIONS

RPO#	DESCRIPTION	QTY	RETAIL $
1YY07	Base Corvette Sport Coupe	15,898	$34,595.00
1YY67	Base Corvette Convertible	5,692	41,195.00
AR9	Base Seats, leather	8,935	475.00
AR9	Base Seats, white leather	766	555.00
AQ9	Sport Seats, leather	11,267	1,100.00
AQ9	Sport Seats, white leather	622	1,180.00
AC1	Power Passenger Seat	18,067	305.00
AC3	Power Driver Seat	20,626	305.00
CC2	Auxiliary Hardtop (convertible)	976	1,995.00
C2L	Dual Removable Roof Panels (coupe)	4,204	950.00
24S	Removable Roof Panel, blue tint (coupe)	6,203	650.00
64S	Removable Roof Panel, bronze tint (coupe)	4,288	650.00
C68	Electronic Air Conditioning Control	19,550	205.00
FX3	Selective Ride and Handling, electronic	5,740	1,695.00
G92	Performance Axle Ratio	2,630	50.00
MN6	6-Speed Manual Transmission	5,330	0.00
NN5	California Emission Requirements	2,401	100.00
UJ6	Low Tire Pressure Warning Indicator	3,353	325.00
UU8	Stereo System, Delco-Bose	2,685	823.00
U1F	Stereo System with CD, Delco-Bose	16,794	1,219.00
V56	Luggage Rack (for convertible)	765	140.00
Z07	Adjustable Suspension Package (coupe)	824	2,045.00
Z25	40th Anniversary Package	6,749	1,455.00
ZR1	Special Performance Package (coupe)	448	31,683.00

• A 350ci, 300hp engine, 4-speed automatic transmission, removable body color roof panel (coupe) or soft top (convertible), and black cloth seats were included in the base price.
• RPO Z07 included RPO FX3, heavy-duty suspension and heavy-duty brakes. Available with manual or automatic transmission.
• RPO ZR1 included unique bodywork (doors, rear quarters, rear facia, and rear upper panel) to accept Goodyear Z-rated P315/35ZR17 tires on 11-inch wide rear rims. RPOs AC1, AC3, AQ9, C68, FX3, LT5 (32-valve engine exclusive to the ZR-1), U1F, UJ6, and a specially laminated "solar" windshield were included. Available with coupes only.
• The RPO K05 engine block heater was available with base engines and sold for Canada export only.
• The RPO Z25 40th Anniversary Package included Ruby Red exterior and interior, and special trim. It was available with coupe, convertibles, and with RPO ZR1(220 sold).

1993 COLORS

CODE	EXTERIOR	QTY	SOFT TOP	INTERIORS
10	Arctic White	3,031	Bg-Bk-W	Bk-Lb-Lg-R-W
41	Black	2,684	Bg-Bk-W	Bk-Lb-Lg-R-W
43	Bright Aqua Metallic	1,305	Bg-Bk-W	Bk-Lb-Lg-W
45	Polo Green II Metallic	2,189	Bg-Bk-W	Bk-Lb-W
53	Competition Yellow	517	Bg-Bk-W	Bk-Lb-Lg-W
68	Ruby Red	6,749	Rr	Rr
70	Torch Red	3,172	Bg-Bk-W	Bk-Lb-Lg-R-W
73	Black Rose Metallic	935	Bg-Bk-W	Bk-Lb-Lg-W
75	Dark Red Metallic	325	Bg-Bk-W	Bk-Lb-Lg-W
80	Quasar Blue Metallic	683	Bg-Bk-W	Bk-Lb-Lg-W

• Only interior-exterior combinations shown were considered acceptable.
• Restrictions applied to some soft top and interior color combinations.
• Ruby Red exterior/interior colors were exclusive to the 40th Anniversary Package. Convertibles included a Ruby Red soft top. Other new colors for 1993 were Competition Yellow (53) and Torch Red (70).

Interior Codes: 103=W/L, 143=Lg/L, 19C=Bk/C, 193=Bk/L, 643=Lb/L, 703=R/L, 793=Rr/L.

Abbreviations: Bg=Beige, Bk=Black, C=Cloth, L=Leather, Lb=Light Beige, Lg=Light Gray, R=Red, Rr=Ruby Red, W=White.

1994 CORVETTE
Production: 17,984 coupe, 5,346 convertible, 23,330 total

1994 NUMBERS

Vehicle: 1G1YY22P9R5100001 thru 1G1YY22P9R5122882
1G1YZ22J9R5800001 thru 1G1YZ22J9R5800448 (ZR1)
• For convertibles, sixth digit is a 3.
• Ninth digit is a check code and varies

Suffix: ZWA: 350ci, 300hp, at   ZWC: 350ci, 405hp, mt
ZWB: 350ci, 300hp, mt

Block: 10125327: 350ci, 300hp   10199001: 350ci, 405hp

Head: 10174389: 350ci, 405hp, lh, ep   10207643: 350ci, 300hp
10174390: 350ci, 405hp, rh   10225121: 350ci, 405hp, lh

Abbreviations: at=automatic transmission, ci=cubic inch, ep=early production, hp=horsepower, lh=left hand, mt=manual transmission, rh=right hand.

1994 FACTS

• After years of planning under the direction of National Corvette Museum Foundation president Dan Gale, the National Corvette Museum opened to the public on September 2, 1994, in Bowling Green, Kentucky.
• The exterior design for 1994 was carried over from 1993, but two new exterior colors were available, Admiral Blue and Copper Metallic. Also, new non-directional wheels were included with ZR-1 models.
• Power output of the base LT1 engine remained 300hp, but several refinements were added. A new sequential fuel injection system improved response, idle quality, driveability and emissions by firing injectors in sequence with the engine's firing order. A more powerful ignition system reduced engine start times, especially in cold temperatures.
• The standard 4-speed automatic transmission was redesigned with electronic controls for improved shift quality and rpm shift-point consistency. Also, a safety interlock was added which required depression of the brake pedal in order to shift from "park."
• A passenger-side airbag and knee bolster, new seat and door trim panel designs, "express down" driver's power window, and a redesigned two-spoke airbag steering wheel were new inside. New white instrument graphics turned to tangerine at night. The tire jack was relocated from the exterior spare tire well to a compartment behind the passenger seat.
• For 1994, all seats were leather. Base and optional "sport" styles were available. Both featured less restrictive bolsters to accommodate a wider range of occupant sizes and for improved entry and exit. Controls for base seats with optional power assist were console-mounted with individual controls for driver and passenger. With sport seats, a single set of power assist controls for both seats was console-mounted. Also, individual motors adjusted the lumbar support for sport seats and these controls (and the side bolster control) were relocated from the seat to the console for 1994. Reclining mechanisms for all 1994 seats were manual.
• The rear window for convertibles was changed from plastic to glass and included an in-glass defogger.
• RPO FX3 spring rates were lowered to improve ride quality; recommended tire pressures were reduced from 35psi to 30psi (except ZR1).
• Air conditioning systems were revised to use R-134A refrigerant, a non-ozone depleting CFC substitute.
• Optional Goodyear Extended Mobility Tires (RPO WY5) had special bead construction to permit use with no air pressure. The low tire pressure warning system (RPO UJ6) was required because if the tire was run deflated more than about fifty miles, damage could result. However, the safe driving range was substantially further.

1994 OPTIONS

RPO#	DESCRIPTION	QTY	RETAIL $
1YY07	Base Corvette Sport Coupe	17,984	$36,185.00
1YY67	Base Corvette Convertible	5,346	42,960.00
AQ9	Sport Seats	9,023	625.00
AC1	Power Passenger Seat	17,863	305.00
AC3	Power Driver Seat	21,592	305.00
CC2	Auxiliary Hardtop (convertible)	682	1,995.00
C2L	Dual Removable Roof Panels (coupe)	3,875	950.00
24S	Removable Roof Panel, blue tint (coupe)	7,064	650.00
64S	Removable Roof Panel, bronze tint (coupe)	3,979	650.00
FX3	Selective Ride and Handling, electronic	4,570	1,695.00
G92	Performance Axle Ratio	9,019	50.00
MN6	6-Speed Manual Transmission	6,012	0.00
NG1	New York Emission Requirements	1,363	100.00
UJ6	Low Tire Pressure Warning Indicator	5,097	325.00
U1F	Stereo System with CD, Delco-Bose	17,579	396.00
WY5	Tires, Extended Mobility	2,781	70.00
YF5	California Emission Requirements	2,372	100.00
Z07	Adjustable Suspension Package (coupe)	887	2,045.00
ZR1	Special Performance Package (coupe)	448	31,258.00

• A 350ci, 300hp engine, 4-speed automatic transmission, removable body-color roof panel (coupe) or soft top (convertible), Delco stereo system with cassette, and leather seats were included in the base price.
• Preferred Equipment Group One included electronic air conditioning control, Delco-Bose stereo system with cassette, and power driver seat (RPO AC3) for $1,333.00.
• RPO G92 was available without restriction.
• RPO WY5 required RPO UJ6; not available with RPOs Z07 or ZR1.
• RPO Z07 included RPO FX3, heavy-duty suspension and heavy-duty brakes. Available with manual or automatic transmission.
• RPO ZR1 included unique bodywork (doors, rear quarters, rear facia, and rear upper panel) to accept Goodyear Z-rated P315/35ZR17 tires on 11-inch wide rear wheels (front and rear wheel design for 1994 was new and unique to the ZR-1). Electronic air conditioning control and RPOs AC1, AC3, AQ9, C68, FX3, LT5 (32-valve engine exclusive to the ZR-1), U1F, UJ6, and a specially laminated "solar" windshield were included. Available with coupes only; availability limited.
• The RPO K05 engine block heater was available with base engines and sold for Canada export only.

1994 COLORS

CODE	EXTERIOR	QTY	SOFT TOP	INTERIORS
10	Arctic White	4,066	Bg-Bk-W	Bk-Lb-Lg-R
28	Admiral Blue	1,584	Bg-Bk-W	Bk-Lb-Lg
41	Black	4,136	Bg-Bk-W	Bk-Lb-Lg-R
43	Bright Aqua Metallic	1,209	Bg-Bk-W	Bk-Lb-Lg
45	Polo Green Metallic	3,534	Bg-Bk	Bk-Lb
53	Competition Yellow	834	Bg-Bk-W	Bk-Lb-Lg
66	Copper Metallic	116	Bg-Bk-W	Bk-Lb-Lg
70	Torch Red	5,073	Bg-Bk-W	Bk-Lb-Lg-R
73	Black Rose Metallic	1,267	Bg-Bk-W	Bk-Lb-Lg
75	Dark Red Metallic	1,511	Bg-Bk-W	Bk-Lb-Lg

• Exterior, interior and soft top combinations were recommended as most desirable, but other combinations could be ordered.
• Admiral Blue (28) and Copper Metallic (66) were new colors for 1994. All others carried over from 1993. Copper Metallic availability was limited.
• All interiors were leather and all interior colors were available in both base and sport seats.

Interior Codes: 143=Lg/L, 193=Bk/L, 643=Lb/L, 703=R/L.
Abbreviations: Bg=Beige, Bk=Black, Lb=Light Beige, Lg=Light Grey, R=Red, W=White.

1995 CORVETTE

Production: 15,771 coupe, 4,971 convertible, 20,742 total

1995 NUMBERS

Vehicle: 1G1YY22P7S5100001 thru 1G1YY22P7S5120294
1G1YZ22J0S5800001 thru 1G1YZ22J0S5800448 (ZR1)
• For convertibles, sixth digit is a 3.
• Ninth digit is a check digit and varies.

Suffix: ZUC: 350ci, 300hp, at   ZUF: 350ci, 300hp, mt
ZUD: 350ci, 405hp, mt

Block: 10125327: 350ci, 300hp   10199001: 350ci, 405hp

Head: 10174390: 350ci, 405hp,rh, ep   10225121: 350ci, 405hp, lh
10207643: 350ci, 300hp   10225122: 350ci, 405hp, rh

Abbreviations: at=automatic transmission, ci=cubic inch, ep=early production, hp=horsepower, lh=left hand, mt=manual transmission, rh=right hand.

1995 FACTS

• The 1995 exterior was distinguished from 1994 by restyling of the front fender "gill" air vents. A new exterior color, Dark Purple Metallic, was added, but 1994's Copper Metallic and Black Rose Metallic were deleted.
• Corvette paced the Indianapolis 500 race in 1995. A replica, Dark Purple and White (convertible only) with special accents, sold 527 units.
• Optional Sport Seats had stronger "French" seam stitching. A readout for automatic transmission fluid temperature was added to the instrument display. Out of sight were numerous Velcro straps to reduce rattles, and a stronger radio mount for less CD skipping. A drip tube was designed into the A-pillar weatherstrip for improved water intrusion control.
• The base LT1 engine continued with the same 300hp and 340 lb-ft torque ratings, but there were refinements. Late in 1994 production, connecting rods were changed to a powdered-metal design to improve both strength and weight uniformity. Fuel injectors were revised to better cope with alcohol-blend fuels and to reduce fuel dripping after engine shutdown. The engine cooling fan was modified for quieter operation.
• This was the ZR-1's last year. Mercury Marine in Stillwater, Oklahoma, completed all LT5 engines in November 1993. Tooling, owned by GM, was removed from Mercury Marine's factory and all engines, specially sealed, were shipped to Corvette's Bowling Green assembly plant for storage until needed. Before September 1, 1993, all internal engine warranty repair was done by Mercury Marine. Between September 1, 1993 and December 31, 1993, internal repairs were done by Mercury Marine if engines had under 12,000 miles or 12 months service. Chevrolet handled service not performed by Mercury Marine, including all after January 1, 1994. Total 1995 ZR-1 production was predetermined at 448 units, the same as 1993 and 1994. Total ZR-1 production for 1990 through 1995 was 6,939.
• Clutch controls in the four-speed automatic transmission were improved for smoother shifting, and its torque converter was both lighter and stronger. The 6-speed manual was redesigned by replacement of the reverse lockout with a high-detent design for easier operation.
• The larger brake package, included previously with Z07 and ZR-1 performance options, was included for 1995 with all models. And all 1995's had the latest anti-lock/traction control (ABS/ASR-5) system.
• The extended mobility "run flat" tires introduced as a 1994 option minimized the need for a spare tire. So 1995's RPO N84 created a delete spare option which reduced weight and included a credit of $100.00.
• Base suspension models had lower front and rear spring rates.
• Windshield wiper arms were redesigned with revised contact angles and higher contact force to reduce chatter at all speeds, and lift at high speeds.

1995 OPTIONS

RPO#	DESCRIPTION	QTY	RETAIL $
1YY07	Base Corvette Sport Coupe	15,771	$36,785.00
1YY67	Base Corvette Convertible	4,971	43,665.00
AG1	Power Driver Seat	19,012	305.00
AG2	Power Passenger Seat	15,323	305.00
AQ9	Sport Seats	7,908	625.00
CC2	Auxiliary Hardtop (convertible)	459	1,995.00
C2L	Dual Removable Roof Panels (coupe)	2,979	950.00
24S	Removable Roof Panel, blue tint (coupe)	4,688	650.00
64S	Removable Roof Panel, bronze tint (coupe)	2,871	650.00
FX3	Selective Ride and Handling, electronic	3,421	1,695.00
G92	Performance Axle Ratio	10,056	50.00
MN6	6-Speed Manual Transmission	4,784	0.00
NG1	New York Emission Requirements	268	100.00
N84	Spare Tire Delete	418	100.00
UJ6	Low Tire Pressure Warning Indicator	5,300	325.00
U1F	Stereo System with CD, Delco-Bose	15,528	396.00
WY5	Tires, Extended Mobility	3,783	70.00
YF5	California Emission Requirements	2,026	100.00
Z07	Adjustable Suspension Package (coupe)	753	2,045.00
Z4Z	Indy 500 Pace Car Replica	527	2,816.00
ZR1	Special Performance Package (coupe)	448	31,258.00

• A 350cI, 300hp engine, 4-speed automatic transmission, removable body-color roof panel (coupe) or soft top (convertible), Delco stereo system with cassette, and leather seats were included in the base price.
• Preferred Equipment Group One included electronic air conditioning control, Delco-Bose stereo system with cassette, and power driver seat (RPO AG1) for $1,333.00.
• RPO WY5 required RPO UJ6; not available with RPOs Z07 or ZR1.
• RPO Z07 included RPO FX3, special springs, stabilizers and bushings, 17x19 1/2" wheels and P275/40ZR17/N black-letter tires. Required AG1 and AG2. Available with manual or automatic transmission, but required G92 with automatic transmission..
• RPO Z4Z (convertible only) included special Dark Purple and Arctic White paint, white convertible top, special graphics and trim.
• RPO ZR1 included unique bodywork (doors, rear quarters, rear facia, and rear upper panel) to accept Goodyear Z-rated P315/35ZR17 tires on special-design 11-inch wide rear wheels. Electronic air conditioning control and RPOs AG1, AG2, AQ9, C68, FX3, LT5 (32-valve engine exclusive to the ZR-1), U1F, UJ6, and a specially laminated "solar" windshield were included. Available with coupes only.

1995 COLORS

CODE	EXTERIOR	QTY	SOFT TOP	INTERIORS
05	Dark Purple Metallic	1,049	Bg-Bk-W	Bk-Lb-Lg
05/10	Dark Purple/White	527	W	BkPc
10	Arctic White	3,381	Bg-Bk-W	Bk-Lb-Lg-R
28	Admiral Blue	1,006	Bg-Bk-W	Bk-Lb-Lg
41	Black	3,959	Bg-Bk-W	Bk-Lb-Lg-R
43	Bright Aqua Metallic	909	Bg-Bk-W	Bk-Lb-Lg
45	Polo Green Metallic	2,940	Bg-Bk	Bk-Lb
53	Competition Yellow	1,003	Bg-Bk-W	Bk-Lb-Lg
70	Torch Red	4,531	Bg-Bk-W	Bk-Lb-Lg-R
75	Dark Red Metallic	1,437	Bg-Bk-W	Bk Lb-Lg

• Exterior, interior and soft top combinations were recommended as most desirable, but other combinations could be ordered.
• All interiors were leather and all interior colors were available in both base and sport seats.

Interior Codes: 143=Lg, 193=Bk, 194=Bk-Pc, 643=Lb, 703=R.
Abbreviations: Bg=Beige, Bk=Black, Lb=Light Beige, Lg=Light Grey, Pc=Pace Car Replica, R=Red, W=White.

1996 CORVETTE

Production: 17,167 coupe, 4,369 convertible, 21,536 total

1996 NUMBERS

Vehicle: 1G1YY2257T5100001 thru 1G1YY2251T5120536
1G1YY2251T5600001 thru 1G1YY2251T5601000 (Grand Sport)
- For convertibles, sixth digit is a 3.
- Eighth digit is a P for LT1, 5 for LT4.
- Ninth digit is a check digit and varies.

Suffix: ZXA: 350ci, 300hp, at (LT1)   ZXD: 350ci, 330hp, mt (LT4)

Block: 10125327: all

Head: 10207643: 350ci, 300hp, at   12551561: 350ci, 300hp, at, lp
10239902: 350ci, 330hp, mt, ep   12555690: 350ci, 330hp, mt

Abbreviations: at=automatic transmission, ci=cubic inch, ep=early production, hp=horsepower, lp=late production, mt=manual transmission.

1996 FACTS

• A new version of Chevy's 350-cubic-inch small block, RPO LT4, became optional exclusively with 1996 Corvettes. Rated at 330-horsepower, 30 more than the base LT1, the LT4 had higher compression (10.8:1 vs 10.4:1), new aluminum head design, Crane roller rocker arms, revised camshaft profile, and other major and minor tweaks. The LT4's redline increased to 6300 rpm (5700 rpm for LT1), so LT4-equipped models had 8000 rpm tachometers instead of the base 6000 rpm. LT4 was available with all Corvette models, but only with manual transmissions.

• LT1 engines were mated only to automatic transmissions which had improved friction materials for the intermediate clutch and front/rear bands, improved shift quality and more durable torque converters.

• "Grand Sport" (RPO Z16) included the LT4 engine, distinctive Admiral Blue paint with white center stripe, and special detailing. The previous year's ZR-1-style five-spoke 17" wheels were used, but painted black. Like the ZR-1, tires for Grand Sport coupes were P275/40ZR17 front and P315/35ZR17 rear. But Grand Sport coupes had rear fender flares rather than the ZR-1's wider rear panels. Convertible Grand Sport tires were P255/45ZR17 front, P285/40ZR17 rear, with no fender flares. Interior choices were limited to black, or a red-black combination. Corvettes with the Grand Sport option had separate serial number sequences.

• LT1 and LT4 engines had a new throttle body for 1996. Those for LT4 engines had red "Grand Sport" lettering, regardless of the application.

• "Collector Edition" (RPO Z15) included Sebring Silver paint and special trim. ZR-1-style 17" five-spoke wheels were used, but painted silver with P255/45ZR17 front and P285/40ZR17 rear tires. Black, red or gray interiors were available, but soft top color choice was limited to black.

• RPO F45, Selective Real Time Damping, was priced the same ($1,695) as 1995's FX3 Selective Ride option, but was substantially different. Using data from wheel travel sensors and the Powertrain Control Module, a controller calculated the damping mode that would provide optimum control via special shock absorbers. It could alter each shock individually (unlike the earlier system which changed all shocks simultaneously) every 10 to 15 milliseconds, or about every foot of roadway travelling at 60 mph.

• Performance Handling Package (RPO Z51) previously optional from 1984 thru 1990, returned in 1996 with different content but similar intent. It included Bilstein shock absorbers with stiffer springs and thicker stabilizer bars. If ordered with an automatic transmission, a 3.07:1 axle was required. Tires were P275/40ZR17 on 17x9.5" aluminum wheels, except for Z51 Grand Sports which had P315/35ZR17 rear tires on 17x11" wheels. Z51 was limited to coupes.

• 1996's On-Board-Diagnostics were much more sophisticated and complex, the number of diagnostic codes increasing from 60 to 140.

1996 OPTIONS

RPO#	DESCRIPTION	QTY	RETAIL $
1YY07	Base Corvette Sport Coupe	17,167	37,225.00
1YY67	Base Corvette Convertible	4,369	45,060.00
AG1	Power Driver Seat	19,798	305.00
AG2	Power Passenger Seat	17,060	305.00
AQ9	Sport Seats	12,016	625.00
CC2	Auxiliary Hardtop (convertible)	429	1,995.00
C2L	Dual Removable Roof Panels (coupe)	3,983	950.00
24S	Removable Roof Panel, blue tint (coupe)	6,626	650.00
64S	Removable Roof Panel, bronze tint (coupe)	2,492	650.00
F45	Selective Real Time Damping, electronic	2,896	1,695.00
G92	Performance Axle Ratio	9,801	50.00
LT4	350 cubic-inch, 330 horsepower Engine	6,359	1,450.00
MN6	6-Speed Manual Transmission	6,359	0.00
N84	Spare Tire Delete	986	-100.00
UJ6	Low Tire Pressure Warning Indicator	6,865	325.00
U1F	Compact Disc Delco-Bose (reqs PEG 1)	17,037	396.00
WY5	Tires, Extended Mobility	4,945	70.00
Z15	Collectors Edition	5,412	1,250.00
Z16	Grand Sport Package ($2,880 w/convertible)	1,000	3,250.00
Z51	Performance Handling Package	1,869	350.00

• A 350ci, 300hp engine, 4-speed automatic transmission, removable body color roof panel (coupe) or soft top (convertible), Delco stereo system with cassette, and leather seats were included in base prices.
• RPO LT4 included (and was available only with) RPO MN6
• Preferred Equipment Group (PEG) 1 included electronic air conditioning control, Delco-Bose stereo with cassette, and RPO AG1 for $1,333.00.
• RPO F45 required RPOs AG1 and AG2.
• RPO WY5 required RPO UJ6; not avail with RPO Z16 coupe or Z51.
• RPO Z15 included 17" 5-spoke wheels painted silver, black brake calipers with silver "Corvette" lettering, Sebring Silver exterior paint, special emblems, P255/45ZR17 front tires, P285/40ZR17 rear tires, and perforated sports seats with "Collector Edition" embroidery.
• RPO Z16 included Admiral Blue paint with white stripe, red left-fender hash marks, 17" 5-spoke aluminum wheels painted black, black brake calipers with silver "Corvette" lettering, P275/40ZR/17 front and P315/35ZR/17 rear tires (coupe), rear wheel flares (coupe), black floor mats, and perforated sport seats with "Grand Sport" embroidery.
• RPO Z51 had Bilstein shocks, special front and rear springs, stabilizers and bushings, 17x9.5"wheels with P275/40 ZR 17 tires. (Z16 with Z51 had 17x11" rear wheels with P315/35ZR17 tires). Z51 required AG1 and AG2. Available with manual or automatic, but automatic required G92.

1996 COLORS

CODE	EXTERIOR	QTY	SOFT TOP	INTERIORS
05	Dark Purple Metallic	320	Bg-Bk-W	Bk-Lb-Lg
10	Arctic White	3,210	Bg-Bk-W	Bk-Lb-Lg-R
13	Sebring Silver Metallic	5,412	Bk	Bk-Lg-R
28	Admiral Blue	1,000	W	Bk-R/Bk
41	Black	3,917	Bg-Bk-W	Bk-Lb-Lg-R
43	Bright Aqua Metallic	357	Bg-Bk-W	Bk-Lb-Lg
45	Polo Green Metallic	2,414	Bg-Bk	Bk-Lb
53	Competition Yellow	488	Bg-Bk-W	Bk-Lb-Lg
70	Torch Red	4,418	Bg-Bk-W	Bk-Lb-Lg-R

•Other combinations could be ordered, except for codes 13 and 28 which could not deviate from combinations shown.
•All seating was leather and all interior colors were available in base and sport seats except for codes 13 and 28 which were sport seat only.

Interior Codes: 143=Lg, 144=Lg-Ce, 193=Bk, 194=Bk-Ce, 195=Bk-Gs, 643=Lb, 703=R, 704=R-Ce, 705=R/Bk-Gs.

Abbreviations: Bg=Beige, Bk=Black, Ce=Collectors Edition, Gs=Grand Sport, Lb=Light Beige, Lg=Light Gray, R=Red, R/Bk=Red and Black, W=White.

1997 CORVETTE

1997 NUMBERS

Vehicle: 1G1YY22G1V5100001 thru 1G1YY22G1V51-----
  • Eighth digit is engine code: G=350ci, 345hp (LS1)
  • Ninth digit is a check digit and varies.

Suffix: ZYC: 350ci, 345hp, mt   ZYD: 350ci, 345hp, at

Block: 12550592: 350ci, 345hp

Head: 10215339: 350ci, 345hp

Abbreviations: at=automatic transmission, ci=cubic inch, hp=horsepower, mt=manual transmission.

1997 FACTS

• The 1997 was the most thoroughly "all-new" model in Corvette history. Unlike past new-generation models which had carryover engines and drivelines, this Corvette had a completely new engine driving a rear transaxle, a Corvette first. Virtually all interior, exterior and suspension components were redesigned for this vehicle.

• The rear transaxle combined a GM-built, electronically-controlled four-speed automatic transmission, or a Borg-Warner six-speed manual with Computer-Aided Gear Selection (CAGS) with a limited-slip axle built by Getrag. Along with near-equal front-to-rear weight distribution (51.4/48.6 with automatic), relocating the transmission to the rear greatly improved the interior environment by enlarging the footwells.

• The 1997 was larger in most measures. Wheelbase increased from 96.2" to 104.5", length from 178.5" to 179.6", width from 70.7" to 73.6", height from 46.3" to 47.8," track by 4.4" in front and 2.9" at the rear. The net effect was to push the wheels more to the corners for increased stability and interior space. Weight was reduced overall by about eighty pounds.

• Somewhat reminiscent of the 1963-1967 series, the 1997 Corvette's interior featured large analog speedometer and tachometer gauges flanked by secondary instruments, with "black" lighting. Seats, by Lear Corporation, were a new design and available in standard base or optional sport. The handbrake was relocated from left of the driver to the center console. Stepover height was reduced by over three inches.

• Build of the LS1 engine was assigned to GM's engine plant in Romulus, Michigan. Most previous Corvette small-block V8's were built in Flint.

• LS1 had the same 4.4" bore spacing and 350ci displacement as the engine family it replaced, but otherwise was new and state-of-the-art in pushrod V8 design. The block was closed-deck aluminum alloy with cast-in cylinder liners. Rather than end at the centerline of the crankshaft, the LS1's block had a deep skirt that extended past the main bearing caps. The four-bolt mains were also cross-bolted to the block for rigidity. The low skirts dictated a flat, shallow cast-aluminum oil pan with special side reservoirs. The pan acted as an engine structural member. Output was 345hp at 5600 rpm, torque 350 lb-ft. at 4400 rpm and redline at 6000 rpm. Premium fuel was recommended and LS1's came filled with 5x30 Mobil 1 synthetic oil. An assembled LS1 was 44 lbs lighter than 1996's LT4.

• LS1's composite intake manifold saved weight and improved air flow. Aluminum valve covers had separate ignition coils mounted close to each spark plug. Spark timing signals were sent by crankshaft and camshaft sensors. Dual knock sensors were mounted under the intake manifold. Firing order was revised from 1-8-4-3-6-5-7-2 to 1-8-7-2-6-5-4-3.

• Engine heads were cast alloy with identical ports. Four bolts held the head to the block. Valves, roller rocker arms, and pushrods were positioned in one plane. The camshaft was hollow for reduced mass. The exhaust manifold was two-layer stainless steel with an air-space insulator to quickly warm the catalytic converter for reduced start-up emissions..

1997 FACTS *cont...*

• Wheel size was 17x8.5" front, 18x9.5" rear. Tire size was P245/45ZR17 front, P275/40ZR18 rear. Suspension consisted of short-long arm (SLA) design at each corner, also known as double wishbone or double A-arm. Springs were composite front and rear, transversely mounted.

1997 OPTIONS

RPO#	DESCRIPTION	RETAIL $
1YY07	Base Corvette Sport Coupe	$37,495.00
AAB	Memory Package	150.00
AG2	Power Passenger Seat	305.00
AQ9	Sport Seats	625.00
B34	Floor Mats	25.00
B84	Body Side Moldings	75.00
CC3	Removable Roof Panel, blue tint (coupe)	650.00
C2L	Dual Removable Roof Panels	950.00
CJ2	Dual Zone Air Conditioning	365.00
D42	Luggage Shade and Parcel Net	50.00
F45	Selective Real Time Damping, electronic	1,695.00
G92	Performance Axle Ratio	100.00
MN6	6-Speed Manual Transmission	815.00
NG1	Massachusetts/New York Emissions	170.00
T96	Fog Lamps	69.00
UN0	Delco Stereo System with CD	100.00
U1S	Remote Compact 12 Disc Changer	600.00
V49	Front License Plate Frame	15.00
YF5	California Emissions	170.00
Z51	Performance Handling Package	350.00

• A 350ci, 345hp engine (LS1), 4-speed automatic transmission, removable body-color roof panel, Delco stereo system with cassette, and leather seats were all standard features.
• RPO AAB (Memory Package) remembered outside-rear-view-mirror, radio, heater-vent-air conditioning control, and power driver seat settings. RPO CJ2 was required.
• RPO AQ9 (Sport Seats) required RPO AG2 (Power Passenger Seat).
• RPO C2L (Dual Removable Roof Panels) included standard body-color roof panel plus blue-tint transparent panel.
• RPO F45 (Selective Real Time Damping) included driver-adjustable ride control system. Not available with RPO Z51.
• RPO G92 (Performance Axle Ratio) provided 3.15:1 ratio with automatic transmission (2.73:1 standard with automatic transmission; 3.42:1 standard with manual transmission).
• RPO U1S (Remote CD Changer) could be ordered with standard Delco cassette stereo system or with RPO UN0 (Delco Stereo System with CD).
• RPO Z51 (Performance Handling Package) included stiffer springs and stabilizer bars. Required RPO G92 with automatic transmission; not available with RPO F45.

1997 COLORS

CODE	EXTERIOR	WHEELS	INTERIORS
10	Arctic White	Alloy	B-Lg-R
13	Sebring Silver Metallic	Alloy	B-Lg-R
23	Nassau Blue Metallic	Alloy	B-Lg-R
41	Black	Alloy	B-Lg-R
53	Light Carmine Red Metallic	Alloy	B-Lg
70	Torch Red	Alloy	B-Lg-R
87	Fairway Green Metallic	Alloy	B-Lg-R

• Exterior-interior combinations were recommended as most desirable, but any combination could be ordered.
• Codes 10, 13, 41 and 70 were the only colors available early in production.
• Seating was leather; all interior colors available in base and Sport Seats.

Interior Codes: 193=B, 923=Lg, 943=R.
Abbreviations: B-Black, Lg=Light Gray, R=Firethorn Red.

NOTES

Owner Name _____

Address/Phone _____

_____

Corvette Description _____

_____

_____

_____

_____

Owner Name _____

Address/Phone _____

_____

Corvette Description _____

_____

_____

_____

_____

_____

Owner Name _____

Address/Phone _____

_____

Corvette Description _____

_____

_____

_____

_____

_____

NOTES

Owner Name _____

Address/Phone _____

_____

Corvette Description _____

_____

_____

_____

_____

_____

Owner Name _____

Address/Phone _____

_____

Corvette Description _____

_____

_____

_____

_____

_____

Owner Name _____

Address/Phone _____

_____

Corvette Description _____

_____

_____

_____

_____

_____

1953 CORVETTE

Wheelbase: 102" **Track:** 57" front, 58.8" rear *William Landis photo*
Length: 167.3" **Width:** 69.8" **Height:** 51.5" (over windshield)
Curb Weight: 2,886 lbs **Tire Size:** 6.70x15"

1954 CORVETTE

Wheelbase: 102" **Track:** 57" front, 58.8" rear *Author photo*
Length: 167.3" **Width:** 69.8" **Height:** 51.5" (over windshield)
Curb Weight: 2,886 lbs **Tire Size:** 6.70x15"

1955 CORVETTE

Wheelbase: 102" **Track:** 57" front, 58.8" rear *Author photo*
Length: 167.3" **Width:** 69.8" **Height:** 51.5" (over windshield)
Curb Weight: 2,805 lbs (V8) **Tire Size:** 6.70x15"

1956 CORVETTE

Author photo

Wheelbase: 102" **Track:** 57" front, 58.8" rear
Length: 168" **Width:** 70.5" **Height:** 51" (over hardtop)
Curb Weight: 2,875 lbs **Tire Size:** 6.70x15"

1957 CORVETTE

Author photo

Wheelbase: 102" **Track:** 57" front, 58.8" rear
Length: 168" **Width:** 70.5" **Height:** 51" (over hardtop)
Curb Weight: 2,849 lbs **Tire Size:** 6.70x15"

1958 CORVETTE

Chevrolet photo

Wheelbase: 102" **Track:** 57" front, 58.8" rear
Length: 177.2" **Width:** 72.8" **Height:** 51" (over hardtop)
Curb Weight: 2,926 lbs **Tire Size:** 6.70x15"

1959 CORVETTE

Wheelbase: 102" **Track:** 57" front, 58.8" rear   *Author photo*
Length: 177.2" **Width:** 72.8" **Height:** 51" (over hardtop)
Curb Weight: 2,975 lbs **Tire Size:** 6.70x15"

1960 CORVETTE

Wheelbase: 102" **Track:** 57" front, 58.8" rear   *Chevrolet photo*
Length: 177.2" **Width:** 72.8" **Height:** 51" (over hardtop)
Curb Weight: 2,985 lbs **Tire Size:** 6.70x15"

1961 CORVETTE

Wheelbase: 102" **Track:** 57" front, 58.8" rear   *Chevrolet photo*
Length: 177.2" **Width:** 72.8" **Height:** 51.5" (over hardtop)
Curb Weight: 3,035 lbs **Tire Size:** 6.70x15"

112

1962 CORVETTE

Wheelbase: 102" **Track:** 57" front, 58.8" rear   *John Amgwert photo*
Length: 177.2" **Width:** 70.4" **Height:** 51.5" (over hardtop)
Curb Weight: 3,065 lbs **Tire Size:** 6.70x15"

1963 CORVETTE

Wheelbase: 98" **Track:** 56.25" front, 57.0" rear   *Author photo*
Length: 175.1" **Width:** 69.6" **Height:** 49.8 (coupe)
Curb Weight: 3,015 lbs (coupe) **Tire Size:** 6.70x15"

1964 CORVETTE

Wheelbase: 98" **Track:** 56.25" front, 57.0" rear   *Author photo*
Length: 175.1" **Width:** 69.6" **Height:** 49.8 (coupe)
Curb Weight: 3,125 lbs (coupe) **Tire Size:** 6.70x15"

1965 CORVETTE

Wheelbase: 98" **Track:** 56.8" front, 57.6" rear *Author photo*
Length: 175.1" **Width:** 69.6" **Height:** 49.8" (coupe)
Curb Weight: 3,135 lbs (coupe) **Tire Size:** 7.75x15-inch

1966 CORVETTE

Wheelbase: 98" **Track:** 56.8" front, 57.6" rear *W. Morton photo*
Length: 175.1" **Width:** 69.6" **Height:** 49.8" (coupe)
Curb Weight: 3,140 lbs (coupe) **Tire Size:** 7.75x15-inch

1967 CORVETTE

Wheelbase: 98" **Track:** 56.8" front, 57.6" rear *Author photo*
Length: 175.1" **Width:** 69.6" **Height:** 49.8" (coupe)
Curb Weight: 3,155 lbs (coupe) **Tire Size:** 7.75x15-inch

1968 CORVETTE

Author photo

Wheelbase: 98" **Track:** 58.3" front, 59" rear
Length: 182.5" **Width:** 69" **Height:** 47.8" (coupe)
Curb Weight: 3,210 lbs (coupe) **Tire Size:** F70x15-inch

1969 CORVETTE

Author photo

Wheelbase: 98" **Track:** 58.7" front, 59.4" rear
Length: 182.5" **Width:** 69" **Height:** 47.8" (coupe)
Curb Weight: 3,245 lbs (coupe) **Tire Size:** F70x15-inch

1970 CORVETTE

Author photo

Wheelbase: 98" **Track:** 58.7" front, 59.4" rear
Length: 182.5" **Width:** 69" **Height:** 47.8" (coupe)
Curb Weight: 3,285 lbs (coupe) **Tire Size:** F70x15-inch

1971 CORVETTE

Wheelbase: 98" **Track:** 58.7" front, 59.4" rear *Chevrolet photo*
Length: 182.5" **Width:** 69" **Height:** 47.8" (coupe)
Curb Weight: 3,202 lbs (coupe) **Tire Size:** F70x15-inch

1972 CORVETTE

Wheelbase: 98" **Track:** 58.7" front, 59.4" rear *Author photo*
Length: 182.5" **Width:** 69" **Height:** 47.8" (coupe)
Curb Weight: 3,305 lbs (coupe) **Tire Size:** F70x15-inch

1973 CORVETTE

Wheelbase: 98" **Track:** 58.7" front, 59.5" rear *Author photo*
Length: 184.6" **Width:** 69" **Height:** 47.8" (coupe)
Curb Weight: 3,416 lbs (coupe) **Tire Size:** GR70x15-inch

1974 CORVETTE

Wheelbase: 98" **Track:** 58.7" front, 59.5" rear *Chevrolet photo*
Length: 185.5" **Width:** 69" **Height:** 47.8" (coupe)
Curb Weight: 3,388 lbs (coupe) **Tire Size:** GR70x15-inch

1975 CORVETTE

Wheelbase: 98" **Track:** 58.7" front, 59.5" rear *Mark Erwin photo*
Length: 185.2" **Width:** 69" **Height:** 48.1 (coupe)
Curb Weight: 3,529 lbs (coupe) **Tire Size:** GR70x15-inch

1976 CORVETTE

Wheelbase: 98" **Track:** 58.7" front, 59.5" rear *Chevrolet photo*
Length: 185.2" **Width:** 69" **Height:** 48.1
Curb Weight: 3,541 lbs **Tire Size:** GR70x15-inch

117

1977 CORVETTE

Wheelbase: 98" **Track:** 58.7" front, 59.5" rear
Length: 185.2" **Width:** 69" **Height:** 48.1"
Curb Weight: 3,534 lbs **Tire Size:** GR70x15-inch

Chevrolet photo

1978 CORVETTE

Wheelbase: 98" **Track:** 58.7" front, 59.5" rear
Length: 185.2" **Width:** 69" **Height:** 48"
Curb Weight: 3,572 lbs **Tire Size:** P225/70R15

Author photo

1979 CORVETTE

Wheelbase: 98" **Track:** 58.7" front, 59.5" rear
Length: 185.2" **Width:** 69" **Height:** 48"
Curb Weight: 3,503 lbs **Tire Size:** P225/70R15

Chevrolet photo

1980 CORVETTE

Wheelbase: 98" **Track:** 58.7" front, 59.5" rear
Length: 185.3" **Width:** 69" **Height:** 48"
Curb Weight: 3,336 lbs **Tire Size:** P225/70R15

Author photo

1981 CORVETTE

Wheelbase: 98" **Track:** 58.7" front, 59.5" rear
Length: 185.3" **Width:** 69" **Height:** 48"
Curb Weight: 3,307 lbs **Tire Size:** P225/70R15

Chevrolet photo

1982 CORVETTE

Wheelbase: 98" **Track:** 58.7" front, 59.5" rear
Length: 185.3" **Width:** 69" **Height:** 48"
Curb Weight: 3,342 lbs **Tire Size:** P225/70R15

Author photo

1984 CORVETTE

Wheelbase: 96.2" **Track:** 59.6" front, 60.4" rear *Author photo*
Length: 176.5" **Width:** 71" **Height:** 46.7"
Curb Weight: 3,192 lbs **Tire Size:** P255/50VR16

1985 CORVETTE

Wheelbase: 96.2" **Track:** 59.6" front, 60.4" rear *Author photo*
Length: 176.5" **Width:** 71" **Height:** 46.7"
Curb Weight: 3,224 lbs **Tire Size:** P255/50VR16

1986 CORVETTE

Wheelbase: 96.2" **Track:** 59.6" front, 60.4" rear *Chevrolet photo*
Length: 176.5" **Width:** 71" **Height:** 46.7" (coupe)
Curb Weight: 3,239 lbs (coupe) **Tire Size:** P255/50VR16

120

1987 CORVETTE

Wheelbase: 96.2" **Track:** 59.6" front, 60.4" rear *Author photo*
Length: 176.5" **Width:** 71" **Height:** 46.7" (coupe)
Curb Weight: 3,216 lbs (coupe) **Tire Size:** P255/50VR16

1988 CORVETTE

Wheelbase: 06.2" **Track:** 59.6" front, 60.4" rear *Chevrolet photo*
Length: 176.5" **Width:** 71" **Height:** 46.7" (coupe)
Curb Weight: 3,245 lbs (coupe) **Tire Size:** P255/50ZR16

1989 CORVETTE

Wheelbase: 96.2" **Track:** 59.6" front, 60.4" rear *Chevrolet photo*
Length: 176.5" **Width:** 71" **Height:** 46.7" (coupe)
Curb Weight: 3,238 lbs (coupe) **Tire Size:** P275/40ZR17

1990 CORVETTE

Wheelbase: 96.2" **Track:** 59.6" front, 60.4" rear *Chevrolet photo*
Length: 176.5" **Width:** 71" **Height:** 46.7" (base coupe)
Curb Weight: 3,288 lbs (base coupe) **Tire Size:** P275/40ZR17

1991 CORVETTE

Wheelbase: 96.2" **Track:** 59.6" front, 60.4" rear *Chevrolet photo*
Length: 178.6" **Width:** 71" **Height:** 46.7" (base coupe)
Curb Weight: 3,288 lbs (base coupe) **Tire Size:** P275/40ZR17

1992 CORVETTE

Wheelbase: 96.2" **Track:** 57.7" front, 59.1" rear *Chevrolet photo*
Length: 178.5" **Width:** 70.7" **Height:** 46.3" (base coupe)
Curb Weight: 3,338 lbs (base coupe) **Tire Size:** P275/40ZR17

1993 CORVETTE

Wheelbase: 96.2" **Track:** 57.7" front, 59.1" rear   *Chevrolet photo*
Length: 178.5" **Width:** 70.7" **Height:** 46.3" (base coupe)
Curb Weight: 3,333 lbs **Tire Size:** P255/45ZR17 (F), P285/40ZR17 (R)

1994 CORVETTE

Wheelbase: 96.2" **Track:** 57.5" front, 59.1" rear   *Chevrolet photo*
Length: 178.5" **Width:** 70.7" **Height:** 46.3" (base coupe)
Curb Weight: 3,309 lbs **Tire Size:** P255/45ZR17 (F), P285/40ZR17 (R)

1995 CORVETTE

Wheelbase: 96.2" **Track:** 57.5" front, 59.1" rear   *Chevrolet photo*
Length: 178.5" **Width:** 70.7" **Height:** 46.3" (base coupe)
Curb Weight: 3,203 lbs **Tire Size:** P255/45ZR17 (F), P285/40ZR17 (R)

1996 CORVETTE

Wheelbase: 96.2" **Track:** 57.5" front, 59.1" rear   *Chevrolet photo*
Length: 178.5" **Width:** 70.7" **Height:** 46.3" (base coupe)
Curb Weight: 3,298 lbs **Tire Size:** P255/45ZR17 (F), P285/40ZR17 (R)

1997 CORVETTE

Wheelbase: 104.5" **Track:** 62.1" front, 62" rear   *Chevrolet photos*
Length: 179.6"   **Height:** 47.8"
Width: 73.6" (vehicle), 78.9 (mirrors)
Curb Weight: 3,221 lbs (automatic), 3,216 lbs (manual)
Tire Size: P245/45ZR17 front, P275/40ZR18 rear
Wheel Size: 17x8.5" front, 18x9.5" rear
Overhang: 38.7" front, 36.3" rear
Windshield Slope Angle: 65.5 degrees

CORVETTE & CAMARO LITERATURE

The following Corvette and Camaro books are available from Michael Bruce Associates by mail. To order, enclose check or money order along with a brief description of the books you wish. Add a total of $3 shipping for each order (no quantity limit) shipped to the same address. All books are shipped in rigid containers for protection, not in padded bags. Your satisfaction is guaranteed unconditionally. Wholesale discounts are available for quantities of ten books or more. Please write for details.

Michael Bruce Associates, Inc.
Post Office Box 396
Powell, Ohio 43065

THE GLORY DAYS OF CORVETTE ROAD RACING

California Screamin' The Glory Days of Corvette Road Racing: A blend of off-the-wall personalities, seat-of-the-pants driving, self-taught skills, and fire-breathing, near raceworthy Corvettes lurking in Chevrolet showrooms, created a special period in Corvette racing history.

Rushed into production in 1953 with six-cylinder engines and Powerglide transmissions, the first Corvettes were anything but race cars. But by 1957, fuel-injected, four-speed, ripsnorting Corvettes were chewing up race tracks all over the country. In production-class sports car racing, they were *the* cars to beat.

With its moderate weather, a handful of first-rate tracks and an abundance of not-so-first-rate tracks carved from airfields and parking lots, and a car-crazy culture, California during the glory years was the center of the Corvette racing universe.

The Corvette's transformation from lamb to lion, the triumphs and tragedies of the racers who rode these beasts...it's all here. Softbound, 160 pages, 11"x8.5", 201 photos, $19.95.

Secrets of
Corvette
Detailing

show, street & sale

Secrets of Corvette Detailing: Corvette detailing? Is that so much different from detailing other automobiles? You bet. Sure, glass is glass and paint is paint; Corvettes are made of many of the same materials as other cars, but the final product is different. More importantly, the attitude of Corvette owners is different. What Corvette owners consider original, correct and proper for their automobiles is a world apart from the attitudes of other marques' owners. It's this owner-attitude factor that dictates a different detailing approach for Corvettes. Apply this book's techniques to other cars. But don't apply the detailing things done to other cars to Corvettes.

Corvette owners think long term. They want their Corvettes to look good today and twenty years from now. This book shows how to detail without destroying, with true *factory* originality always the goal.

You'll find the concepts, engine and chassis detailing, interior detailing, exterior detailing, even proper fuel and storage considerations. For show, resale or just improving and preserving your street-driven *Corvette, Secrets of Corvette Detailing* is the book you need. Softbound, 96 pages, 8"x10", 198 photos. $14.95.

125

Camaro White Book: This is the companion to the famous *Corvette Black Book*. Now Camaro lovers can have their own pocket bible of Camaro facts.

Introduced in 1985, completely rewritten and resized in 1993, and revised again for 1997, this new edition covers 1967-1997 models. It lists facts, numbers, codes, and the complete option scoop. For Camaros, options can be the difference between collectable and ho-hum. This book presents options in a comprehensive, yet easy to locate year-by-year format.

The *Camaro White Book* also tells you how many of each Camaro factory option Chevrolet sold each year so you can determine what's really rare and what isn't.

Not the old incomplete, inaccurate data charts you've seen reprinted elsewhere, this book is start-from-scratch, thoroughly researched and beautifully printed. Softbound, 128 pages, 40 photos, $12.95.

Illustrated Corvette Buyer's Guide: Written by Mike Antonick (author of the *Corvette Black Book*), published by Motorbooks International, this fourth edition of the *Illustrated Corvette Buyer's Guide* includes all models from 1953 through 1997. This is considered *the* standard reference work for anyone interested in purchasing a Corvette. Each model's heritage, its good and bad points, and what each is like to drive and own is described. There's an exclusive five-star rating system for best buys, typical mechanical bugs, even cautions for avoiding the dreaded "bogus" Corvette. Best of all, the "numbers match" terminology one sees in every Corvette ad is fully explained.

This book is an obvious must for anyone intending to purchase a Corvette, but even the most astute enthusiast will love the delightful four-decade tour through the evolution of a modern marvel. Soft cover, 176 pages, 230+ photos, 7.5"x9.25", $17.95.

Illustrated Camaro Buyer's Guide: Written by Mike Antonick (author of the *Camaro White Book*), published by Motorbooks International, this new third edition of the *Illustrated Camaro Buyer's Guide* covers 1967 through 1994 models.

With millions produced, one wonders if there are any truly collectible Camaros. And, how to pick them from such a multitude? Yes, there are many *very* collectible Camaros; some of which are plenty rare. This excellent book sorts out all of the four generations, years, models, and options.

A five-star rating system gives you the inside line on future appreciation. Weak points on certain models and special mechanical and authenticity cautions are explained. A lot of enthusiasts think the Camaro market is today where the Corvette market was ten years ago. In other words, now may be the best time to find that special Camaro. Softbound, 176 pages, 7.5"x9.5", 231 photos, $16.95.

Remember, to order any of these books, enclose check or money order along with a brief description of the books you wish. Add a total of $3 shipping for each order (no quantity limit) shipped to the same address. All books are shipped in rigid containers for protection, not in padded bags. Your satisfaction is unconditionally guaranteed.

Michael Bruce Associates, Inc.
Post Office Box 396
Powell, Ohio 43065

BLACK BOOK ORDER FORM

Send _____ copies of the

Corvette Black Book 1953-1997

@ $12.95 each $ _____.____

Ohio residents add .75 sales tax ____.____

Postage/hard shipping container ___3.00___

Check or money order enclosed $ ____.____

Name _____

Street _____

City _____ State _____ Zip_____

Mail Order To: **Michael Bruce Associates, Inc.**
Post Office Box 396
Powell, Ohio 43065

- >✄

BLACK BOOK ORDER FORM

Send _____ copies of the

Corvette Black Book 1953-1997

@ $12.95 each $ _____.____

Ohio residents add .75 sales tax ____.____

Postage/hard shipping container ___3.00___

Check or money order enclosed $ ____.____

Name _____

Street _____

City _____ State _____ Zip_____

Mail Order To: **Michael Bruce Associates, Inc.**
Post Office Box 396
Powell, Ohio 43065

**BLACK BOOK
ORDER FORM**

**BLACK BOOK
ORDER FORM**